The Existentialist Theology of Paul Tillich

The
Existentialist Theology
of
Paul Tillich

by

Bernard Martin, Ph.D.

Bookman Associates :: New York

MANUFACTURED IN THE UNITED STATES OF AMERICA BY
UNITED PRINTING SERVICES, INC.
NEW HAVEN, CONN.

Preface

One of the most striking phenomena on the philosophical landscape in America in the mid-twentieth century is the measure of intellectual respectability that is once again being accorded theology and religious thought by many philosophers. For the emergence of this phenomenon no one, perhaps, is more responsible than Paul Tillich. Acclaimed as one of the two or three greatest living Protestant theologians and as one of the foremost interpreters of the Christian faith in our time, he is also widely recognized as a philosopher of unusual ability and scope. Because of his competence in both theology and philosophy and of his lifelong interest in the problems of their relationship to one another, he has produced works that have genuine philosophical as well as theological significance, works that have further made many philosophers aware that theology need not necessarily be dismissed as alien in spirit and intention to the philosophical enterprise.

For the philosopher, the primary significance of Tillich's work lies in the fact that he has not been content to set forth an independent and self-contained exposition of Christian theology, but has sought rather to relate this theology to contemporary philosophical currents and to show that it makes significant contact with, and is relevant to, the fundamental questions about human existence that people both inside and outside the Christian Church are asking.

The correlation of philosophy and theology in Tillich's work appears most markedly in his anthropology, an exposition and critique of which is here undertaken. For Tillich, as for many other contemporary theologians, the doctrine of man is of central importance and constitutes the basis of his whole theological system. This book concentrates on Tillich's anthropology, but since this cannot be understood without a knowledge of his doctrine of Reason and Revelation, God, the Christ, and "the

New Being," it provides in fact a summation and criticism of the fundamental elements of his entire theology.

Not only in the theological field, but in almost all other intellectual circles today, the problem of man has come increasingly to be recognized as the one in most urgent need of reconsideration. What Max Scheler wrote over thirty years ago is even more true at present.

> In no other period of human knowledge has man ever become more problematic to himself than in our own day. We have a scientific, a philosophical and a theological anthropology that know nothing of each other. Therefore we no longer possess any clear and consistent idea of man. The ever-growing multiplicity of the particular sciences that are engaged in the study of man has much more confused and obscured than elucidated our concept of man.[1]

The great merit of Tillich's work lies in the fact that he has made one of the few attempts in our time to bridge the gaps between the various anthropologies which Scheler mentions—the scientific, philosophical and theological—and to construct a doctrine of man that will include, and do justice to, their various insights. Whether his attempt has been an altogether successful one is, of course, an open question; but the very fact of his having undertaken such a venture makes it worthy of serious consideration.

In all his work, including his anthropology, Tillich of course writes primarily as a theologian. Our own basic concern in this study, however, will not be with the adequacy of the purely theological side of his doctrine. The question whether he has done justice to the content of the classical Christian teaching about man must be left for decision to those who are more expert in the knowledge of the Christian faith and its theological expression. We shall here approach his anthropology primarily from a philosophical point of view and seek to evaluate its general validity and significance from that perspective. Let it be said also at this point that the author of this study has

---

[1] Max Scheler, *Die Stellung des Menschen im Kosmos* (Darmstadt: Reichl, 1928), pp. 13ff.

theological commitments quite different from those of its subject. He is a believing Jew and a rabbi, and the influence of his
Jewish beliefs will be apparent in his critique of some of Tillich's
doctrines. Nevertheless, it is the author's hope that his own
theological convictions have not prevented him from achieving
an adequate and sympathetic understanding of Tillich's religious position or debarred him from maintaining a generally
objective philosophical attitude in his criticisms of that position.

Of few men is it so true as of Tillich that his thought cannot
be understood without a knowledge and appreciation of his
life. Tillich's theology is "existential," in the sense that it stems
not only from his intellect but from his life, from the crucial experiences of his personal existence. Hence, our first chapter is
biographical. It sets forth the major facts of Tillich's life and
seeks to explain what incidents and experiences of his personal
historical destiny have been of basic importance in molding his
thought, as well as the crucial intellectual influences upon it.

We have already indicated that the philosopher's interest in
Tillich lies primarily in the fact that he has sought to correlate
philosophy and theology. He has lived and thought, as he himself puts it,[2] on the borderland between these two disciplines.
In our second chapter we shall therefore consider his own views
on the nature of philosophy and theology, respectively, and the
method of correlating them that he professes to follow in his
mature systematic work, particularly in the development of his
anthropology.

It is Tillich's contention that all anthropological questions
must be considered from a threefold perspective. He maintains
that three different aspects are involved in all genuine theological thinking about man, namely, "essential goodness, existential
estrangement, and the possibility of something, a 'third,' beyond
essence and existence, through which the cleavage is overcome
and healed."[3] This threefold theological division of human
nature, according to Tillich, is also to be found in the philosoph-

---

[2] In the autobiographical statement at the beginning of his *The Interpretation of History*, pp. 30-41.
[3] "The Theological Significance of Existentialism and Psychoanalysis,"
in *Theology of Culture*, p. 119.

ical tradition, where, he suggests,[4] it assumes the form of the idea that man's essential and existential nature point to his teleological nature. The crucial importance of recognizing the distinction between these three aspects of human nature is insisted upon. The failure properly to distinguish them, Tillich claims,[5] has been a fertile source of confusion in the anthropological thought of many contemporary psychologists and philosophers.

In accordance with the foregoing, we shall show, in our third chapter, how this tripartite scheme is applied in Tillich's discussion of that basic anthropological problem to which he devotes especially great attention, namely, the nature of human rationality. We shall here consider Tillich's threefold picture of what he terms reason in essence, reason in existence, and "ecstatic" or "saved" reason as operative in revelation. We shall also consider in this chapter his general epistemology and theory of knowledge.

In our fourth chapter we shall be dealing with the heart of Tillich's anthropology, his analysis of man's essential ontological structure, of the fundamental elements and categories which enter into it, and of the types of anxiety which he regards it as necessarily producing. We shall here observe how, following the Existentialist and *Lebensphilosophie* traditions, he utilizes anthropology as the entrance and key to general ontology.

Our fifth chapter will proceed to an examination of Tillich's characterization of man's existential situation. Here we shall be concerned with what he calls man's condition of estrangement, his "existential disruption" as contrasted with the "essential finitude" of his created being, and the "existential despair" to which this disruption leads as contrasted with the "essential anxiety" produced by finitude.

In our sixth chapter we shall discuss Tillich's views on the "saving" or teleological forces which he sees as overcoming man's essential anxiety and existential despair. Though Tillich insists that he is here presenting "answers" derived from the Christian

---

[4] *Loc. cit.*

[5] *Ibid.*, pp. 119-22. Cf. *Systematic Theology*, II, 53-55.

revelation concerning God and the Christ, these answers, we believe, are worth considering from a philosophical point of view, particularly inasmuch as he himself puts forth the claim that the *logos* manifest in the Christian revelation is identical with the universal *logos*, i.e., that the Christian revelation yields the same truth about being as that yielded by the philosophy which is the product of ontological reason in its essence.

Each of chapters two through six concludes with a section in which the attempt is made, in brief compass, to criticize and evaluate the fundamental ideas presented in the exposition.

I wish to express my gratitude to Professor Harry M. Tiebout, Jr., of the Department of Philosophy at the University of Illinois, who first aroused my interest in Paul Tillich and encouraged my study of his work. Much of the material in the present volume was written as a doctoral dissertation under Professor Tiebout's supervision. I am indebted also to other members of the Department, particularly professors Max Fisch, D. W. Gotshalk, B. J. Diggs, and A. R. Turquette, under whose tutelage my philosophical studies were pursued.

Thanks are also due to The University of Chicago Press for granting permission to quote from Paul Tillich, *Systematic Theology*, Vols. I and II (Copyright 1951, 1957, by The University of Chicago), and to Charles Scribner's Sons for permission to quote passages from Paul Tillich, *The Interpretation of History* (Part I, translated by N. A. Rosetski; Parts II, III, and IV, translated by Elsa L. Talmay; New York: Charles Scribner's Sons, 1936).

—BERNARD MARTIN

St. Paul, Minnesota
November, 1962

Contents

The Existentialist Theology of Paul Tillich

CHAPTER ONE

The Life of Paul Tillich

PAUL TILLICH was born on August 20, 1886 in the village of Starzeddel in the German province of Brandenburg near the Silesian border, where his father served as a minister of the Prussian Territorial Church. Four years after his birth, the family moved to the trans-Elbian town of Schönfliess. Here the father held the position of superintendent of a group of Lutheran parishes. From his fourth to his twelfth year the young Paul Tillich lived in the walled medieval town, surrounded by historical landmarks.

Residing in Schönfliess, with its Gothic church and town hall but set in the countryside amidst fields and woods, was—he believes—the stimulus to the creation of his lifelong romantic attitude toward both history and nature. "To grow up in towns in which every stone is witness of a period many centuries past," he writes, "produces a feeling for history, not as a matter of knowledge, but as a living reality in which the past participates in the present."[1] And of his attachment to nature he writes, "Nearly all great memories, and all strong longings are interlaced with landscapes, with the soil and with weather, with corn fields and the smell of autumnal potato foliage, with the forms of clouds, with wind, flowers, and woods."[2]

Both his father and mother, he tells us,[3] were strong personalities, but of contrasting types and representing different Germanic traditions and attitudes toward life. It is to their opposite influence that he ascribes the fact that he himself has always lived on the boundary between two temperaments.

I have never doubted . . . that the union of a father from the Mark and a mother from the Rhineland implanted in me the

tension between eastern and western Germany: in the East
a meditative bent tinged with melancholy, a heightened consciousness of duty and personal sin, a strong sense for authority,
and feudal traditions are still alive; while the West is characterized by zest of living, sensuous concreteness, mobility,
rationality, and democracy. It would not be possible, of course,
to allocate these two groups of characters to my father and
mother respectively. Yet it would seem that it was by way of
them that these contradictory qualities were rooted in me—my
life, inward and outward, to be enacted on their battleground.[4]

Tillich also tells us[5] of his youthful struggle against the intellectual and religious authoritarianism of his conservative father.
In this struggle he found that his best weapon was philosophy,
for his father was extremely fond of philosophical argumenta-
tion. In his metaphysical discussions with him, Tillich achieved
the happiest instances of a positive relationship with his father,
but through these he also managed to arrive at an independent
religious and intellectual standpoint. "It is this difficult and
painful break-through to autonomy," he declares, "which has
made me immune against any system of thought or life which
demands the surrender of this autonomy."[6]

At the age of twelve Tillich entered a humanistic *gymnasium*
in Königsberg-Neumark, a somewhat larger medieval town than
Schönfliess and not far from it. In 1900 his father was called
to an important church post in Berlin and the family moved to
the capital. Tillich's residence in the German metropolis and,
later in life, in other great cities of the world taught him, he
believes, many significant things. By this means, he writes,

. . . I was saved from romantic enmity against technical civiliza-
tions and was taught to appreciate the importance of the big
city for the critical side of intellectual and artistic life. Later
there was added to this a vital and thoughtful understanding
of the world of Bohemianism, possible only in the large cities,
and also an esthetic appreciation of the internal and external
immensity of the metropolis; and finally I gained personal experience of the political and social movements that are concentrated in the capital.[7]

In Berlin Tillich again enrolled in a humanistic *gymnasium*
from which he graduated in 1904. The basic subjects in the

curriculum of the *gymnasium* were Latin and Greek, and here Tillich developed his lifelong love of the Greek language, Greek culture, and especially Greek philosophy. One of his best courses at the *gymnasium,* he recalls,[8] was that on the pre-Socratic philosophers. Interest in the pre-Socratics was apparently very high in German academic circles at the time. Heidegger, Tillich's great contemporary and later his colleague at the University of Marburg, has also had a lifelong interest in the pre-Socratics, and has maintained that not only were they the finest exemplars of philosophic thought ever to appear but that Western metaphysical speculation after them has followed a road of continuous decline in power and significance.

Following his graduation from the *gymnasium* Tillich studied under the theological faculties at the universities of Berlin, Tübingen, and Halle. In 1909 he took his first, and in 1911 his second, theological examination. In the latter year he also received the degree of Doctor of Philosophy at Breslau, and a year later the degree of Licentiate of Theology at Halle as well as ordination into the Evangelical Lutheran Church of the province of Brandenburg.

Long before embarking on his theological studies, Tillich informs us,[9] he had studied philosophy privately and had acquired a good knowledge of its history as well as a basic acquaintance with the work of Kant and Fichte. At the university he studied Schleiermacher, Hegel, and Schelling, concentrating on the latter's philosophy of religion. His doctoral dissertation at Breslau was entitled *Die religionsgeschichtliche Konstruktion in Schellings positiver Philosophie, ihre Voraussetzungen und Prinzipien* and his thesis for the degree of Licentiate of Theology at Halle was on *Mystik und Schuldbewusstsein in Schellings philosophischer Entwicklung.* The Schelling of the second period was the earliest and perhaps the single greatest influence on the development of both his theological and philosophical views. Writing in 1936 Tillich declared:

> I thought that, fundamentally, I had found the union of theology and philosophy in the philosophical explanation of the Christian doctrine through the older Schelling, in his founding of a Christian philosophy of existence in contrast to Hegel's human-

istic philosophy of essence and in his interpretation of history as the History of Salvation. I must confess that even today I find more "theonomous philosophy" in Schelling than in any of the other idealists.[10]

In the later Schelling, Tillich sees the philosophically decisive break with Hegelian idealism and the beginning of the modern movement of Existentialism, whose greatest figure was Kierkegaard. Schelling, according to Tillich, had seen the chasm which looms before man but had quickly averted his eyes from the terrifying sight; Kierkegaard looked at it unflinchingly. Tillich read Kierkegaard with great avidity and found his psychology and doctrine of man radically shaking in their impact. In the pre-war years the full power of Kierkegaard's vision was not yet generally recognized, but towards the end of the war and in the immediate post-war period Kierkegaard became the saint of the philosophers as well as of the theologians of Germany. His influence upon the thinking of Tillich, as upon that of Heidegger, was immense.

Heidegger himself has contributed very importantly to Tillich's intellectual development. Tillich was teaching theology at the University of Marburg in the 1920's at the same time that Heidegger was expounding his philosophy there and writing his *Sein und Zeit,* the major statement of the Existentialist doctrine of man in our time. Though Tillich has nowhere indicated how close a personal relationship he had at Marburg with Heidegger, the influence of the latter upon his thinking has obviously been of a prime order of magnitude. Of the Heideggerian philosophy he writes:

By its explanation of human existence it establishes a doctrine of man, though unintentionally, which is both the doctrine of human freedom and human finiteness; and which is so closely related with the Christian interpretation of human existence that one is forced to speak of a "theonomous philosophy," in spite of Heidegger's emphatic atheism. To be sure, it is not a philosophy which includes the theological answer and explains it philosophically. Such an undertaking would be idealism and the opposite of the philosophy of existence. However, the philosophy of existence asks the question in a new and radical manner, the answer to which is given in theology for faith.

By means of these ideas . . . the border between theology and
philosophy has been drawn more acutely than in my earlier
philosophy of religion, without abandoning the mutual relation of comprehension.[11]

Aside from Heidegger, the modern German philosopher to
whom Tillich is most indebted is probably Edmund Husserl.
Husserl's *Logische Untersuchungen* appeared to Tillich the
most forceful refutation of positivism and particularly of that
form of it, psychologism, which is of most significance for the
philosophy of religion. For Tillich, Husserl's doctrine was the
most satisfying confirmation of what he claims to have learned
from Kant and Fichte, and to Husserl's phenomenology he
owes, as we shall observe,[12] much of his conception of the
general nature of philosophical reflection.

During the years that Tillich was studying philosophy at
various German universities he was also engaged in intensive
theological studies. Martin Kähler of Halle is singled out by
him[13] as the theologian who had the greatest impact upon his
thinking. It is to Kähler that he acknowledges indebtedness
for his understanding of the fundamental importance of the
Pauline-Lutheran idea of justification through faith. Of it he
writes:

The doctrine of justification on the one hand rends every human
claim in the face of God and every identification of God and
man. On the other hand, it shows how the decadence of human
existence, guilt, and despair, is overcome by the paradoxical
judgment that the sinner is just before God. My Christology and
Dogmatics were determined by the Cross of Christ as the
event of history in which the divine judgment over the world
became concrete and manifest. From this point of view it was
easy for me to make a connection between my own theology
and that of Karl Barth and to accept the analysis of human
existence as given by Kierkegaard and Heidegger.[14]

Kähler had restricted the application of the doctrine to the
sinner justified in his sin. Tillich, however, was to extend it
later on to the situation of the doubter in his doubt. He who
doubts but is ultimately concerned about the object of his doubt
is also justified before God. "The justification of the one who

doubts corresponds to the justification of the one who sins. Revelation is just as paradoxical as forgiveness of sins, and can become an object of possession as little as the latter."[15]

Tillich became very much concerned during his student days with the problem of the historical Jesus and the New Testament. The *religionsgeschichtliche Methode* which had been developed by Wellhausen and Gunkel in their Old Testament studies fascinated him and gave him, he tells us,[16] fundamental insights into the meaning of this literature. His understanding of the New Testament came primarily from Albert Schweitzer's *The Quest of the Historical Jesus* and Rudolf Bultmann's *Synoptische Tradition*. As a result of his studies and reflection, Tillich became convinced that the problem of the historical Jesus is not of fundamental importance for Christian theology. As early as 1911 he wrote a paper in which, he informs us, he "raised and attempted to answer the question, how the Christian doctrine might be understood if the non-existence of the historical Jesus should become historically probable."[17] It has been his contention ever since that not the historical Jesus, but the biblical "picture" of Jesus as the Christ, is the foundation of Christian faith.[18]

Following the conclusion of his theological studies Tillich served briefly as assistant pastor of various parishes of the Old Prussian United Church. When World War I broke out he immediately volunteered as a chaplain and served with the German army from September, 1914 to September, 1918. It took him only a few months to become convinced that the war was an unmitigated disaster and would end in the ruination of all of Europe. At this time the realization also came to him that the unity of the nation was a myth, that Germany was divided into conflicting classes, and that the proletarian masses regarded the Church as the ally of their enemies, the ruling classes. It was this division and conflict that led to the revolution in which imperial Germany collapsed.

Tillich found himself in deep sympathy with the social aspects of the short-lived revolution. He became one of the founders of German religious socialism and, as one of the major theoreticians of the movement, developed some of its key concepts.

The idea of the *Kairos* particularly was elaborated at meetings with his colleagues in the early days of the Religious Socialist movement. Tillich thus explains the concept of *Kairos*:

> The term is meant to express the fact that the struggle for a new social order cannot lead to a fulfillment such as is meant by the Kingdom of God, but that at a special time special tasks are demanded, and one special aspect of the Kingdom of God appears as a demand and expectation. The Kingdom of God will always remain as transcendent; but it appears as a judgment to a given form of society and as a norm to a coming one. Thus, the decision for Socialism during a definite period may be the decision for the Kingdom of God, even though the Socialist ideal remains infinitely distant from the Kingdom of God.[19]

Though religious socialism as an organized movement failed in Germany, Tillich has never repudiated his espousal of it. "If the prophetic message is true," he wrote in 1952, "there is nothing beyond religious socialism."[20]

As a result of his involvement in the social movements of post-war Germany Tillich became profoundly interested in Marx, and he expresses his debt to him for many of his fundamental insights. To Marx he owes first of all, he declares, his recognition of "the ideological character, not only of idealism, but of all systems of thought, religious as well as profane, which as the servants of power hinder, even though unconsciously, the more righteous forms of social reality."[21] From Marx he also learned something that he had previously learned from Kierkegaard, namely, that truth is always bound to the situation of the knower, but in the Marxist doctrine he found a new and different emphasis.

> In the situation of despair in which, according to Kierkegaard, every human being exists, and in the situation of the class struggle in which, according to Marx, historical humanity has lived up to now, every system of harmony is untrue. That leads both Kierkegaard and Marx to the point of connecting truth to a particular psychological or social situation. To Kierkegaard truth is just that subjectivity which does not disregard its despair, its exclusion from the objective world of essence, but which holds on to it passionately; whereas to Marx, truth is found in the class-interest of that class which becomes

conscious of itself as destined to overcome the class struggle, the necessarily non-ideological class. Thus arises the pecular idea, though intelligible from the Christian standpoint, that the greatest possibility of obtaining an un-ideological truth is given at the point of the greatest meaninglessness, of despair, of the broadest self-alienation of human essence.[22]

In Marx's concept of economic materialism Tillich again found another confirmation of the Kierkegaardian doctrine of human self-alienation. Economic materialism, he maintains, "confirms the theological insight, neglected by idealism, that man lives on earth and not in heaven; philosophically expressed, in existence and not in essence."[23]

In general Tillich regards Marx as one of the great modern unveilers of the truth about human existence. He compares him in this respect to Freud, who also laid bare many of the secret springs of human behavior. Both men refuted the sham, harmonizing idealism of the nineteenth century. While this or that element of Marxism and of psychoanalysis may be invalid or obsolete, the general power of both doctrines in unveiling human existence and destroying ideology cannot be denied. In addition to its unveiling power, Tillich sees in Marxism a genuine prophetic passion, a demand and expectation that society be radically reformed and reconstructed. In this it is sharply distinguished from idealism which, because of its mystical and sacramental roots, tends to be conservative in its social outlook.

It is far from an unqualified endorsement, however, that Tillich has given Marxism. His attitude towards Marx, he writes, "has always been dialectical, combining a Yes and a No. The Yes was based on the prophetic, humanistic and realistic elements in Marx's passionate style and profound thought, the No on the calculating, materialistic and resentful elements in Marx's analysis, polemics, and propaganda."[24] It is a tribute to Tillich's intellectual integrity and courage that still today, when even the most guarded and qualified approval of any aspect of Marxism lays one open to opprobrium and danger, he will not repudiate the positive insights that he claims to have derived from his reading of Marx.

Immediately following the end of the war, Tillich began his academic career in Germany. From 1919 to 1924 he served as a *Privatdozent* of theology at the University of Berlin. His intellectual interests had already begun to range far and wide. In his lectures in Berlin he sought to relate religion to art, politics, depth psychology, philosophy and sociology. It was a general "theology of culture" that he was attempting to develop. This enterprise began with one of his earliest scholarly papers, *Über die Idee einer Theologie der Kultur*, which he read in 1919 before the Berlin branch of the *Kant-Gesellschaft*.

The environment in Berlin during the post-war years was most conducive to the work Tillich had undertaken, for society and culture were in ferment. "The social structure," he recalls, "was in a state of dissolution, the human relations with respect to authority, education, family, sex, friendship and pleasure were in a creative chaos."[25] Two new movements particularly, in addition to religious socialism, engaged Tillich's interest and attention at this time and have continued to do so until the present: modern art and psychoanalysis. In the works of the Expressionists Tillich saw form-destroying power, creative ecstasy, and a manifestation of the depth of reason—precisely the elements which, as we shall observe,[26] he emphasized in elaborating his doctrine of revelation. Epressionist painting also opened up for Tillich the road to an appreciation of expressionist literature, particularly the works of Hoffmannsthal, George, Werfel and Rilke. "The strongest impression," he writes, "was made on me by Rilke's late poetry. Its profound psychoanalytical realism, the mystical fulness, the form charged with metaphysical content, all that made this poetry the expression of what in the concepts of my philosophy of religion, I could seize only abstractly."[27] Not only the new painting and literature, but also the new depth psychology of Freud and his disciples, struck Tillich as little short of revelatory. We have already observed how he came to regard psychoanalysis as unveiling many deep and long-repressed truths about the human situation.

Though it was an academic career that Tillich was pursuing during these years, he did not isolate himself from the practical problems either of society or of the church. We have already noted his involvement in the work of the Religious Socialist movement. Tillich also interested himself profoundly in the efforts that were being made to reform the ritual of the Protestant Church. He joined the so-called *Berneuchener* movement led by Wilhelm Stahlin and Karl Ritter, which sought not only to bring about a new understanding of ritual, sacrament, and symbol, but also to provide a clearly defined theological basis for the ceremonial forms of the Church. His own contributions to this enterprise have been highly significant ones.

In 1925 Tillich became professor of theology at Marburg. Here, as we have already indicated,[28] he encountered Heidegger and his existentialist doctrine of man. Here also he began work, he tells us,[29] on his massive *Systematic Theology*, the first volume of which appeared in America twenty-six years later, in 1951. During the years from 1925 to 1933 Tillich served as a professor of theology at Leipzig and at Marburg, as a professor of the science of religion at Dresden, and as a professor of philosophy at Frankfurt-am-Main. His academic posts alone testify to his continuing concern with both philosophy and theology and their interrelationships. As he himself puts it, "A constant change of faculties and yet no change in the subject! As a theologian I tried to remain a philosopher, and conversely so."[30]

Tillich's growing reputation in German academic circles, his many books and articles, and his frequent public lectures and speeches soon made him an important figure in the intellectual life of Germany. His open and passionate opposition to the developing National Socialist movement led to increasing conflict with the Nazis, and upon the accession of Hitler to the German chancellorship in 1933, Tillich was immediately dismissed from his post at the University of Frankfurt. In the fall of that year he left Germany with his family and came to the United States.

From his exile in America, Tillich wrote an open letter to his former friend and colleague, the theologian Emanuel Hirsch, who had become an ardent follower of the "German Christian" compromise with Nazism. Hirsch had declared the Nazi movement a "holy storm," a "power full of blessing," in which "the

work of the Almighty Lord" was to be seen and in whose
Weltanschauung "Germans of Evangelical faith should find
their sustaining natural historic dwelling place."[31] Though
Hirsch used much of the same terminology as Tillich had used
in his defense of religious socialism and though Hirsch's identification of the present will of God with Nazism was strikingly
similar to Tillich's identification of God's present will with
religious socialism in his concept of *Kairos*, Tillich could not
but regard his erstwhile friend's doctrine as a "demonic" distortion of Christianity, and he passionately denounced it as such.

Nor was Tillich much happier with the position taken by
Karl Barth and his associates in the so-called Barmen Declara-
tion, in which they repudiated Hirsch's Nazi Christianity and
proclaimed that the God of the Christians is to be found only
in the Bible and nowhere else. For Barth the universe is godless
and profane, and the Christian is ultimately unconcerned with
it. While Tillich also refused to consecrate any political or
economic order as "unbrokenly divine," he came to believe that
Barth's surrender of all concern for the dominations and powers
that rule the universe constituted a removal of them from all
moral and religious criticism and was therefore destructive.

Tillich came to America under the sponsorship of the Niebuhr
brothers. Richard Niebuhr had translated his book *Die Religiöse Lage der Gegenwart* and supplied it with an interpretative
introduction, thus preparing a reputation for him among American theologians. Reinhold Niebuhr invited him to become his
colleague on the faculty of the Union Theological Seminary.
It was not easy for Tillich to begin a new career and learn a
new language at the age of forty-seven, but his adjustment to
the American environment was a rapid one. A steady stream
of articles and books flowed from his pen, and personal appearances on the lecture platform soon made him a familiar
figure in America.

There is little doubt that contact with a wide variety of
theologians and philosophers in America and acquaintance with
new philosophical and theological tendencies have influenced
Tillich's reflection. Yet the major outlines of his thought seem
to have been fairly well fixed long before he left Germany.

Study of the work of the empirical and process theologians and of that of the pragmatist and naturalist philosophers has not greatly affected his views. Details have changed but the broad aspects have remained unaltered. Kierkegaard and Heidegger remain his philosophic heroes, and the existentialist doctrine of man continues to be for him the most valuable and enlightening account that has been given of the human predicament in modern times.

In 1956 Tillich retired from Union Theological Seminary and went to Harvard as a "university professor." There today, at the age of seventy-six, he continues his teaching and writing, sallying forth frequently to lecture at various colleges and universities. There also he is engaged in the work of completing his *Systematic Theology*, the last volume of which is yet to be published. What has already appeared of this monumental work makes it evident that it is one of the great theological documents in the history of Christendom—comparable, in a sense, to the works of Augustine, Aquinas, Luther, Calvin, Schleiermacher, and Barth. Though it is not a *Summa* in the sense of Aquinas' great work, for Tillich holds that Protestantism cannot pretend to any final truth if it be true to its own fundamental principle, it is a system which includes in itself much of the most vital thought of the twentieth century and seeks to relate it to classical Christian doctrine. In time Tillich's philosophical theology is bound to become dated and obsolete, but for the present it provides a guide and stimulus for which all those concerned with religious problems, both inside and outside Christianity, should be profoundly grateful.

CHAPTER TWO

Philosophy and Theology in Tillich's System

IN HIS *Systematic Theology*,[1] which is his *magnum opus* and the culmination of his lifetime of intellectual endeavor, Tillich draws a sharp distinction between philosophy and theology and ascribes a separate function to each, particularly in connection with the doctrine of man.

Philosophy is here described as *"that cognitive approach to reality in which reality as such is the object."*[2] Philosophy in general is identified by Tillich with ontology, which he defines as "an analysis of those structures of being which we encounter in every meeting with reality."[3] Tillich's conception of the nature of ontology or philosophy derives largely from Husserl's phenomenology, according to which the task of the philosopher is disinterestedly to analyze certain basic "essences" or "structures" given in experience to human consciousness while "bracketing" the question of the particular existence of the knower and of the objects known. But Tillich, unlike Husserl, seems to believe that there is also a philosophy which is a general kind of reflection, unanchored to any particular standpoint or subject matter.

> The philosopher looks at the whole of reality to discover within it the structure of reality as a whole. He tries to penetrate into the structures of being by means of the power of his cognitive function and its structures. . . . There is no particular place to look to discover the structure of being; there is no particular place to stand to discover the categories of experience. The place to look is all places; the place to stand is no place at all; it is pure reason.[4]

27

The truth of the results of such general ontological analysis may be established, according to Tillich, not experimentally but "experientially." The way of experiential verification is characterized by him as "the way of an *intelligent recognition* of the basic ontological structures within the encountered reality, including the process of encountering itself."[5]

Theology, as Tillich understands it, is also fundamentally an ontological inquiry.[6] Its concern, however, is not with "*the structure* of being *in itself*," but rather with "the *meaning* of being *for us*."[7] From this basic difference in perspective between philosophy and theology, Tillich holds, stem other important differences. The philosopher seeks to maintain towards being the "detached objectivity" characteristic of the scientific investigator, while the theologian is existentially involved in it, looking at it with passion, fear and love.[8] This is so because in studying being the theologian is really concerned with "being-itself," or the infinite, ultimate and unconditional power of being which determines human being or non-being.[9] Again, according to Tillich, the philosopher, as we have seen, in seeking truth about the structure of being "looks at the whole of reality" and tries to grasp "the universal *logos*," while the theologian "must look where that which concerns him ultimately is manifest," that is, "at the *logos* manifesting itself in a particular historical event."[10] Lastly, the philosopher, whose interest is predominantly theoretical, deals with the categories of being "in relation to the material which is structured by them" while the theologian, whose dominant interest is soteriological, deals with these categories in relation to "the quest for a 'new being.' "[11]

From the foregoing, Tillich concludes that "there is no common basis between theology and philosophy."[12] He does admit, to be sure, that every specific philosophy is in actuality colored by theological elements, but this is an accident deriving from the fact that every philosopher is not only a philosopher but also a "hidden theologian," in the sense that he is a human being with an ultimate concern and with existential involvements, the influence of which he cannot, *qua* human being, altogether escape, though, *qua* philosopher, he attempts to do so.[13] Essentially, however, philosophy and theology in themselves are distinct and sharply separated from each other, and there is no possibility either of synthesis or conflict between them.[14]

How, then, does Tillich himself relate philosophy and theology in his own system, particularly in the construction of his doctrine of man? The task of philosophy, he declares, is to provide an analysis of human existence and to develop the questions implied in it, while the theological task is to show that final answers to these questions are given only in the symbols of revelation, and particularly, the Christian revelation.[15] According to the division of labor prescribed by what he calls "the method of correlation," philosophy asks questions about man and theology answers them by explaining the significance of the symbols given in revelation.[16] While Tillich is willing to admit[17] that, in respect to form, the answer may be dependent on the question asked, he strongly contends that, as far as their content is concerned, question and answer are separate and independent.[18] The substance of the answer cannot be derived from the question through philosophical reflection; to suppose that it could, i.e., to identify reason and revelation, was the mistake of idealistic philosophy.[19] The reason why philosophy cannot answer its own questions is that these arise from its analysis of the structure of being as this manifests itself under the conditions of existence. The structure revealed under these conditions exhibits contradiction, conflict, incompleteness, ambiguity and distortion. Only revelation, which goes *beyond* this structure and, through the transparency of some finite medium to the unconditional, discloses the depth or ground of being, can give answers to the problems which become apparent in the analysis of the structure of being. And revelation is not at the philosopher's, or any man's, disposal; it is "spoken to" man from beyond and not by man to himself.[20]

It should be added that, while Tillich declares that the analysis of human existence and the development of the questions implicit therein is essentially a philosophical task and that the theologian, when performing it, operates autonomously as a philosopher, refusing to tell himself what is theologically true and allowing his act of seeing to be "determined only by the object as it is given in his experience," he does understand

and admit that the theologian's work even here is partially focused by his ultimate concern and his commitment to the revelation whose symbols he expounds.[21]

Though Tillich thus sharply distinguishes philosophy and theology, it is his contention that ultimately there is no disagreement between philosophy and the revelation which the Christian theologian sets forth.

> The Christian claim that the *logos* who has become concrete in Jesus as the Christ is at the same time the universal *logos* includes the claim that wherever the *logos* is at work it agrees with the Christian message. No philosophy which is obedient to the universal *logos* can contradict the *concrete* logos, the Logos "who became flesh."[22]

Beyond this, Tillich, as we shall see, also claims that no contradiction is possible between the knowledge of revelation and empirical or scientific knowledge of any kind, because these lie on different levels and deal with different dimensions of experience.[23]

The distinction between Tillich's approach to the problem of the relation between philosophy and theology, or revelation, and that of the later[24] Karl Barth is worth noting briefly. While Barth rejects autonomous philosophy and denies reason and experience in theology, Tillich affirms them as having a proper place in the theological enterprise. While Barth emphasizes the "Word of God" which stands over against man and which is to be "thrown" at him, Tillich speaks, as we shall see,[25] of the New Being in which man participates with his entire being and in all his functions, including his reason. While Barth declares that revelation is in no way dependent upon man, Tillich, though agreeing that the content of revelation is "given" to man as an objective reality and is not produced by philosophical or theological reflection, holds that revelation, or the self-manifestation of God, is nevertheless dependent upon its reception by man and that no "pure" doctrine of revelation, apart from its human reception, is possible.[26]

The sharp distinction between philosophy and theology which Tillich sets forth in connection with "the method of correlation" in his *Systematic Theology*, it might also be noted here, has not been made by him throughout his intellectual career. In his earlier work he tended to contrast philosophy and theology not in terms of a clear-cut difference in their substance and content but rather in terms of a general difference in their attitude and intention. In his *Das System der Wissenschaften nach Gegenständen und Methoden*, published in 1923, Tillich described theology as "theonomous" philosophy or "theonomous" metaphysics. The difference between autonomous, or non-religious, philosophy and theonomous philosophy, or theology, is here described as being simply that the former is primarily concerned with the conditioned and finite, regarding the unconditional only insofar as it gives these their ground, while the latter turns towards the unconditional for its own sake, using the conditioned forms to grasp the unconditional through them.[27] Though they thus differ, synthesis between them is possible and even necessary. Tillich here declares that the highest task of theonomous philosophy is "to pass beyond its own independence, bringing to expression its unity with autonomous philosophy."[28]

In his earlier period, Tillich tended to regard all philosophy or metaphysics, insofar as it does to some extent seek the unconditional ground behind everything finite, as having "a religious attitude always and necessarily."[29] As late as 1941, in his essay "Philosophy and Theology" included in *The Protestant Era*, he declared that "the division between philosophy and theology [is] impossible"[30] and described the theological attitude of ultimate concern as giving "the impulse to philosophy."[31] Here a theology which denies entirely its philosophical concern was characterized by Tillich as being "as poor and distorted as philosophy without a theological impulse."[32] In his article "The Relation of Metaphysics and Theology," published in 1956,[33] Tillich in general reaffirms the position maintained in his *Systematic Theology* but shows some signs of returning to his earlier views, as when he declares that "there is a theological element in metaphysics itself" and that "theology must use concepts . . . taken . . . from a metaphysical system."[34]

Whatever may be the shifts to and fro in Tillich's thinking on the relationship of philosophy and theology, it is the relationship implied in the method of correlation and described in his *Systematic Theology* that largely determines his latest and most mature work. Whether this way of conceiving the relationship is a valid one remains a question. Whether Tillich himself, in his constructive work, has been able to follow the procedure dictated by his avowed methodology and his conception of the proper roles of philosophy and theology is another question, the answer to which will become fully apparent only after an exposition of his thought, though we shall here attempt to give an outline of this answer. First, however, a few comments on Tillich's conception of the nature of philosophy and theology as such are in order.

If Tillich chooses to identify the philosophical enterprise with general ontology, we need not quarrel with him. The diversity of competing definitions of the nature of philosophy on the contemporary scene is an obvious, even if regrettable, phenomenon; and Tillich is free to select his own definition. It is clear, however, that his conception of ontology as a general intuiting of the "structure of reality as a whole" from "no particular place" but from "pure reason"[35] alone is an impossible one, and one, furthermore, which he himself abandons when he comes to develop his own ontology. Here Tillich takes, as we shall see,[36] the subject-object relation in the cognitive experience of man as a "key" to ontology, and assumes that this relation is not a unique and restricted one but one that may be used to describe being in general. Tillich's selection of this relation and, more generally, of human *Dasein*, or "being-there," as illuminatory of all being may be a useful one, leading him, as it does, to an interesting and valuable ontological analysis. But he should recognize that he has, in fact, chosen a particular standpoint and is not intuiting the "structure of reality as a whole" from "no particular place."

It is difficult also to accept Tillich's doctrine that the basic difference between the ontological inquiry which is philosophy and the ontological inquiry which is theology is that the former is concerned with "the structure of being in itself" and the latter with "the meaning of being for us."[37] He himself, in developing his philosophical ontology, does so, as Dorothy Emmet has pointed out,[38] by extrapolating from the teleological categories we experience in our own lives. He might defend this procedure by saying that this is the "hidden" theological element in his philosophy; but to say this is surely to explain in a rather peculiar way the simple fact, which he declines to acknowledge, that the philosopher *as philosopher* may be just as much concerned with the "meaning" as with the "structure" of being.

Again, there would seem to be no good reason why the philosopher must look "at the whole of reality" and the "universal *logos*" and refrain from looking "at the *logos* manifesting itself in a particular historical event," reserving the consideration of the latter for the theologian.[39] Why should not a philosopher take a concrete historical event as the starting-point for his philosophizing, particularly when that event has, as Tillich claims the event Jesus as the Christ to have, a *logos* or rational character?

It seems to us that, in point of fact, Tillich himself *does* "philosophize" as a Christian. The analysis which he gives of man's essential being and of his existence, and which we shall describe below, is presumably, if the method of correlation be taken to mean what he says it means, a fundamentally philosophical undertaking. Tillich admits that in performing this philosophical task the theologian may have his vision partially focused by his own ultimate concern and his personal commitment to the revelation he represents. But, in Tillich's case, the focusing seems to us to be considerably more than partial. It is true that his analysis borrows heavily from nineteenth- and twentieth-century existentialist philosophies, particularly Heidegger's philosophy of Being and Non-being,[40] and from the findings of modern depth psychology; but in its total structure it shows the unmistakable and heavy influence of specifically Christian thought. What is the entire first half of the second volume of his *Systematic Theology* if not a reinterpretation—in philosophical terminology, to be sure—of the classical Christian doctrine of sin? A philosopher of the naturalist or idealist school, without Christian convictions, would certainly not describe the human situation in the way Tillich does. Here, obviously, the sharp separation of the functions of philosophy and theology implied in the method of correlation breaks down. Tillich's own analysis of man's situation is not, as he explicitly claims, a philosophical enterprise but rather, as he himself occasionally recognizes and admits, a mixture of elements borrowed from both philosophical and theological sources. To say this is not, of course, to prejudge the validity of this analysis. That is a question we shall have to examine later.

The breakdown of Tillich's sharp distinction between philosophy and theology will become even more evident when we consider what he regards as the essentially theological aspect of his system, the "answers" to man's existential questions. These, it is his contention, are given only in the symbols of the Christian revelation which it is the business of the theologian to elaborate. But, in fact, Tillich *does,* as we shall see, give philosophical answers to existential questions and *does not* confine himself to theological or revelatory sources. His book *The Courage To Be* provides an obvious and important example. Here Tillich, after giving a philosophical description of man's finitude and the "ontological anxiety" resulting therefrom, proceeds to show how this anxiety is overcome by man's "ontological courage" derived from his participation in "being-itself."[14] Nowhere is there any reference to a Christian or other specifically religious revelation as the source of this solution. On the contrary, the courage with which every human being finds himself enabled to confront crises and threats to his existence is held to be itself the means of attaining truth about being and being-itself.

> *The courage to be in all its forms has, by itself, revelatory character.* It shows the nature of being, it shows that the self-affirmation of being is an affirmation that overcomes negation.[42]

> . . . everything that is participates in being-itself, and everybody has some awareness of this participation, especially in the moments in which he experiences the threat of non-being.[43]

Aside from this work, even in the purportedly theological passages of his *Systematic Theology,* i.e., in the second half of each major section where Tillich gives the answers to the existential questions developed in the first half, the reader may often be left to wonder whether these answers are not as much the product of the author's philosophical reflection as of his Christian faith. Is not the statement that "God is being-itself," which Tillich, as we shall see, holds to be the basic and only non-symbolic, or literal, statement that may be made about God, more the result of philosophical analysis than of Christian revelation? And is not the analysis that we shall observe him to give of the attributes of the divine life on the basis of the elements of the ontological structure, despite his specific disclaimer, a philosophical analysis more than an explication of revelatory experience?

Furthermore, philosophy, surely, cannot admit that it is able to do no more than raise questions about human existence and that the answers thereto are beyond its competence to attain. And theology, surely—if it believes that it has ultimate answers to man's questions through revelation—must claim the right not only of setting forth these answers but also of reformulating the questions in their light. Not only do philosophy and theology, as we shall see, so "behave" in Tillich's system; he himself, on occasion, acknowledges their *right* to do so. Thus, in reply to the question whether philosophy has not arguments of its own which solve the antinomies of existential reason without the "Christian hypothesis" and whether it has not also arguments of its own against atheism, Tillich says, "I answer in the affirmative, in so far as philosophy is theonomous, using 'ecstatic' and not calculating reason."[44] Here Tillich, in referring to theonomous philosophy, seems to be returning to his early position on the relationship of philosophy and theology.[45] But it is hard to understand, after his insistence that "ecstatic" reason is the mark of revelation, how he can speak of it in connection with philosophy. As far as theology and the *questions* of human existence are concerned, it will be recalled that here also Tillich admits[46] that these questions should be formulated under the impact of God's answers, though insisting that the unity of human questions and divine answers thereby implied belongs only to man's essential being and not to his existential state.

Whatever the relation between philosophy and theology may be in Tillich's constructive work, it will become clear, after our exposition, that it is not appropriately to be described as that of "question-and-answer." The method of correlation as he defines it is, it seems to us, a largely misleading description of his own procedure.

Tillich himself, in an autobiographical statement, has said, "as a theologian I tried to remain a philosopher and conversely."[47] This attempt to practice philosophy and theology *simultaneously* is what is very much in evidence in his mature work, particularly in his anthropology, and it is this, we suggest, that gives distinction and importance to his work.

In an age when philosophy and theology have become increasingly dissociated and the practitioners of each tend to look askance at the other, Tillich has made a sustained attempt to combine their insights and to show their relevance for one another. Against the more rabidly anti-philosophical, "Kerygmatic" theologians of the Barthian school, he insists that systematic theology—if it is to be something more than a collation of Scriptural passages—cannot dispense with the tools of philosophical terminology and analysis. More than this, his "apologetic" theology is a serious attempt to show that the doctrines of classical Christianity *do* make some significant contact with the basic questions that are being asked today about human existence, particularly the questions raised in the philosophies of the Existentialists, whom he takes to be the most acute and relevant exponents of the human condition on the contemporary scene, and that these insights and doctrines are not simply an independent system of divine truths that must be "thrown" at man. It may be permissible to doubt that Tillich's attempt accomplishes all that he claims for it, but its significance and value is beyond question.

Our general conclusion is, that as far as philosophy and theology are concerned, Tillich combines and interpenetrates insights from both realms of thought, and that both in his professedly ontological analyses and in his professedly theological interpretations. The question of the validity of these particular analyses and interpretations is, however, one that we must look into below.

CHAPTER THREE

Human Reason and Revelation

I. Introduction

TO NO SINGLE TOPIC in the doctrine of man does Tillich give more serious and sustained attention than to the nature and limits of human rationality. His discussion of this topic must surely remain, by reason both of the scope of the problems included in it and of the depth of Tillich's treatment of them, one of the most important and valuable features of his anthropology.

It is Tillich's fundamental contention that man's reason no more escapes the universal transition or "fall" from an essential to an existential state than does any other aspect of his life, and that reason, too, requires "salvation," which, in its case, comes through revelation.[1] In accordance with his professed method of correlating philosophical questions with theological answers,[2] he first presents what purports to be a philosophical description of the structure and functions of human reason in its essential state and of the contradictions and conflicts by which it is beset in its existential state, and then attempts to show, in what is professedly a theological discussion, that these conflicts and contradictions are "overcome" and reason itself is "reintegrated" and "healed" only in the Christian revelation.

We shall examine, in this chapter, Tillich's doctrine of reason in all the three aspects of it which he distinguishes: reason in essence, reason in existence, and "ecstatic"[3] reason as manifest in revelation. First, however, we must be clear what Tillich means when he uses the word reason, more specifically, what scope he assigns to human reason and what functions of man's spiritual life he intends to include within it. Tillich himself distinguishes two major concepts of reason, and declares that it is the broad "ontological" concept of reason developed in the philosophical tradition, rather than the limited "technical" concept, that encompasses all of the functions that he personally considers rational; and that it is reason as understood by the former concept rather than the latter that is, therefore, the subject of his analysis.[4] The distinction between the two concepts of reason denoted by these names requires some discussion.

The technical concept, Tillich maintains,[5] has been present in all stages of man's intellectual history but has become the predominant understanding of the nature of reason only in modern times, primarily as a result of the decline of German idealism and the emergence of British empiricism. This understanding of reason limits it to the capacity for reasoning or calculating, in the ordinary senses of these terms. Among all the realms of man's spiritual life only the cognitive is recognized as a proper sphere of activity for reason, and within this realm reason is limited to a strictly instrumental function. Its only role is to discover means for the attainment of ends which are derived from "somewhere else."[6] What Tillich means by technical reason appears to be, in general, that kind of reason with which modern logicians, semanticists and students of scientific method have largely concerned themselves. It is reason as the instrument which makes possible the verification of empirical knowledge, the establishment of logically consistent and deductively valid forms of argument, and the semantic clarification of the meanings of words and statements.

Tillich does not deny the logical or methodological validity of such reason. On the contrary, he is willing to ascribe an important function to it even in theology.[7] What he does challenge is the claim, made by contemporary Logical Positivism and other philosophical schools, that technical reason is the exhaustive and only legitimate expression of man's rationality. He is disturbed also by the relegation, on the part of technical reason, of all noncognitive functions to the realm of mere emotion or subjectivity and by its failure to exercise any direction over norms, values and ends. In this he sees a danger that a vacuum will be created which can be filled only by non-rational or irrational forces.

In the ontological concept of reason, which he declares to be the dominant one in the classical philosophical tradition from Parmenides to Hegel, Tillich finds what he deems to be a much more adequate expression of the full and proper range of human rationality. Reason, in that ontological understanding of it which is exemplified, according to Tillich, in the great metaphysical systems of Western philosophy, is defined as "the structure of the mind which enables the mind to grasp and transform reality."[8] According to this understanding, reason is not restricted to a merely cognitive function; it is also effective in the aesthetic, practical and technical activities of the mind.[9] Beyond this, ontological reason differs from technical reason in that it does not regard emotion and passion as intrinsically irrational and does not, therefore, exclude them in its exercise. Unlike technical reason again, ontological reason does not confine itself to deliberation about means but concerns itself also with ends, values and norms. Indeed, not only such things but structures, *Gestalt* processes, and meanings as well, can be grasped, Tillich contends,[10] only by ontological reason. When technical reason does condescend to deal with these, it inevitably reduces them to something less than their full reality.

The proper relationship of technical reason to ontological reason, Tillich concludes,[11] is that of adjunct and instrument; technical reason should be "the companion of ontological reason" and its techniques of calculation and deliberation should be used "to fulfill the demands of reason."

It is, then, with reason in its broad sense, with ontological reason, that Tillich is concerned. Now, this reason must first of all be understood, he urges,[12] as both subjective and objective, that is to say, incarnate in both mind and reality. Tillich declares that it is the common assumption of all philosophers from Parmenides on that both the mind and reality have a *logos*, or rational, structure which are somehow related. A correspondence between the subjective reason individualized in the mind and the objective reason embodied in reality is presupposed in all rational functions, no matter who the employer of reason may be or to what area of reality he applies it.

> Reason in the philosopher grasps the reason in nature. Reason in the artist grasps the meaning of things. Reason in the legislator shapes society according to the structures of social balance. Reason in the leaders of a community shapes communal life according to the structures of organic inter-dependence.[13]

Tillich points out that a variety of theories have been set forth in the history of philosophy to account for the relation between what he calls "the *logos* structure of the grasping-and-shaping self and the *logos* structure of the grasped-and-shaped world."[14] He sees weaknesses in all of the traditional explanations of the relationship between mind and reality—those offered by philosophical realism, idealism, dualism and monism—but declines to issue a personal verdict concerning their relative adequacy;[15] he is content to rest his own belief in the general coincidence of the subjective and objective sides of ontological reason on what he regards as the consensus of the classic philosophical tradition.

The subject-object structure of reason is connected by Tillich[16] with the self-world correlation, which, as we shall see,[17] he regards as the basic ontological fact, or the fundamental articulation of all being. Without reason or the *logos* of being, it is his contention, the self would not be a structured center and the world would not be a structured whole. It is only because the *logos* of being becomes incarnate both in the self as subjective reason and in the world as objective reason that there is real being, instead of the mere potentiality of being, and that a real self and a real world exist in interdependence.

Since it is man who is Tillich's central interest here, it is, of course, with subjective reason, i.e., reason in the human mind, that he primarily concerns himself. To his description, then, of ontological reason on its subjective side and its essential state we must now turn.

II. The Structure and Functions of Ontological Reason in its Essential State

There are, according to Tillich, two major types of activity exercised by ontological reason. These he terms the activity of "grasping" or "receiving" and the activity of "shaping" or "reacting."[18] The two-fold operation of reason arises from the fact that it is always actualized in an individual self which is related to a world or environment from which it not only receives but towards which it also reacts. When ontological reason receives reasonably, says Tillich,[19] it grasps some thing or event in the sense of understanding it, or penetrating to its depth or essential nature, and then expressing it. When it reacts reasonably, it transforms some given material into a "*Gestalt*, a living structure which has the power of being."[20]

In the essential state of reason the activities of grasping and shaping are distinguishable, but they are not actually separated and in conflict with each other, as is the case with reason in existence.[21] The unity of these activities which is maintained in essential reason is, however, according to Tillich, not entirely lost even in existential reason. The word "experience," for example, points to this unity; one connotation of this word, he declares,[22] is the unity of insight and action. The modern philosophy of Instrumentalism also reflects the union between knowledge and action. Beyond this, the interrelationship that exists between myth and cult[23] in existential reason points, according to Tillich,[24] to the essential unity of knowledge and action. Myth, which is an expression of reason on its grasping side, and cult, which is an expression of reason on its shaping side, are interdependent and inclusive of each other. "Cult includes the myth on the basis of which it acts out the divine-human drama, and myth includes the cult of which it is the imaginary expression."[25]

Having distinguished the grasping and shaping activities of ontological reason, Tillich goes on to note that each of these activities gives rise to two rational functions. The four functions within ontological reason which his analysis leads him to distinguish are (1) the cognitive, (2) the aesthetic, (3) the organizational or legal, and (4) the organic or communal.[26] The first two belong to the receptive side of reason and the last two to the reactive side. Tillich is careful to deny that any clearly defined or permanent system of rational functions is possible, and he offers his own four-fold division as only a preliminary description. There are no sharp limits, he warns,[27] between the functions which he distinguishes, and considerable change and development have taken place in their growth in the course of history.

The cognitive and aesthetic functions, as has already been noted, pertain to the receptive side of reason. The distinction between them arises from a basic polarity which Tillich finds in reason, that between its formal and emotional elements.[28] The cognitive function is characterized by the fact that in its exercise the emphasis is on form and detachment on the part of the knower, while the element of *eros* or emotional union, though not wholly absent, is minimal. In the aesthetic function the relative importance of the roles of form and emotion is reversed. Between these two functions of receptive reason in their extreme forms there are many transitional stages. Thus, for example, philosophy, while it should be considered as an expression of the cognitive function along with technical science, is nevertheless closer to the aesthetic function than is science because of the greater degree of emotional participation involved in it; and the writing of a novel, though it should be included along with music as an expression of the aesthetic function, is closer to the cognitive function than the composition of a piece of music because, generally at least, there is more of the formal and less of the emotional element involved in writing novels than in composing music.

In the reactive or shaping activity of reason the two functions are constituted, as we have seen, by what Tillich calls the organizational or legal and the communal or organic functions. Here again the distinction is made on the basis of the polarity of form and emotion.[29] The organizational function is predominantly formal and includes such things as commercial law; the communal function is predominantly emotional and includes activities such as friendship and personal communion. Between these two functions and sharing more equally in the character of both,

according to Tillich, are such things as national community
and government.

What Tillich wishes to emphasize, contrary to the understanding of reason held by those who restrict it to the technical concept, is that all of the four functions which he has distinguished
are equally rational in the view of the ontological understanding
of reason. As he himself puts it,

> Music is no less rational than mathematics. This emotional ele-
> ment in music opens a dimension of reality which is closed to
> mathematics. Communion is no less rational than law. The
> emotional element in communion opens a dimension of reality
> which is closed to law. . . . This is the meaning of Pascal's
> sentence about the "reasons of the heart which reason cannot
> comprehend." Here "reason" is used in a double sense. The
> "reasons of the heart" are the structures of aesthetic and com-
> munal experience (beauty and love); the reason "which cannot
> comprehend them" is technical reason.[30]

It is important to note that in essential reason, according to
Tillich, the two functions belonging, on the one hand, to its
grasping side, and the two functions belonging, on the other, to
its shaping side are distinguishable from each other but not
separated. Their actual separation is a mark of existential or
disrupted reason. Even under the conditions of existence, however, the essential union of the cognitive and aesthetic functions
of reason is reflected in the transitional activities mentioned
above, such as philosophy and literature. It is also reflected pre-
eminently in myth. "The union of the cognitive and aesthetic
functions," Tillich writes, "is fully expressed in mythology, the
womb out of which both of them were born and came to independence and to which they tend to return."[31] Of the essential
unity between the legal and communal functions of reason
Tillich finds a strong reflection under the conditions of existence
in the religious cult community.[32]

Underlying the four rational functions discussed above, according to Tillich, is a polar structure which is fundamentally
constitutive of ontological reason. His description of this structure and of its three basic polarities is a centrally significant
part of his theory of reason.

The first polarity which Tillich distinguishes is that of the formal and emotional elements of reason. These elements, he contends,[33] are present in every rational act. In essential reason they are maintained in an unbroken unity. Under the conditions of existence, however, form and emotion are dissociated. The result is the separation, already mentioned above, of reason's grasping and shaping activities and the further separation of the cognitive from the aesthetic, and of the legal from the communal, functions of reason. Their separation in existence, or the exclusive emphasis on one at the expense of the other, also creates, as we shall see in the next section of this chapter, further conflicts within each function. Beyond this, as we shall note later in the fourth section, it creates special difficulties for the cognitive function of reason and poses a fundamental problem for knowledge.

The second polarity which Tillich finds within ontological reason is that of its static and dynamic elements. This polarity, he holds,[34] is present in both objective and subjective reason. It is an expression of the fact that the rational structures of both reality and the mind are characterized by duration within change and change in duration. The static pole maintains reason's structural identity within the changing processes of life, and the dynamic pole gives reason the power to actualize itself within these processes and to be expressive of their changes. Against those who question the existence of a dynamic element in objective reason on the grounds that if reality changes—as it obviously does—this is possible only because the structure of reality is itself basically unchangeable, Tillich takes his stand with the philosophy of emergent evolution. "Reality itself," he declares, "creates structural possibilities within itself. Life, as well as mind, is creative."[35] If an emergent product of nature does not comply with the demands of objective reason, it is an unsuccessful trial and disappears. The same thing is true of legal forms and social relations, which, again, can endure only if they are in accord with objective reason.[36]

The dynamic element in objective reason necessitates a corresponding dynamic element in subjective reason. Without dynamism in the rational structure of reality there would be no dynamism in the rational structure of the mind. In such a situation there would be only two elements in the rational process: (1) static reality and (2) the activity of the mind which might either grasp and shape this reality adequately or fail to do so and thus fall into what is commonly termed "error." But the fact that there is a dynamic element in both objective and subjective reason and the further fact that this element in either or both may become distorted under the conditions of existence lead, according to Tillich,[37] to the possibility of many kinds of difficulties and dangers other than simple error in the exercise of reason. Something may be defended as a static element of reason which is actually an existential distortion of it, and something may be attacked as a distortion of reason which is really a dynamic element of it. Because of the dynamism inherent in both mind and reality no act of reason, Tillich concludes, can ultimately avoid the character of risk.[38]

The third, and perhaps the most important, polarity which Tillich distinguishes is that of reason's structure and depth. Manifest within the structure of reason, both subjective and objective, is something, he declares,[39] which yet "precedes" this structure and transcends it in power and meaning. This is the depth of reason which, since it both precedes and transcends the structure, cannot be described in rational or literal terms but only by way of metaphor. Such a description of the depth of reason might call it

the "substance" which appears in the rational structure, or "being itself" which is manifest in the *logos* of being, or the "ground" which is creative in every rational creation, or the "abyss" which cannot be exhausted by any creation or by any totality of them, or the "infinite potentiality of being and meaning" which pours into the rational structures of mind and reality, actualizing and transforming them.[40]

In indicating more specifically what the depth of reason is in the various functions in which it actualizes itself, Tillich uses language that is thoroughly Platonic in spirit and intention. Thus, in the cognitive realm the depth of reason is its quality of pointing to "truth-itself," or the ultimately real, through the relative truths in every field of knowledge. In the aesthetic realm it is the quality of pointing to "beauty-itself" through the imperfect creations of art and aesthetic intuition. In the legal or organizational realm it is the quality of pointing to "justice-itself" through the acts and structures of human justice. In the communal realm it is the quality of pointing to "love-itself" through the forms of actualized human love.[41] What Tillich means by the depth of reason, and the relationship of his concept to similar ideas in the philosophical tradition, have been well described by J. H. Randall, Jr.

> Reason . . . points to something that is one step beyond the intelligible structures it actually finds. This farther step is the Source or the One of Neo-Platonism, the Imprinter of the Seal, the Original of the copy of Augustinian thought. For the Platonic tradition this stands one step "above" intellect and *Nous*; following Böhme and Schelling, Tillich locates it one step "below," in the "depths." It is the Standard by which finite human intellectual activity ultimately judges.[42]

Dorothy Emmet throws further light on what Tillich means by the depth of reason when she writes,

> In speaking of the "depth of reason" he is, I think, saying that every rational expression indicates further meaning and possibilities than it expresses. There is thus a kind of bottomlessness about reason. But there is also a quest for perfection in reason which could only be achieved in an intuitive union with reality. Tillich holds that essentially this should be possible; reason and reality should be one. But under the conditions of human knowledge we cannot have this *scientia intuitiva*.[43]

In essence reason in all of its functions, according to Tillich,[44] is transparent toward its own depth, but this transparency disappears under the conditions of existence, and the depth of reason can henceforth be expressed only in the symbolic forms of myth and cult. Tillich rejects the popular understanding of myth as primitive science and cult as primitive morality. Because of the elements of "infinity," transcending science and morality and expressive of ultimate concern, which are present in them and in the attitude of people toward them, they must be considered expressions of that depth of reason which is implicit in every rational act and process. From the point of view of reason in its essence, myth and cult should not be. They are expressions of reason in its fallen state, reason which has lost immediate unity with its own depth; but at the same time they point to this depth.

Myth and cult are supremely important for Tillich's conception of reason. He regards them as the major symbolic expressions pointing, under the conditions of existence, to what reason essentially is. Not only does each in itself reflect for him the unity of structure and depth which he holds to be maintained in essential reason, but the inseparable connection between them, i.e., the myth as the explanation of the cult and the cult as the dramatic expression of the myth, point for him, as we have already seen,[45] to the basic unity of the activity of essential reason, which has not yet been distorted by the separation of its grasping and shaping, or theoretical and practical, aspects. As we have also noted,[46] myth by itself reflects for Tillich the unity maintained in essential reason between its cognitive and aesthetic functions, and cult by itself reflects the unity maintained between its legal and communal functions. Being the expressions of existential reason and at the same time pointing to essential reason, myth and cult are thoroughly ambiguous. Nevertheless, they cannot be overcome, Tillich maintains[47] against Enlightenment theories, by rational knowledge and rational morality. They lie in a completely different dimension from that of the ordinary cognitive and communal functions of reason and cannot, therefore, interfere with them. Only if they are regarded as special rational functions in addition to the others, rather than as symbolic expressions of the depth of reason, do they come into conflict with these functions.[48]

To sum up the discussion thus far, it may be said that Tillich sees the fundamental quality of essential reason in its integrated and unified state. In reason in essence different activities and functions may be analytically distinguished. However, since the opposite elements in each of the polarities of form and emotion, staticism and dynamism, and structure and depth remain connected with each other in an undisrupted tension and no element is emphasized to the exclusion of, or at the expense of, its opposite, these activities and functions are not actually separated from each other. Moreover, there are no destructive conflicts among them or within any of them. Separation and conflict occur only when reason has "fallen" from essence to existence.

III. The Conflicts and Contradictions of Ontological Reason in its Existential State

Even in its essential state, Tillich holds,[49] reason is finite. In the state of existence, however, the finitude of reason is compounded, according to him,[50] through self-contradiction, ambiguity and conflict.

For proving that reason is finite, Tillich does not feel the need to offer any arguments of his own. Its finitude, he maintains, has been effectively demonstrated many times in the history of philosophy, notably by Nicolaus Cusanus and Immanuel Kant.

Kant's critiques, according to Tillich,[51] contain the most profound and comprehensive description of the finitude of reason. In them he has shown how the categories of reason, while enabling man to apprehend the world of phenomena, fail him when it comes to grasping the *noumenon,* or reality-in-itself. The chief characteristic of finitude is temporality, and reason is inextricably bound to the "category"[52] of time, beyond the limits of which it cannot go to reach the eternal. The other categories likewise reflect the imprisonment of man within the boundaries of finitude, an imprisonment which he tries repeatedly, but necessarily without success, to overcome. Only in the realm of moral experience, specifically in his awareness of the demand implicit in the categorical imperative, can man, according to Tillich's interpretation of Kant, approach the possibility of transcending the chain of temporal and causal conditions and apprehending the unconditioned which lies at the depth of reason.

While Tillich is thus content to rely on Kant for demonstrating the finitude of reason, he gives his own description of the contradictions within reason as it actually functions under the con-

ditions of existence. His analysis is based on the observed
conflicts between the opposite elements in each of the three
polarities which he recognizes within reason. That these elements, which in essential reason are held together in an undisrupted tension, become separated[53] under the conditions of
existence and struggle against each other in conflicts that are
destructive of reason itself is illustrated by Tillich through many
examples taken from intellectual and social history. The three
major conflicts within reason which he describes are (1) that
between autonomy and heteronomy produced by the polarity of
structure and depth, (2) that between absolutism and relativism
produced by the polarity of the static and dynamic elements of
reason, and (3) that between formalism and emotionalism, or
irrationalism, produced by the polarity of the formal and emotional elements of reason.

(a) The Conflict Between the Polar Elements of Structure and Depth as the Conflict Between Autonomy and Heteronomy

Every act of essential reason, according to Tillich, is transparent to its depth, which is here united with its structure. But
in reason under the conditions of existence, structure and depth,
as we have seen,[54] are separated; the depth of reason becomes
opaque and can henceforth be symbolized only through myth
and cult. Beyond this, Tillich attempts to show that in the state
of separation destructive conflicts break out between autonomous reason, representing the structure of reason, and heteronomous authorities, representing—or claiming to represent—the
depth of reason.

Reason which completely disregards its depth and seeks only
to actualize its structure is called by Tillich "autonomous" reason.[55] By autonomous reason he does not mean the individual
mind of a person, set in a particular time and place and conditioned by a particular environment, which arbitrarily makes
absolute claims for itself. On the contrary, autonomous reason,
as he defines it, seeks to keep itself uninfluenced by anything
which is merely the expression of an individual's particular situa-

tion and his subjective impressions and strivings. It sees these, as well as all the other contents given to it, as material to be grasped and shaped according to the universal structural laws of reason. The individual whose reason functions autonomously does not affirm his own personality-structure; he subjects himself, rather, to the universal law of reason, implied in the *logos* structure of mind and reality. Autonomous reason is independent, not in the sense of expressing the individual's willfulness, but of refusing to accept anything which transcends reason's own structure, no matter by what authority it is given.

Throughout human history, however, Tillich points out,[56] there have repeatedly arisen heteronomous authorities challenging the independence of autonomous reason and demanding that it subject itself, in one or all of its functions, to laws which are strange to, or outside of, its own structure. The resulting struggle is, according to him, not merely a conflict between reason and non-reason but a conflict within reason itself, for the genuinely heteronomous authorities challenge the independent actualization of reason not in the name of something completely outside of reason but in the name of the depth of reason, which, they claim, is disregarded in autonomous reason. "The basis of a genuine heteronomy," Tillich writes, "is the claim to speak in the name of the ground of being and therefore, in an unconditional and ultimate way."[57] It is in terms of myth and cult, for which it demands recognition as expressions of the depth of reason, that heteronomy generally opposes autonomy.[58]

Under the conditions of existence autonomy and heteronomy struggle with each other and attempt to destroy each other. In the process they tend to destroy reason itself. The resolution of the conflict between them is possible, according to Tillich, only in the recognition that both are rooted in what he calls "theonomous"[59] reason and that each is destructive when their essential unity is broken and they go their separate and conflicting ways. Theonomous reason, as Tillich defines it, is autonomous reason which is united with its own depth rather than oblivious of it. "In a theonomous situation," he writes, "reason actualizes itself in obedience to its structural laws and in the power of its own inexhaustible ground."[60] There have been, he suggests,[61]

some approximations to theonomy in history, as in the classical
synthesis in Clement and Origen and the medieval one in Bona-
ventura, but under the conditions of existence there can be no
complete theonomy. Only saved reason, or revelation, can succeed in reuniting autonomy and heteronomy. Such a reunion
is especially necessary at the present time, Tillich urges, because the autonomy, which, under the influence of technical
reason, has become dominant in modern times but has at the
same time rendered life empty and devoid of ultimate significance, is now being challenged by powerful and destructive
political quasi-heteronomies which seek to fill the vacuum
created by its disregard of the depth of reason.

(b) *The Conflict Between the Static and Dynamic*
Poles of Reason as the Conflict Between
Absolutism and Relativism

Under the conditions of existence, according to Tillich,[62] the
synthesis obtaining within essential reason between its static
pole, which maintains reason's structural identity in the life-
process, and its dynamic pole, which gives reason the power to
actualize itself in the ever-changing processes of life, is disrupted, and the two poles come into conflict with each other.
Tillich sees undue emphasis on the static pole of reason to the
neglect of its dynamic pole as productive of absolutism in
thought and social life, and overemphasis on the dynamic pole
at the expense of the static as productive of a relativism which
inevitably conflicts with this absolutism.

Tillich distinguishes two forms of absolutism, the absolutism
of tradition and the absolutism of revolution. On the surface
these would seem to be wholly different and mutually exclusive
forms but, in fact, because of the impossibility of actually maintaining for any length of time either pole of reason without in-
vasion from the other, they are alternately productive of each
other. The absolutism of tradition seeks to maintain as permanently valid certain forms of moral, political and intellectual
life. These are regarded as the eternal deliverances of reason.
The attempt, however, to maintain these absolutized forms and

to suppress the novelties produced in both thought and reality by the dynamic side of reason leads ultimately to their overthrow by the emergent forms which refuse to be suppressed. The revolutionary attack against the old conservatism which affirmed its absoluteness is itself then made by these emergent forms in the name of another absolutism which establishes itself in the place of the old. The claim of "revolutionary reason" to represent the unchangeable truth then leads to a new traditionalism which again seeks to suppress new forms but is destined, sooner or later, to be itself overthrown by these in another revolution. So the pendulum swings backward and forward between the absolutism of tradition and the absolutism of revolution whenever the static element of reason is split off from its dynamic element and emphasized at the expense of the latter.[63]

Opposed to both of these absolutisms is relativism, of which Tillich again distinguishes two varieties, positivistic and cynical, the former parallel to the absolutism of tradition, the latter to the absolutism of revolution. Tillich finds positivistic relativism importantly emphasized in that development of modern philosophy from Hume to the present which has tended to deny the existence of absolute principles and norms and to claim, rather, that truth can be established only by pragmatic tests and is always relative to a particular group or situation.[64] He points out that in the realms of law and art, for example, positivistic relativism, because of its inclination to accept the merely given and to deny that there are any absolute standards by which this given may be criticized or evaluated, can result in just as firm and unshakeable an attitude of conservatism as that produced by the absolutism of tradition, despite its theoretical opposition to the latter. Positivistic relativism, however, does not necessarily develop into conservative absolutism; it may also transform itself into cynical relativism. This kind of relativism refuses to admit the validity of any rational act whatsoever. Even rational criticism is regarded as inadmissible, since criticism involves the assumption that there are at least *some* permanently valid principles. Such relativism is aware of the self-contradiction involved in using reason to deny reason, but it accepts this contradiction in a cynical attitude of superiority or indifference to the notion that there can be any valid rational norms whatever. The vacuum that it creates is, in time, generally filled by new absolutisms.

In all realms of ontological reason, Tillich declares,[65] the attempt has been made to resolve the conflict between absolutism and relativism resulting from the disruption of the static and dynamic poles by means of "criticism." The method which criticism pursues in seeking to reunite the dynamic and static poles of reason is to accept the contingent or given, i.e., the dynamic, and then to forestall the possibility of any conflict between it and the static by reducing the latter to a pure form. But the critical attempt, which in philosophy is pre-eminently exemplified by Socrates and Kant, must be pronounced a failure, according to Tillich.[66] It failed because the static principles for which the critical philosophy made absolute claims were not as purely formal and devoid of relative content as it supposed. Under their abstract form they always reflected a concrete and relative historical situation. As a result, the critical philosophy in its development became either another absolutism, as in the later Platonic transformation of Socrates, or another relativism, as in the neo-Kantian school of the nineteenth century. Only a revelation which is simultaneously absolute and concrete, Tillich concludes,[67] can finally overcome the conflict between absolutism and relativism.

(c) The Conflict Between the Formal and Emotional Poles of Reason

In its essential state ontological reason unites formal and emotional elements. Under the conditions of existence, however, the unity, according to Tillich, is disrupted. The basic result which he believes to follow from the separation of form and emotion is, as has already been indicated,[68] the breaking of the essential unity between the grasping and shaping activities of reason and the coming of these activities into conflict with each other. This is the conflict, often noted, between theory and practice. Practice, on the one hand, tends to consider theory its inferior and refuses, in its attitude of activism, to wait for the completion of theoretical investigation. Theory, on the other hand, with its infinite horizons, cannot provide a sure basis for concrete action.[69] Though, as we have seen,[70] the separation between the grasping and shaping, or theoretical and practical, activities of reason is regarded by Tillich as never complete, the conflict that does exist between them can be finally overcome, he maintains, only in a revelation which provides a truth "which is present in spite of the infinity of theoretical possibilities" and a good "which is present in spite of the infinite risk implied in every action."[71]

According to Tillich, the separation of form and emotion also tends, as we have noted,[72] to dissociate from each other the cognitive and aesthetic functions belonging to the grasping side of reason and the legal and communal functions belonging to the shaping side of reason. Within each of these functions, it is Tillich's further contention, the conflict between form and emotion continues, producing destructive consequences.

In the cognitive function the exclusive emphasis on form without *eros* leads to the monopolistic claim on the part of technical reason, and the "controlling knowledge"[73] and formalized logic which are connected with it, to be the pattern of all knowledge. No other cognitive method is admitted as valid. This exclusively formal intellectualism, Tillich holds, is a distortion of cognitive reason, in that it prevents it from penetrating into those depths of things and events which are fathomable only through *amor intellectualis*. Formalism in knowledge, or intellectualism, provokes emotional reactions which rightfully demand that there be in the cognitive act union between the knower and the known, as well as control of the latter by the former. But these emotional reactions are themselves distortions of reason insofar as they neglect the necessity of rigorous and technically correct thinking in the attainment of knowledge.[74]

The aesthetic function of reason is another field of battle in the conflict between the polarities of form and emotion. Formalism in art or aestheticism, the attitude of "art for art's sake," emphasizes the form of artistic productions and deprecates or wholly disregards their spiritual substance and meaning. "Aestheticism," writes Tillich,

deprives art of its existential character by substituting detached
judgments of taste and a refined connoisseurship for emotional
union. No artistic expression is possible without the creative
rational form, but the form, even in its greatest refinement, is
empty if it does not express a spiritual substance. . . . The emotional reactions of most people against aestheticism are wrong in
their aesthetic judgment but right in their fundamental intention.[75]

In the legal function of reason, also, the conflict between
form and emotion manifests itself.[76] Formalism in law, or legalism, concerns itself exclusively with abstract structures and
rules and disregards the problem of the adequacy of these forms
to the human reality which they are to shape. Formal rules detached from life can become oppressive and destructive. The
emotional reactions against itself to which legalism gives rise
are valid insofar as they are instinctive recognitions of the demand that law and life be brought into harmony with each
other, but they are themselves distorted insofar as they tend to
overlook the need for form and structure in law.

The communal function of reason is the arena of still another
conflict between the polarities of form and emotion. Here
formalism issues in a conventionalism which demands obedience
to customary personal and social forms, not on the basis of any
claim to intrinsic value in their content and meaning, but merely
as forms. Tillich sees conventional formalism as a destructive
and tragic force in human life.

It tends to destroy the inborn vitality and creativity of every new
being and new generation. It cripples life and replaces love by
rule. It shapes personalities and communities by suppressing the
spiritual and emotional substance which it is supposed to shape.[77]

Yet, despite these destructive tendencies, custom and convention,
Tillich points out, have their own instrumental values in supporting and guiding personal and social life, values to which the
emotional reactions they provoke are generally oblivious.

In all four of the rational functions the result of the formaliza-
tion of reason is identical. An emotional reaction inevitably
arises against formal reason in whatever way it manifests itself,

whether in intellectualism, aestheticism, legalism, or conventionalism. But this emotional reaction solves no problems. It either
uses reason "irrationally," that is, blindly and fanatically, or, if
it repudiates all rational content and becomes nothing more than
subjective feeling, it creates a vacuum into which the forces of
a distorted reason pour. Only in revelation, Tillich concludes,[78]
is the conflict between form and emotion finally overcome and
their unity re-established.

IV. The Special Conflict between Form and Emotion (Distance and Union) in Cognitive Reason in Existence

The cognitive function of reason is implicated, as we have
seen, along with the other three rational functions, in all the
conflicts which result under the conditions of existence from the
tension between the opposing elements of reason's structural
polarities. But aside from these general conflicts from which
it suffers, cognitive reason, according to Tillich, also bears the
burden of a special conflict deriving from its own unique structure. This conflict is given special attention by him and deserves
special discussion here.

The exercise of the cognitive function, i.e., knowing, Tillich
contends,[79] is a form of union. Following the Platonic tradition,
he holds that knower and known, subject and object, must be
united in the act of knowledge. But this union is not direct; it
is mediated through detachment and separation. In order to
be united with the object of his knowledge, the knower must
also be separated from it and "look" at it "from a distance." The
requirement of maintaining between subject and object the relationship both of union and distance, participation and separation, poses the basic problem of knowledge. In that form of
knowledge which is generally called "understanding" these elements are balanced and their unity preserved.[80] But their separation from each other, and the tendency to concentrate on
satisfying the demands of one element to the relative neglect
of the other, are very common. The result of such separation and
concentration, according to Tillich, is the emergence of two
major types of knowledge, each of which is genuine and im-

portant but, nevertheless, one-sided and in need of being re-integrated with the other type.

The type of knowledge yielded by that exercise of cognition in which the attitude of detachment and distance is predominant is called by Tillich, following Max Scheler, "controlling knowledge."[81] Such knowledge is the outstanding product of technical reason. In it there is a measure of union between subject and object, for without some union there would be no knowledge at all; but it is a union in which the subject seeks only to control and manipulate the object and refuses to allow it to reveal whatever it possesses of the quality of subjectivity or self-relatedness. Controlling knowledge applied, say, to a metal is generally quite adequate. Little of the truth about it is missed thereby, for the degree of a metal's subjectivity is minimal. But to seek to know man completely through controlling or objectifying knowledge is a misguided venture which can yield only a distorted picture.

A truly objective relation to man is determined by the element of union; the element of detachment is secondary. It is not absent; there are levels in man's bodily, psychic, and mental constitution which can and must be grasped by controlling knowledge. But this is neither the way of knowing human nature nor is it the way of knowing any individual personality in past or present, including one's self. Without union there is no cognitive approach to man.[82]

The second type of knowledge, that in which the element of union is predominant, is termed by Tillich "receiving knowledge."[83] The cognitive attitude that is here characteristic emphasizes the intuitive "participation" of the subject in the object. It does not seek to dismiss emotion from the cognitive act, as does controlling knowledge, but rather makes it the vehicle of union. It is only receiving knowledge, Tillich insists,[84] that can yield a true insight into such realms of reality as life, spirit, personality, community, meanings, values and ultimate concerns.

Controlling knowledge, because of its practical success, precision, and susceptibility to public and repeatable verification, has tended to assert the imperialistic claim that it possesses the only proper method of dealing with any realm of reality. The result, when applied to man, has been disastrous.

Man actually has become what controlling knowledge considers him to be, a thing among things, a cog in the dominating machine of production and consumption, a de-humanized object of tyranny or a normalized object of public communications.[85]

The philosophic movements of modern times—notably Romanticism, *Lebensphilosophie* and Existentialism—which have protested against the totalitarian claim of controlling knowledge, though justified in their motive, have lacked effectiveness, Tillich declares,[86] because they could not solve the problem of verification. He himself attempts to outline a theory of verification that will do justice to receiving as well as controlling knowledge. While denying the claim of Logical Positivism and related schools that the term "truth" must be restricted to analytic statements or to experimentally confirmed propositions, Tillich admits that "statements which have neither intrinsic evidence nor a way of being verified have no cognitive value."[87] But he insists that neither logical analysis nor scientific experimentation— nor, for that matter, pragmatism—exhausts the methods of verification.

Truth, Tillich holds, must first be recognized as more than a quality of judgments. Judgments, insofar as they express or fail to express reality, may be true or false, but basically truth is concerned with reality. Tillich places himself squarely within the tradition of epistemological realism when he declares:

The truth of something is that level of its being the knowledge of which prevents wrong expectations and consequent disappointments. Truth, therefore, is the essence of things as well as the cognitive act in which their essence is grasped. The term "truth" is, like the term "reason," subjective-objective. A judgment is true because it grasps and expresses true being; and the really real becomes truth if it is grasped and expressed in a true judgment.[88]

Now the true being of certain realms of reality may be adequately grasped, Tillich admits,[89] by controlling knowledge and the repeatable scientific experiment which is its major mode of verification. But he will not grant that the experimental method is the only proper type of verification. In addition to the experimental, there is another legitimate method of verification, the "experiential."[90] Experiential verification occurs "within the life-process itself."[91] Unlike experimental verification, "it need not halt and disrupt the totality of a life-process in order to distill calculable elements out of it."[92] The experiential method, Tillich holds,[93] corresponds to the cognitive attitude of receiving knowledge, as the experimental method corresponds to that of controlling knowledge. The essence of the experiential method is "the creative union of two natures, that of knowing and that of the known."[94] To such things as life-processes, which have the character of totality, spontaneity and individuality, the application of the experimental method is insufficient. It may yield a great deal of valuable knowledge, but its limits are indicated by the fact that it must necessarily isolate and dissect. In relation to life-processes this method must be supplemented by the experiential, the method of "participation" and "intuition." The same necessity obtains, Tillich declares,[95] in relation to historical knowledge and the knowledge of philosophical principles and norms. Philosophical systems, though repeatedly refuted in terms of controlling knowledge and rational criticism, survive and are verified by "their efficiency in the life-process of mankind. They prove to be inexhaustible in meaning and creative in power."[96]

The experiential method of verification, Tillich maintains,[97] avoids the fallacies of both rationalism and pragmatism, neither of which distinguish receiving from controlling knowledge and both of which are largely determined by the cognitive attitude characteristic of the latter, while at the same time it "somehow" combines the valid elements in each. Receiving knowledge and the experiential method of verification, he is willing to admit,[98] do not give the same kind of certainty as controlling knowledge and the experimental method, but it is only the former that are appropriate to most of the truly significant problems. This poses the basic difficulty of cognitive reason.

Knowledge stands in a dilemma; controlling knowledge is safe but not ultimately significant, while receiving knowledge can be ultimately significant but it cannot give certainty.[99]

The recognition of this problem must lead, Tillich concludes, either to skepticism or to the quest for revelation,

> for revelation claims to give a truth which is both certain and of ultimate concern—a truth which includes and accepts the risk and uncertainty of every significant cognitive act, yet transcends it in accepting it.[100]

Whether Tillich's experiential method of verification really adds anything to the rationalistic and pragmatic methods, and whether the problem he has described is solvable only through revelation, are questions which must be left to the concluding critical section of this chapter.

V. Ecstatic Reason Or Reason In Revelation

It is Tillich's basic contention that the conflicts and contradictions of reason in existence, and particularly of its cognitive function, are finally overcome only in the situation of revelation in which reason becomes "ecstatic" or "self-transcending."

Revelation, according to Tillich's definition, is the manifestation of the "mystery" of the "ground of being" or "being-itself," mediated through an objective "miracle" and received through the subjective "ecstasy" of the mind.[101] All of these terms require discussion and explanation.

A mystery, Tillich holds,[102] is not something presently unknown which may become known in the future through a given cognitive approach. Nor is the term mystery properly applied to realms of reality such as qualities, *Gestalten*, meanings, or values; these, though not to be grasped by the ordinary methods of experiment or quantitative analysis, are not opaque to other, more adequate, methods. A mystery is something which "cannot lose its mysteriousness even when it is revealed."[103] A mystery, when revealed, does not become dissolved into ordinary knowledge, for such knowledge is bound to the subject-object structure of experience, and mystery characterizes a dimension which "precedes" this structure.[104] The ultimate mystery, according to Tillich, appears when "reason is driven beyond itself to its 'ground and abyss,' to that which 'precedes' reason, to the fact that 'being is and non-being is not' (Parmenides), to the original fact (*Ur-Tatsache*) that there is *something* and not *nothing*."[105]

Being-itself, or the ground of being, is the ultimate mystery. In the revelation of this mystery there are two sides, a negative and a positive. The negative side is expressed in the "ontological shock" that seizes the mind when it realizes that the "stigma" of finitude, or the threat of non-being, is in all things, and in the whole of reality. Here the "abysmal element in the ground of being" is revealed.[106] On the positive side, the mystery "appears as ground and not only as abyss. It appears as the power of being, conquering-non-being. It appears as our ultimate concern. And it expresses itself in symbols and myths which point to the depth of reason and its mystery."[107]

Neither the "ontological shock," though it is expressed in the basic philosophical question—the question of being and non-being—nor the positive revelatory experience in which the conquest of non-being by the ground or power of being becomes manifest, is the product of ordinary reason. On the contrary, both are the results of reason which has reached its extreme boundary, where it has been "thrown out of its normal balance, shaken in its structure."[108] The experience in which this occurs is called by Tillich "ecstasy," and the reason which has been thus shaken in its structure "ecstatic reason." Ecstasy is not to be confused with overexcitement or enthusiasm. Though it has a psychological and subjective side, it is not merely psychological or subjective. It is an objective state in which the mind actually transcends its ordinary situation.[109] But the ecstatic state, Tillich insists, is not irrational or anti-rational. Ecstatic reason is not the negation of ordinary reason but its fulfillment. What happens in ecstatic reason is that the mind "transcends the basic condition of finite rationality, the subject-object structure";[110] but ecstatic reason remains reason and does not negate what is ordinarily called rational.[111] The experience of ecstasy, Tillich further maintains, cannot be voluntarily induced. The ascetic and meditative practices of the mystics are merely preparatory; the actual experience of ecstasy is "due exclusively to the manifestation of the mystery in a revelatory situation," wherein the mind is "grasped" by "the ground of being and meaning."[112]

Ecstasy, Tillich admits, is similar to "demonic possession" in one respect, namely, that in both "the ordinary subject-object structure of the mind is put out of action."[113] But demonic possession destroys the rational structure of the mind, whereas divine ecstasy affirms and elevates it, while at the same time transcending it. In demonic possession the ethical norms and logical principles of ordinary reason are denied; in ecstatic reason they are affirmed. In the state of demonic possession, Tillich holds,[114] the mind is not really "beside" or "beyond" itself; instead, it has been seized by some partial elements which seek to make themselves masters of the whole and thereby destroy its rational structure.

The ecstatic experience is correlated with that objective event in which the mystery of being reveals itself and which Tillich calls a "miracle." A miracle, as he defines it, is not a supernatural interference with, or suspension of, the natural order; it is a "sign-event" which "produces astonishment" and "points to the mystery of being."[115] Miracles are essentially the expressions of that finitude, or threat of being overcome by non-being, to which everything is inescapably subject.

> As ecstasy presupposes the shock of nonbeing in the mind, so sign-events presuppose the stigma of nonbeing in the reality. In shock and stigma, which are strictly correlated, the negative side of the mystery of being appears.[116]

Tillich points to the fact that in many miracle stories there is included a description of the "numinous"[117] dread felt by those who participate in the miraculous events and are witnesses of them. Non-being has here been revealed to them, and this dread is the concomitant of the revelation.

There is no such thing as a public and "objective" miracle. For any event to become a miracle it must be received in an ecstatic experience. Actually, in order to be considered a miracle an event must fulfill three conditions.

> A genuine miracle is first of all an event which is astonishing, unusual, shaking, without contradicting the rational structure of reality. In the second place, it is an event which points to the mystery of being, expressing its relation to us in a definite way.

In the third place, it is an occurrence which is received as a sign-event in an ecstatic experience.[118]

Because of the essential correlation between ecstasy and miracle, it is possible to interchange these terms. "One can say that ecstasy is the miracle of the mind and that miracle is the ecstasy of reality."[119]

Revelation, or the manifestation of the mystery of being, can occur, Tillich maintains,[120] through any medium. In principle there is nothing debarred from becoming an instrument of revelation. On the contrary, since every person and every thing participates to some degree in "being-itself," or the ground and meaning of being, it may by that very fact become a medium of revelation. Revelation occurs when anything becomes transparent to its own depth, to being-itself as distinguished from the structure of being. Natural objects, historical events, groups, and individual persons—all have been, and may be, media of revelation. So may words, when these point beyond their ordinary sense both in denotation and expressiveness.

In the situation of revelation, language has a denotative power which points through the ordinary meaning of words to their relation to us. In the situation of revelation, language has an expressive power which points through the ordinary expressive possibilities of language to the unexpressible and its relation to us.[121]

But against the position of mystics, philosophical idealists and spiritualists[122]—Tillich denies that there is any such thing as "inner revelation" occurring "in the depths of the soul" through an "inner word," spoken by man to himself or recalling and making actual and a matter of consciousness what is potentially present in man.[123] Man in the state of existential estrangement from the ground of being, Tillich insists,[124] cannot by himself attain the message of the New Being. This must be spoken to him in revelation. Nothing, however—neither natural objects nor historical events nor groups nor persons nor words—can be a medium of revelation unless it appears in a "miraculous" constellation which shakes the mind and serves as a sign-event, and unless it is existentially received in a state of ecstasy.

What kind of knowledge does Tillich believe the revelatory situation to produce? The "knowledge of revelation,"[125] he tells us, is not ordinary knowledge or an addition thereto. "Knowledge of revelation does not increase our knowledge about the structures of nature, history, and man."[126] It has nothing to do with scientific or practical knowledge and can neither supplement nor interfere with them, just as they cannot supplement or interfere with it. Receivable only in the special revelatory situation described above and communicable only to those who participate existentially in this situation, revelation does not give information about the nature of finite beings and their relation to one another but rather partially unveils the mystery of being-itself.[127]

Knowledge of revelation is fundamentally knowledge of God. As such, Tillich holds,[128] it is analogous or symbolic knowledge. It is mediated by what medieval philosophy and theology called the *analogia entis,* the "analogy of being" between the finite and the infinite. But this does not mean that the philosopher or theologian can himself create, through the *analogia entis,* a rational or natural theology; the *analogia entis* points rather to the form in which all knowledge of God, being necessarily mediated through finite objects or persons, must be expressed. The term "religious symbol" is similar in that it likewise points "to the necessity of using material taken from finite reality in order to give content to the cognitive function in revelation."[129]

It is Tillich's contention that the necessity of using the *analogia entis* and finite objects in order to express whatever knowledge of God is given in revelation does not in any way diminish the cognitive value of revelatory knowledge. The truth value of revelation, he maintains,[130] cannot be judged by criteria similar to those used in ordinary knowledge; it must be judged by its own implicit criterion, which is itself given in revelation. Both the classic example of revelation and of the criterion which is to be used in judging its truth are to be found, according to Tillich,[131] in the event which he calls "Jesus as the Christ." This event, he contends, both on the basis of his "critical phenomenological" approach[132] and his ultimate concern as a Christian theologian, is the final revelation, in the sense of being "the decisive, fulfilling, unsurpassable revelation, that which is the criterion of all the others."[133] Within this revelatory event is also to be found the basic criterion which justifies its claim to be the final one, namely, "that a revelation is final if it has the power of negating itself without losing itself."[134]

Tillich believes that revelations, though genuine, can be—and, in man's corrupted state, are—distorted. They give rise to idolatry, understood as the identification of a finite object in which the divine manifests itself with the divine itself, and to the confusion of preliminary with ultimate concerns.[135] Hence, the need for a final revelation in which the tendency to idolatry and the elevation of the preliminary to the ultimate is overcome through the rejection, by the medium of revelation, of all claims for itself. The revelation which is the event Jesus as the Christ, qualifies for finality by negating itself, inasmuch as the historical man Jesus, who is the finite medium of revelation, overcomes, according to Tillich, all of his finite conditions by sacrificing them and himself as well. Completely united with God while participating in all the ambiguities of human life, he nevertheless makes no claim whatever for himself but becomes entirely "transparent to the mystery he reveals."[136] Not Jesus, but the Christ "as the one who sacrifices what is merely 'Jesus' in him"[137] is the bearer of the final revelation. The surrender of all claims on behalf of his own person or doctrine makes the finite Jesus the medium of a revelation that is universal without being heteronomous. Jesus, Tillich declares, "stands the double test of finality; uninterrupted unity which the ground of his being and the continuous sacrifice of himself as Jesus to himself as the Christ."[138] It is to this sacrifice that the Cross, the basic symbol of Christianity, points.

According to Tillich, the final revelation in Jesus as the Christ "overcomes" all of the conflicts arising in reason under the conditions of existence as a result of the separation of its polarities. It overcomes, first, the conflict between autonomy and heteronomy deriving from the separation of the poles of structure and depth. Inasmuch as Jesus is completely united with, and transparent to, the ground of being, the depth of reason is maintained.

> The presence of the divine ground as it is manifest in Jesus as the Christ gives a spiritual substance to all forms of rational creativity. It gives them the dimension of depth, and it unites them under symbols expressing this depth in rites and myths.[139]

But also, inasmuch as Jesus sacrifices his finite person and makes no claims for himself, heteronomy is prevented "from establishing itself against rational autonomy."[140] Instead of either autonomy or heteronomy, the situation of theonomy is established in religion and culture. In this situation reason is neither subject to revelation nor independent of it, but autonomous and heteronomous reason are united. The cognitive function of reason does not merely pursue knowledge for its own sake, nor does it develop heteronomously authoritative doctrine; it seeks in all things, rather, the depth of reason, "the truth of being as being, the truth which is present in the final revelation."[141] The aesthetic function of reason in the situation of theonomy does not produce works of art in which the depth of aesthetic reason is lost, nor does it subject itself to religious or political authorities. "Through its autonomous artistic forms it points," Tillich declares, "to the New Being which has appeared in final revelation."[142] The legal function of reason avoids both the autonomous tendency to interpret laws in technical-utilitarian terms and the heteronomous claim that they are divinely sanctioned and untouchable; it seeks, instead, to relate all laws to what Tillich calls "the justice of the Kingdom of God" and to the *logos* of being as manifest in the final revelation.[143] Finally, the communal function of reason neither autonomously relegates human relations to the realm of natural process nor accepts ecclesiastically or politically dictated communal forms; what it seeks rather to do is to relate all human relations "to the ultimate and universal community, the community of love, transforming the will to power by creativity and the libido by *agape*."[144] These, Tillich maintains, are the results when the poles of structure and depth in reason are reintegrated through the final revelation and theonomous reason is established, as, he claims,[145] it is, though fragmentarily and ambiguously, in the community of the New Being or the Church.

The final revelation, Tillich further maintains, also "overcomes" the conflict between absolutism and relativism which derives from the tension between the static and dynamic poles of reason. It does this by presenting a "concrete absolute"—the picture of Jesus as the Christ. A personal life, "the most concrete of all possible forms of concreteness," is here "the bearer of that which is absolute without condition and restriction."[146]

> The paradoxical Christian claim is that this picture has unconditional and universal validity, that it is not subject to the attacks of positivistic or cynical relativism, that it is not absolutistic, whether in the traditional or the revolutionary sense, and that it cannot be achieved either by the critical or by the pragmatic compromise. It is unique and beyond all these conflicting elements and methods of existential reason.[147]

No special trait of this picture can or should be used, Tillich holds,[148] as authority for absolute laws, absolute ethics, absolute doctrines, or absolute ideals of personal and social life. Jesus sacrifices all personal claims and thereby makes himself completely transparent to the mystery of God, with whom he is in unbroken unity. Only one absolute law can be derived from the final revelation, or the picture of Jesus as the Christ, and that is the "law of love." In love absolutism and relativism are united and the conflict between them overcome.

> Love is always love; that is its static and absolute side. But love is always dependent on that which is loved; and therefore it is unable to force finite elements on finite existence in the name of an assumed absolute. The absoluteness of love is its power to go into the concrete situation, to discover what is demanded by the predicament of the concrete to which it turns. Therefore, love can never become fanatical in a fight for an absolute, or cynical under the impact of the relative. This refers to all realms of rational creativity. Where the paradox of final revelation is present, neither cognitive nor aesthetic, neither legal nor communal, absolutes can stand. Love conquers them without producing cognitive skepticism or aesthetic chaos or lawlessness or estrangement.[149]

Though Tillich claims that love overcomes the conflict between relativism and absolutism even in the theoretical realm, he gives particular emphasis to its capacity for overcoming this conflict in the practical realm. Love makes decision and action possible by surrendering the claim that "right" decisions are attainable.

> There are no right decisions; there are trials and defeats and successes. But there are decisions which are rooted in love, which by resigning the absolute do not fall into the relative. They are not exposed to the revenge of the excluded possibilities because they were and still are open for them. No decision can be annihilated; no action can be undone. But love gives meaning even to those decisions and actions which prove to be failures. The failures of love do not lead to resignation but to new decisions beyond absolutism and relativism.[150]

The final revelation, Tillich concludes, also "overcomes" the general conflict between formalism and emotionalism in all the functions of reason and, particularly, the special conflict between the requirements of detachment and union in the cognitive function. This revelation, he suggests, might be subsumed under what classical philosophy and theology called *gnosis*, which has implications of mystical and sexual, as well as cognitive, union.[151] *Gnosis* does not contradict *epistēmē*—detached scientific knowledge—because "the same *Logos* who taught the philosophers and legislators is the source of final revelation and teaches the Christian theologians."[152] Though Tillich admits the possibility and even the very real and constantly actualized danger that emotion may distort truth, he insists that the final revelation is beyond the alternatives of formal detachment and emotional union.

> . . . that which can be grasped only with "infinite passion" (Kierkegaard) is identical with that which appears as the criterion in every act of rational knowledge. . . . The ultimate concern about the final revelation is as radically rational as it is radically emotional, and neither side can be eliminated without destructive consequences.[153]

VI. Criticism and Evaluation

There is little doubt that Tillich has performed a valuable service in joining other noted philosophers[154] in recalling that classical concept of the range of human rationality which he terms "ontological" and in emphasizing that man's reason is not only properly involved in many human activities beyond cognition but that reason also need not exclude emotion. Though it may be doubted whether Tillich has been altogether fair to the actual practice of scientists in general in his suggestion that they restrict themselves in their work entirely to what he terms technical reason and controlling knowledge, there is little question that he is justified in denying the extreme claims made by some scientists and by the Logical Positivists and analytic philosophers for these specialized methods.

Our first major difficulty with Tillich's doctrine of ontological reason arises in connection with his contention that there is a correspondence or coincidence between its subjective and objective sides. The meaning of subjective reason is relatively clear, but that of objective reason seems to us thoroughly ambiguous. Is objective reason what Tillich sometimes calls "the *logos* of being," the objective rational structure of reality which is "there," to be discovered by the inquiring mind; or is it perhaps only the logical structure of organized knowledge and interpretation superimposed, as Kant would say, on an ultimately unknowable reality by the human mind? If it is the former, is there any ground, beyond a vague appeal to the "common assumption of all philosophers" from Parmenides on,[155] for favoring the Hegelian doctrine of the coincidence of the real and the rational in preference to the Kantian critical view? If it is the latter, then should not Tillich explicitly adopt the classic idealist explanation according to which the correspondence between the mind and reality is there because the constructive activity of the mind, or subjective reason, has put it there? Or is it, perhaps, Tillich's view that the "structures" of objective reason are intuited by a Husserlian phenomenological method and that the question of their actual existence is to be bracketed? A definite stand, it would seem, is required here on Tillich's part, if ambiguity and misunderstanding are to be avoided.

Furthermore, Tillich has left it uncertain, to us at any rate, whether he regards the coincidence of its subjective and objective sides as a characteristic only of reason in essence or also of reason in existence. The general trend of his thought seems strongly to indicate that as far as existential reason, or reason estranged from its depths, is concerned, he accepts the Kantian doctrine of its radical incapacity to grasp ultimate reality, but the matter is by no means as clear as we would wish.

With Tillich's classification of the activities and functions of ontological reason we are not inclined to quarrel. They are useful and enlightening, though, as he himself admits, there can be no clearly defined or permanent system of rational functions. We cannot, however, but question his contention that "music is no less rational than mathematics" or that "communion is no less rational than law."[156] Music may have its own rational form of structure[157] and it may "open a dimension of reality which is closed to mathematics,"[158] but it seems fairly clear that the possibilities of its cognitive use are very limited by comparison with those of mathematics. With all due respect to the rational character of the other functions, which Tillich is quite right in emphasizing since it has often been overlooked or denied, we should still be inclined to insist that cognition is *the* pre-eminent rational function.

It is in his description of the three fundamental polarities of human reason that we encounter more serious problems. First of all, we assume that Tillich would not regard these as the only polarities in the structure of reason, but it is disappointing to see that he fails to mention any others.[159] His analyses of the polarities of form and emotion and of the static and dynamic elements of reason are a significant contribution, and their value in illuminating many intellectual problems, both of the historical past and of the present, is to be acknowledged. But in his description of the third and most basic of the polarities, that of structure and depth, we find a number of difficulties.

Just what is the "depth of reason"? Tillich's language in describing it, while admittedly metaphorical, would appear to indicate that he follows the tradition of Augustinian Platonism[160] in identifying it with God, though Tillich's God is more than the Augustinian Ultimate Truth or Logos, since he also manifests himself as "the power of being" in all things. His use of the word "theonomy" to describe the union of structure and depth is another indication that it is just such an identification that he intends. Knowledge and truth are not merely regarded, as they have been by many philosophers, as ultimately dependent upon God, but God himself, at least in one of his aspects, is identified with what Plato called "truth-itself."[161]

If, however, Tillich's "depth of reason" is not to be identified with God but rather to be interpreted naturalistically as merely a way of saying that reality is inexhaustible and must forever elude full comprehension on the part of man's finite reason, then Tillich should cease speaking about the coincidence of subjective and objective reason. It seems to be his conviction, however, that reality *is* fully fathomable both in reason in essence (which is, of course, more a normative than a descriptive idea) and in revelation.[162] With regard to reason in essence, he writes, "Essentially reason is transparent towards its depth in each of its acts and processes."[163] And concerning revelation, he declares, "Revelation is the manifestation of the depth of reason and the ground of being."[164] With Tillich's normative statement that mind and reality *should* be one we would not wish to disagree. The question of the truth of his claim, however, that in revelation they *are* actually one must be looked into further below.[165]

In Tillich's discussion of the conflict between autonomy and heteronomy, deriving from the tension between the polarities of structure and depth, another problem arises. Our difficulty here lies in the notion of heteronomous reason as representing the depth of reason. Does heteronomous reason *actually* represent the depth of reason, or does it only *claim* to do so? Tillich is not at all clear on this point. He seems to suggest that "genuine" heteronomies do represent the depth of reason, but no criteria are given by which genuineness is to be determined. Furthermore, the question may be raised whether the struggle between autonomy and heteronomy is really, as Tillich asserts, a struggle *within* reason. The general drift of his discussion seems to imply that heteronomy is not a representative of the pole of depth in the same way as autonomy is a representative of the pole of structure, but rather something which has usurped the place vacated through the loss of the dimension of depth in reason in existence. False heteronomies (and false myths and cults), at any rate, are such usurpers, and no standards are given by which to distinguish the false from the true. In the case of the former the conflict is still real, but it is a conflict between reason and non-reason and not within reason. In Tillich's entire discussion of the conflict between autonomy and heteronomy, it seems to us, there is perhaps present more than a little of the general ambiguity of the Protestant attitude toward Catholicism.

Tillich's analysis of the conflict between the polarities of form and emotion in all the functions of reason, and particularly of the special conflict between the requirements of detachment and union in the cognitive function, also presents a number of problems. We readily acknowledge the validity and importance of the general distinction which he here makes between controlling and receiving knowledge, and we are willing to concede that he has given a fairly adequate description of the former and of its limitations. We are prepared to agree also with his denial of the Positivistic claim that logical analysis and scientific experimentation are the only proper methods of verification. But what about receiving knowledge? Tillich's doctrine that knowledge involves emotional participation and a union of the subject and object is not without honorable intellectual antecedents; it derives ultimately, through a long chain of tradition, from Plato's *Symposium,* where the object of knowledge and the object of love are identified. But what does it mean to say, for example, that "without a union of the nature of the historian with that of his object, no significant history is possible"?[166] How can there be a "union" between two entities so radically different from each other as "the nature of a historian" and, say, a historical document? And what can "union" mean here? If Tillich means by this that the historian must bring to his reading of a historical text not only a knowledge of the relevant facts and complete philological competence but also the qualities of imagination, insight and empathy, we readily agree. But if he means that there must be an emotional concern and a positive commitment on the part of the historian to the ideas expressed in the document, we deny that this is necessary in order to "understand" it properly and assert, to the contrary, that it may well lead to radical misunderstanding. But perhaps Tillich means to say that "objective" truth is here impossible of attainment in any case, and that an emotional, intuitive approach is more capable of making the document "come alive" than a critical, factual and detached approach.

Our real difficulty, however, lies in what Tillich calls the "experiential method" of verifying "receiving knowledge." Does this method, as Tillich describes it, actually advance beyond pragmatism? We fail to see that it does. What does "efficacy in the life-process of mankind,"[167] which Tillich claims as the verifying test of philosophical principles and systems, mean and wherein does it go beyond pragmatism? Tillich may be right in his contention that pragmatism is "largely determined by the attitude of controlling knowledge and tied up with the alternatives implied in it,"[168] but we cannot accept his unexplained and dogmatic assertion that his experiential method of verification "somehow combines the pragmatic and the rational elements without falling into the fallacies of either pragmatism or rationalism."[169]

We conclude that Tillich's epistemology and theory of verification are quite weak. But perhaps this is due less to lack of logical power than to a conviction on Tillich's part that absolute knowledge and absolute truth are finally unattainable by man. Is this Tillich's real view? We must consider his doctrine of revelation and his claims concerning the capacities of ecstatic reason before we can answer this question.

We have already indicated Tillich's indebtedness to Rudolf Otto for his doctrine of revelation, an indebtedness which he has himself acknowledged.[170] We may add here that we are persuaded that the phenomenological approach to revelation (and God) through man's experience of what Otto calls "the holy" or "the numinous" and Tillich calls "the unconditional," rather than through the traditional philosophical and theological arguments, is thoroughly justified as the most valid and promising approach to the problem. Tillich's doctrine of revelation, be it also noted, is a much more "human" and "philosophical" one than that, say, of Karl Barth, who refuses to admit that the divine self-manifestation is in any way dependent upon man. For Tillich, the content of revelation is also completely independent of man, but its reception is definitely conditioned by human existence. For Tillich, we may also add, revelation is in no sense supernatural. Both "ecstasy" and "miracle" are natural events. Events which are called miracles are extraordinary only in the sense of being experienced as particularly weighted with the sense of the depth and mystery of existence.

We do not here intend to criticize Tillich's entire doctrine of revelation as outlined above.[171] We wish rather to call attention to certain problems in its crux, namely, the situation of the individual in which, Tillich believes, the revelation of "the mystery of being" may occur: the experience of ecstasy, or the transformation of ordinary reason into ecstatic reason.

That a "shaking" of the mind is a dominant characteristic of revelatory experiences as recorded in the world's religious literature is certainly to be granted. Tillich describes the result of this shaking as a transcendence of "the basic condition of finite rationality, the subject-object structure."[172] This transcendence, apparently, creates a kind of immediate awareness in which there is no consciousness of a separation or gulf between a perception, or an idea, and its object. Such awareness can occur, as Dorothy Emmet points out, even "in a low form of sense perception."[173] Tillich believes that the subject-object structure is transcended both in the ecstasy of revelatory experience and in demonic possession.[174] But this creates a problem. How are ecstasy and demonic possession to be distinguished? Tillich holds that they are differentiated by the fact that in demonic possession "the ethical and logical norms of ordinary reason" are denied while in ecstasy they are affirmed. This, however, is a notoriously difficult criterion to apply. Was the revelation to the biblical Abraham of the divine command to sacrifice his son, we may ask (following Kierkegaard), demonic possession or ecstasy? And even if it be allowed that "the ethical and logical norms of ordinary reason" constitute clear-cut and easily applicable criteria, how does ecstatic reason in revelation basically differ from ordinary reason, aside from an emotional "shaking," seeing that it merely affirms and elevates the principles of ordinary reason?

Indeed, Tillich admits[175] that reason plays an important part in "the revelatory situation." In his discussion of what he calls "universal revelation," he insists that the rational creations of the philosophers and their rational criticism of "distorted revelations" contribute, along with mysticism and prophetism, to the emergence of new revelatory constellations. His explicit claim is that the participation of reason in revelation is "indirect," but it would seem, in view of his concept of ecstatic reason as affirming and elevating the principles of ordinary reason, that he should grant a much closer affinity between this reason and the ecstatic reason of revelation.

Much of Tillich's doctrine of ecstasy and ecstatic reason is undoubtedly valid. He seems to be perfectly correct in his assertion that there have been, and are, certain situations in which people find themselves shaken and grasped by a feeling of what might be called the mystery of existence, and, if he wishes to call such experiences ecstatic and the mental situation in which they occur ecstatic reason, he is certainly justified in doing so. There seems to be little doubt, furthermore, that in such experiences reason may be more creative than it ordinarily is and its power of insight greatly heightened. If Tillich wishes to call this revelation, there is again no good reason why he should not do so. But, we repeat, to claim that ecstatic or revelatory reason and ordinary reason are radically different seems unjustified in view of Tillich's own admissions.

The question of the cognitive value of ecstatic reason, and particularly of the validity of Tillich's claim that the ecstatic reason which receives the final, or Christian, revelation overcomes the conflicts and contradictions of ordinary reason, must still be examined; but first a comment concerning the relationship of "ecstatic" reason to "theonomous" reason may be in order. In general, the relationship appears to be one of identity. Ecstatic reason is held by Tillich to open the way to an apprehension of the depth of reason, or the unconditional element in every act of reason, without contradicting the structure of reason; and the-onomous reason is defined as a union of structure and depth. The major distinction seems to be that when speaking of ecstatic reason Tillich insists upon the necessity of its correlation with an objective "miracle" received in an existential attitude, whereas when speaking of theonomous reason he does not mention these prerequisites. His final conclusion seems to be that both theon-omous reason and ecstatic reason appear only in the revelatory situation, wherein ordinary reason is transformed and "saved."[176]

It is Tillich's contention, as we have seen, that the knowledge of revelation has nothing to do with ordinary knowledge and can neither support it nor come into conflict with it. If this is merely a way of saying, as it in part undoubtedly is, that knowledge of God or the unconditional is *sui generis* and incommensurable with the knowledge of finite beings, we readily agree. But is it really true that the knowledge of revelation cannot conflict with ordinary or scientific knowledge? We cannot help wondering if Tillich would assert, as he should if he wishes to be consistent, that the Christian revelation would in no way be affected if, *per impossibile*, scientific research definitely proved that the man Jesus never existed. This, it would seem, is a historical conclu-sion that he could not accept in view of his insistence that Jesus as the Christ is not a mere category or idea but a reality which has actually occurred in time and space.

We come now to the question whether the final revelation, as Tillich conceives it, does actually overcome the conflicts and contradictions of existential reason. We must first confess that we cannot pretend to a full comprehension of what Tillich means by the criterion according to which he judges the revelation of Jesus as the Christ to be the final one, namely, "that a revelation is final if it has the power of negating itself without losing itself";[177] and we must add that, insofar as we do understand this criterion and its application to the revelation in question, it seems to us that in negating himself Jesus does in fact lose himself, or perhaps more accurately, in being negated by Tillich he is in fact largely lost by Tillich.

Tillich maintains that the revelation of Jesus as the Christ overcomes the conflict between autonomy and heteronomy deriving from the separation of the poles of structure and depth in reason by reuniting these poles and establishing a situation of theonomy. In this situation reason's autonomous structure is affirmed, according to Tillich, since Jesus sacrificed himself and surrendered all personal claims, thereby preventing heteronomy "from establishing itself against rational autonomy."[178] That the affirmation of autonomous reason would, in fact, be guaranteed by such sacrifice and surrender, *if it occurred,*[179] we are prepared to admit; but we cannot help wondering if the price is not too high and if most Christian theologians would not ask whether, in Tillich's doctrine that Jesus negates all personal claims for himself, Jesus is not lost as the unique person classical Christian thought has considered him to be throughout the centuries. Our real difficulty at this point, however, is with the second half of Tillich's claim, namely, that through the complete union of Jesus as the Christ with, and his transparency to, God or the ground of being, the depth of reason, "the truth of being as being,"[180] is revealed. If the depth of reason were truly and completely revealed, then it would seem that myth and cult would have been done away with, for these, according to Tillich,[181] are ambiguous, hiding, as well as pointing to, the depth of reason. But they are not done away with even in the final revelation.

> The presence of the divine ground as it is manifest in Jesus as the Christ gives a spiritual substance to all forms of rational creativity. It gives them the dimension of depth, and it unites them under *symbols expressing this depth in rites and myths.*[182]

So it would appear that we are still left, as in existential reason, with nothing more than symbols and rites and myths; and since we are given no clear-cut criteria by which to distinguish the true (or valid) among these from their opposites, how can we know with certainty that those of the Christian revelation are among the former?

We fail also to see that the final revelation overcomes the conflict between absolutism and relativism. A "concrete absolute" may well be a possible solution to this conflict, but we are not persuaded that Tillich's conception of Jesus as the Christ is such an absolute. A personal life may certainly be called concrete, but if the picture of Jesus as the Christ cannot serve as authority for any absolute—neither absolute laws nor absolute ethics nor absolute doctrines nor absolute ideals of personal and social life —wherein lies what Tillich calls its "unconditional and universal validity"?[183] The "law of love," which Tillich claims is the only absolute derivable from the final revelation, is rather peculiarly termed an absolute. Tillich, in calling it such, takes refuge in the word "paradox" and not in the straightforward sense in which he ordinarily defines it, namely, as that which is contrary to popular opinion or general expectation,[184] but in the sense of logical meaninglessness. The absoluteness of love is said to be "its power to go into the concrete situation, to discover what is demanded by the predicament of the concrete to which it turns"[185]—which is to say that the absoluteness of love derives from its turning to the predicament of relativities in which it can never be sure what is really "demanded." Furthermore, we may point out that Tillich, in his full ontological analysis of love,[186] has pointed out that love presupposes power and justice and is presupposed by them. These three activities are interdependent. Why, then, is one singled out here as *the* "absolute" and the others not even mentioned?

It seems to us that the conception of Jesus as the Christ which Tillich offers as the solution to the problem of the conflict between absolutism and relativism is, in fact, not greatly different from the "critical" doctrines which he cites[187] as having attempted, but without success, to solve this problem. All of the relative or contingent elements in the life of Jesus are regarded by Tillich as without essential significance; Jesus, he argues,[188] sacrificed the finite conditions of his being and, indeed, his whole life, and refused to make any claims for himself or his own doctrines. Only as the Christ, that is, as "the one who sacrifices what is merely 'Jesus' in him"[189] could he be the bearer of the final revelation. The Cross, which makes Jesus the Christ, functions in Tillich's system—it would appear—in very much the same fashion as a "critical" principle, preventing the relative and contingent from asserting their claims. It may be questioned, however, whether Tillich's "critical" Christology as he elaborates it is finally as devoid of relative content as he believes. If it is not, then it is no more successful than the Socratic or Kantian critical principles.

We cannot see, either, that the final revelation has overcome the conflict between formalism and emotionalism. Tillich tells us that "that which can be grasped only with 'infinite passion' is identical with that which appears as the criterion in every act of rational knowledge."[190] This criterion, we take it, is the depth of reason, or Truth-Itself, or God, or the Unconditional. But we have seen that this is *not* fully grasped, even in final revelation received with "infinite passion," but is still veiled by the symbols of myth and cult.

Tillich's final position is, apparently, a relativistic one. He appears to be quite skeptical of man's ability to attain absolute truth. Yet he is sufficiently acute to see that complete relativism depends logically upon the positing of at least one absolute, just as a thoroughgoing doctrine of symbolism depends upon the positing of at least one non-symbolic truth. Such an absolute for Tillich is God or the Unconditioned, and this is not attainable by anyone. No human life, not even that of Jesus, can overcome the relativity and ambiguity implicit in its finitude. Only by surrendering all finite claims can Jesus even bear witness to the absolute.

It thus appears that in his *Systematic Theology* Tillich has not really advanced beyond the position he had reached many years earlier in his essay "Kairos and Logos."[191] Here Tillich maintained that

> the judgment of absolute unequivocal truth can be only the fundamental judgment about the relationship of the Unconditioned and the conditioned . . . the content of this judgment is just this, that *our subjective thinking never can reach the unconditioned truth, that it must always remain in the realm of ambiguity.*[192]

Referring to this as "the judgment which constitutes truth as truth,"[193] Tillich declared that "the absolute standpoint is therefore a position which can never be taken; rather it is the guard which protects the Unconditioned."[194] From this he concluded that there is a need in the intellectual realm, as in the moral, for a kind of "justification through faith."

> We have characterized the absolute standpoint as a guardian standpoint, as one which is not actually a position, but only a battle, constantly changing with the opponent, against any standpoint that wants to set itself up as unconditioned. But the guardian is at the same time the one who points to the sanctuary which he guards. His existence itself is an indication. The absolute standpoint, that is, the point from which relativism is overcome, is possible only as an indication and defence at the same time. Thus the basic principle of Protestantism, the principle of justification through faith, is applied to the question of truth.[195]

Our final conclusion is that in Tillich's thinking both about human reason and about revelation there is an interpenetration of insights derived from the philosophical tradition and from Christian theology. His analysis of human reason is obviously made in the light of his doctrine of revelation. It is clear that the "questions" about reason that are raised in this analysis are put in such a way that the "answers" of revelation are relevant to them, but this seems to us in no way to diminish the considerable value of the analysis. The doctrine of revelation that he sets forth, on the other hand, is clearly influenced by philosophical considerations. Tillich takes great pains to develop a "non-supernatural" theory of revelation that will not be as philosophically objectionable as most traditional theories have been. The result is certainly a valuable one, even if it does not make possible the extensive cognitive claims on behalf of revelation that the traditional theories do. Where we must dissent from Tillich, however, is in his contention that what he calls the final revelation in Jesus as the Christ has been shown to have overcome the conflicts and contradictions of human reason. Tillich seems to us not to have proved his case and, beyond this, not to have sufficiently considered the question whether there may not be, besides the "answer" of revelation as he describes it, rational and non-self-defeating methods of adjusting these conflicts and contradictions.

CHAPTER FOUR

The Structure of Man's Being

I. Introduction

IN THIS CHAPTER we shall be concerned with Tillich's analysis of the fundamental structure of man's being. This analysis is given within the context of his general ontology, in which he correlates the philosophical questions implied in the problems of being, especially the problem of the finitude of man and all other beings, with the theological or revelatory answer of God, understood as being-itself or the ultimate and infinite ground or power of being.

Tillich's general ontology is thoroughly anthropological both in its foundation and center, for he believes, following many representatives of recent Existentialism, that man's being is the key to the nature of being in general. "Man," he writes, "occupies a pre-eminent position in ontology, not as an outstanding object among other objects, but as that being who asks the ontological question and in whose self-awareness the ontological answer can be found."[1] In and through man, it is Tillich's contention, all levels of being are united and approachable.

The analysis of man's being, rather than that of non-human entities, must be the basis of ontology, according to Tillich,[2] because while every being participates in the structure of being, only man has an immediate *awareness* of this structure. It is not because he regards man as a more easily accessible object of scientific knowledge, Tillich explains, that he approaches the problem of being by way of a phenomenological analysis of human experience rather than by way of an objective study of nature or any of the physical objects within it. Quite the contrary. Man is recognized by him as the most difficult object encountered in the cognitive process. Nevertheless, the being of man must be taken as the key to the nature of being in general because man is the only being who is aware of the "structures" which make possible cognition, or the subject-object scheme of experience.

Underlying Tillich's entire ontology is the assumption that the epistemological subject-object distinction is ultimate not only for human *knowledge* but for *all being*. The nature of being, he assumes, is revealed in the conditions of knowing. "The truth of all ontological concepts is their power of expressing that which makes the subject-object structure possible. They constitute this structure; they are not controlled by it."[3] Since man himself lives and acts and knows through the conditions which make cognition possible, his reflective self-awareness opens the door to universally valid ontological knowledge. When man analyzes the structures which make his own experience possible, the resultant concepts are not of anthropological significance alone but can be applied, at least by analogy, to all beings.

These concepts descriptive of the structure of man's experience are, according to Tillich,[4] *a priori*, not in the sense that they are known prior to experience but rather in the sense that they determine its nature. Though their explicit formulation is the product of a critical phenomenological analysis of experience, they are themselves presupposed in every actual experience, of which they are the necessary conditions. In calling them *a priori* Tillich does not mean to suggest that they constitute a static and unchangeable system. He acknowledges that the form of human experience may have changed in the past and may change in the future but insists that, given any form of experience, there must be some stable ontological structure which makes this experience possible and which can be discovered through a critical analysis of it.

Tillich is not unmindful of the objection that could be raised against his analysis by those who, holding that man's nature is continually changing in the historical process and that there is therefore no such thing as a fixed human nature, deduce from this the impossibility of an ontological doctrine of man.[5] He grants their premise that human nature does, in fact, change in history, but denies their conclusion that this invalidates an enterprise such as he here undertakes. Dynamics, he admits, is one of the basic ontological elements in man's being, and he himself gives an important place to it in his description of the ontological structure; but he insists that underlying all the changes which have taken place or may take place in man's nature is the structure of a being *which has a history*. It is with this being, *historical man*, as given in present experience and in historical memory, that his ontology is concerned. In historical man, as distinguished from the animal background which was the biological preparation for him and the superman who may possibly be his biological continuation, Tillich maintains, there is an ontological structure which is at least relatively permanent and *a priori* and which may be critically elaborated.

In developing his anthropological ontology Tillich distinguishes four conceptual levels: (1) the fundamental ontological structure, which he sees in the subject-object, or self-world, correlation; (2) the three major pairs of polar elements which constitute the basic structure of being, i.e., individuality and participation, dynamics and form, and freedom and destiny; (3) the character of finitude which, in unity with freedom and destiny, forms the turning point from essential being to existence or existential being; and (4) the basic categories of being and knowing in which finitude and its accompanying anxiety are reflected.

II. THE BASIC STRUCTURE OF MAN'S BEING: THE SELF-WORLD CORRELATION

Man's primary experience, from which the analysis of the structure of being in general must also take its rise is, according to Tillich,[6] that of *being a self having a world to which he belongs*. The existence of selfhood,[7] he holds, following Augustine, is beyond question. The awareness of self-relatedness or self-centeredness is implied in all human experience. Since it is experienced in every mental act, whether of negation or affirmation, this awareness is implicitly affirmed even when it is explicitly denied. Tillich puts the matter as follows: "A self is not a thing which may or may not exist; it is an original phenomenon which logically precedes all questions of existence."[8] The reality of man's self, Tillich further maintains, is necessarily implied in the very asking of the basic ontological question, What is being itself?

> The ontological question presupposes an asking subject and an object about which the question is asked; it presupposes the subject-object structure of being, which in turn presupposes the self-world structure as the basic articulation of being. The self having a world to which it belongs—this highly dialectical structure—logically and experientially precedes all other structures.[9]

Insofar as man is a self, he is a centered being, in some way separated from, and independent of, all other beings; and he can look and act upon these as opposite himself. Nevertheless, he is simultaneously aware that he also belongs to the things opposite himself and that his self is in some way "in" them. He is conscious that he is part of an environment of beings upon which he acts and which act upon him in mutual determination.

Self-centeredness and belonging to an environment are essential characteristics of all beings, but in man self-centeredness has developed to the point where he "possesses" himself in full self-consciousness and has become an *ego-self* and where, as a result, his environment is no longer of the same largely determining character as in the case of other beings but has become instead a *world*, upon which his own interpretive and organizing activity is exercised. As an ego-self man transcends the complete conditioning of any environment in which he may find himself and relates himself instead to the world, which Tillich defines as "the structural whole which includes and transcends all environments, not only those of beings which lack a fully developed self, but also the environments in which man partially lives."[10] It is basically by reason of his possession of language, which gives him the power to grasp and shape any given environment according to universal norms and ideas, that man can transcend this environment and relate himself to a world inclusive of all possible environments. The fact that man can selectively organize his environment by means of his own ideas and norms invalidates all theories which regard him as completely conditioned by his surroundings.[11]

Self and world are correlated. Without a world, which provides the content for all its acts of self-consciousness, the self would be an empty form. And without self-consciousness, in the actualization of which man stands apart from the world and looks upon it as opposite himself, there would be no world-consciousness. "The self without a world is empty; the world without a self is dead."[12]

The self-world polarity, according to Tillich,[13] is also the basis of the subject-object structure of reason. Without a self or mind, he suggests, there would be no bearer for subjective reason, and without a world looked at by the self or mind there would be no bearer for objective reason. On the other hand, there is a sense in which reason creates both self and world and the possibility of their correlation. "Reason," he writes, "makes the self a self, namely, a structured center; and reason makes the world a world, namely, a structured whole. Without reason, without the *logos* of being, being would be chaos, that is, it would not be being but only the possibility of it (*me on*). But where there is reason there are a self and world in interdependence."[14] Tillich, it might be added here, shows[15] how the subject-object structure of human experience, though intimately connected with the self-world correlation, nevertheless has a tendency to hide the reality of the first polar element of the correlation, that is, selfhood or subjectivity. Everything, whether a stone or man or even God, that is brought into the cognitive relationship is necessarily objectified. This objectification, of course, is a logical one, but it can have the practical consequence of hiding from the view of the knower the subjectivity that inheres in every being and transforming it for him, both in theory and practice, into a mere object, that is, a completely conditioned thing. To regard a mechanical tool, which comes closest to being a thing, as a mere object is to distort its nature, for even a tool is not completely lacking in subjectivity; to regard man as such is, *a fortiori*, to miss some of the most important truths about him.

Both sides of the self-world polarity must be recognized, Tillich insists.[16] By simultaneously affirming the independent reality of self-relatedness and world-relatedness and their correlation with each other as the basic ontological structure, Tillich believes that he is avoiding the errors both of reductive naturalism, with its unsuccessful attempt to derive the ego from the world, and of deductive idealism, with its unsuccessful attempt to derive the world from the ego. He also overcomes, he believes, the Cartesian dualism which gives rise to the impossible task of trying to reunite a completely subjective *res cogitans* with a completely objective and mechanical *res extensa*.

Tillich's solution of the relation of subject and object in his doctrine of the self-world correlation as the basic articulation of all being, it may be observed, is in some respects very close to identity philosophy. He holds that everything, insofar as it is brought into the cognitive relationship, is an object, while at the same time, insofar as there is nothing completely devoid of self-relatedness, it is a subject. Yet it is not really identity philosophy that Tillich expounds here because the polarity of subject and object, self and world, is regarded by him as an irreducible fact, and its ground, he concludes, is beyond the capacity of reason to discover.

> The basic ontological structure cannot be derived. It must be accepted. The question, "What precedes the duality of self and world, or subject and object?" is a question in which reason looks into its own abyss—an abyss into which distinction and derivation disappear. Only revelation can answer this question.[17]

III. The Ontological Elements
Constitutive of Man's Being

Man, whose primary experience of himself is that of being a centered self having a world, discovers, through reflection and critical analysis, three polarities which, according to Tillich, are fundamentally constitutive of this experience and may therefore also be considered the fundamental elements of the structure of his being.[18] These three polarities, within each of which any element is meaningful only insofar as it is seen in relation to its polar opposite, are individualization and participation, dynamics and form, and freedom and destiny. All of them derive from the basic ontological fact, the self-world correlation. Within each of them, Tillich holds, "the first element expresses the self-relatedness of being, its power of being something for itself, while the second element expresses the belongingness of being, its character of being a part of a universe of being."[19]

The polarity of individualization and participation is reflected in the fact that every being not only exists in and for itself as a centered and indivisible self but, at the same time, belongs to realms of reality outside itself in which it participates, whether consciously or unconsciously, directly or indirectly. In man individualization achieves its perfect form and reaches the level of "personality." By reason of the essential interdependence of individualization and participation, participation in man thereby also achieves its perfect form and reaches the level of "communion." Unlike that of sub-human beings, the participation of man's personal being in the universe is potentially infinite. The special character of his personal individuality, the fact that he possesses reason, language and universals, opens up to him the rational structures, laws and forms of all reality. Though he can in principle participate in all levels of being and life, man in fact participates fully and completely only in that level of being and life which he himself is; he has communion only with other persons.[20]

As the ontological elements of individualization and participation are strictly interdependent, so are personality and communion, the special forms which these ontological elements take in man. Following Martin Buber's insight that the ego becomes an "I" only through its meeting with a "Thou,"[21] Tillich declares that "there is no person without an encounter with other persons"[22] and that "the person as the fully developed individual self is impossible without other fully developed selves."[23]

Individualization and participation are interdependent, according to Tillich, at all levels of being. Their polar correlation makes relations possible. "Without individualization nothing would exist to be related. Without participation the category of relation would have no basis in reality."[24] The polarity of individualization and participation also solves the problem of nominalism and realism.[25] Pure nominalism, which admits the ontological reality of individuals only, cannot adequately explain cognition. Even empirical knowledge is dependent, according to Tillich, on the truth expressed in what he calls the "mystical realism" of the medieval tradition which "emphasizes participation over against individualization, the participation of the individual in the universal and the participation of the knower in the known."[26] But this realism, he warns, must not be understood as positing the existence of a second realm of reality behind empirical reality.

The second ontological polarity, that of dynamics and form, appears in man's immediate experience as the polar distinction of vitality and intentionality. Vitality is the special expression in man of a dynamism or potentiality of being which Tillich believes is present in all levels of being.[27] Man's vitality is his special power of being, the dynamic element in him which keeps him alive and at the same time tends to push him beyond the natural basis of his biological existence. The impulse towards self-transcendence in man's vitality distinguishes it from the dynamism or potentiality of other beings.

> The dynamic element in man is open in all directions; it is bound by no *a priori* limiting structure. Man is able to create a world beyond the given world; he creates the technical and the spiritual realms. The dynamics of sub-human life remain within the limits of natural necessity, notwithstanding the infinite variations it produces and notwithstanding the new forms created by the evolutionary process. Dynamics reaches out beyond nature only in man. This is his vitality, and therefore man alone has vitality in the full sense of the word.[28]

The unique character of man's dynamism is dependent upon his intentionality, which is the special expression in human life of the universal ontological element of form.[29] By intentionality Tillich does not understand merely man's ability to act for a consciously conceived purpose but rather his living in tension with, and toward, objectively valid structures. Intentionality means "being related to meaningful structures, living in universals, grasping and shaping reality."[30] Man's intentionality is his power of actualizing reason in the processes of life. By virtue of its correlation with intentionality, man's vitality is not undirected, chaotic and self-contained. The push of vitality towards self-transcendence is directed, through intentionality, towards objective structures and meaningful contents. Vitality is conditioned by intentionality, and *vice versa*.

Vitality and intentionality are the bases of human self-conservation and self-transcendence. In attempting to achieve self-conservation, i.e., to preserve his humanity, man at the same time transcends both nature and himself. When the conjoint operation of his vitality and intentionality result in the creation of new forms in the technical and cultural realms, man transforms nature; living in these creations, he also transforms himself.[31] But though man, through science and culture, can develop indefinitely beyond any given environmental situation, there are structural limits to his biological self-transcendence. He cannot develop beyond the structure that makes his historicity and intentionality possible. If, *per impossibile*, such a development were to take place, man as a being who lives in history and has the power of indefinite cultural self-transcendence would have disappeared. Historicity and intentionality, which are given to man by his freedom, can only be transcended through the destruction of man as he is presently constituted. As Tillich puts it, " 'Super-man,' in a biological sense, would be less than man, for man has freedom, and freedom cannot be trespassed biologically."[32]

Freedom is one side of the third ontological polarity; its opposite side is destiny. Freedom, for Tillich, is the most important of the structural elements of being, because it is through freedom that the essential necessity of being is transcended and the transition to existence, as distinguished from essence, is made possible.[33]

The nature of man's freedom is misunderstood, Tillich declares, if it is regarded as a quality of a thing called his *will*. A thing by definition is something *bedingt*—completely conditioned and determined. When freedom is ascribed to an object or function called "will," the determinist's denial of freedom is quite justified. Furthermore, the indeterminist, while right in his contention that the facts of moral and cognitive consciousness presuppose the power of responsible decision, does not really explain the reality of experienced freedom as long as he accepts the premise on which determinism is based. In merely negating deterministic necessity, the indeterminist, Tillich holds, "asserts something absolutely contingent, a decision without motivation, an unintelligible accident which is in no way able to do justice to the moral and cognitive consciousness for the sake of which it is invented."[34] Theoretically, of course, both determinism and indeterminism refute themselves, because by implication both deny their claim to express truth.[35]

Freedom, according to Tillich, is ascribable not to any one of man's special functions but to himself as a whole personality, i.e., as "that being who is not a thing but a complete self and a rational person."[36] Man's total being as a personal self is free, and every part and function which makes man a personal self, including even the cells of his body, participates in his freedom. In isolation the parts *are* subject to determination, but this does not mean that man's total being is determined.

> . . . it is impossible to derive the determinacy of the whole, including its nonseparated parts, from the determinacy of isolated parts. Ontologically the whole precedes the parts and gives them their character as parts of this special whole. It is possible to understand the determinacy of isolated parts in the light of the freedom of the whole—namely, as a partial disintegration of the whole—but the converse is not possible.[37]

In man's actual experience freedom is manifested in the facts of *deliberation, decision,* and *responsibility.* The self-centered person who "weighs" arguments or motives in the act of deliberation is above these and, as long as he has reached no decision, is not identifiable with any of them but free from all of them. In decision, again, the person who "cuts off" or "excludes" possibilities shows himself, in so doing, to be beyond, and free of, those possibilities which he does not actualize. And the word "responsibility," Tillich concludes, "points to the obligation of the person who has freedom to respond if he is questioned about his decisions. He cannot ask anyone else to answer for him."[38]

But man's freedom, though real, is certainly not absolute. It has its limits and conditions, and these constitute the destiny which, for man, is always in polarity with his freedom. The self which deliberates and makes decisions is not a pure epistemological subject, a disembodied self-consciousness. The concrete, deciding self is the product of many factors. These form its destiny and all of them enter to some degree into the decisions which it makes.

> This refers to body structure, psychic strivings, spiritual character. It includes the communities to which I belong, the past unremembered and remembered, the environment which has shaped me, the world which has made an impact on me. It refers to all my former decisions. Destiny is not a strange power which determines what shall happen to me. It is myself as given, formed by nature, history and myself. My destiny is the basis of my freedom; my freedom participates in shaping my destiny.[39]

Destiny, Tillich insists,[40] is not, like fate, a contradiction to freedom, but rather in polar correlation with it. It points to the conditions and limits of freedom. Furthermore, even insofar as the word destiny has futuristic connotations suggesting what is going to be, language still properly speaks of the freedom of men to realize or fail to realize their destines. For that matter, even fate may be accepted or rebelled against, and as long as there is this alternative man's freedom is affirmed.

The polarity of freedom and destiny, according to Tillich, is fully and properly ascribable only to man, but analogies to it are to be found at every level throughout all of nature. The polarity of spontaneity and law[41] holds sway even at the level of inorganic nature, where individual, self-centered *Gestalten* react spontaneously according to their special structures but within limits set by the laws of nature. Except in the case of the abstract equations of macrophysics, there is never complete determination or necessitation. The inductive generalizations which constitute the laws of nature, insofar as they never go beyond probability to absolute necessity, do not destroy the element of spontaneity or self-determination. By thus affirming freedom[42] throughout all of nature, Tillich again definitely locates man within nature and refuses to make a radical disjunction between them.

IV. MAN'S FINITUDE

Beyond the ontological polarities just discussed, Tillich sees the quality of finitude as the fundamental fact in the being of man as well as in that of every other existent. In unity with freedom and destiny, man's finitude forms the basis for the transition from his essential being to his existence or existential being. Tillich therefore gives a special analysis of finitude in its polarity with infinity, as well as of its relation to being and nonbeing.

Man's finitude lies in the fact that his being is limited by nonbeing. This, indeed, is Tillich's definition of finitude: "being, limited by nonbeing."[43] According to Tillich, not only does man, along with every other existent, participate in nonbeing, but he alone, by virtue of his freedom to transcend every given reality, can actually experience the "shock of nonbeing," envisage nothingness, and ask the ontological question about the mystery of being and nonbeing, that is, why there is something rather than nothing.

The nonbeing in which man participates is, Tillich insists,[44] a reality, in the sense of having a definite ontological character. Nonbeing is not simply a logical concept devised to explain the possibility of negative judgments. The possibility of making negative or erroneous judgments is itself ontologically grounded in man's participation in real nonbeing.

> What is the structure of this being which is able to transcend the given situation and to fall into error? The answer is that man, who is this being, must be separated from his being in a way which enables him to look at it as something strange and questionable. And such a separation is actual because man participates not only in being but also in nonbeing. Therefore, the very structure which makes negative judgments possible proves the ontological character of nonbeing.[45]

Nor is the nonbeing in which man and all other beings participate to be understood as pure nothingness. To understand it as such and to place it in absolute contrast with being is to exclude everything except static being itself. The whole world, with its dynamism and contingency, is thereby excluded. As Tillich puts the matter, "there can be no world unless there is a dialectical participation of nonbeing in being."[46]

Tillich appeals to the philosophic tradition as a witness to the dialectical nature of nonbeing. That nonbeing somehow has positive character was recognized, he holds, by Plato in his concept of *me on*, "that which does not yet have being but which can become being if it is united with essences or ideas."[47] Augustine also, in calling sin "nonbeing," denied actual ontological status to it but at the same time ascribed to it the power of resisting and perverting being. The Judaeo-Christian doctrine of man's creatureliness also assumed the dialectical character of nonbeing, its positive relationship to being. "Being created out of nothing means having to return to nothing. The stigma of having originated out of nothing is impressed on every creature."[48] Modern Existentialism, Tillich points out,[49] has emphasized even more radically the reality of nonbeing and given it an even more positive character and power. Heidegger with his concept of *nichtendes Nichts*, "annihilating nothingness," has shown how nonbeing threatens man inescapably in the form of death, and Sartre has included in nonbeing the threat of ultimate meaninglessness, the destruction of the very structure of being.

According to Tillich, man's finitude, the fact that his being is united with, and limited by, dialectical nonbeing, is manifest in his basic ontological structure and in the elements which have been shown to constitute that structure.

> Selfhood, individuality, dynamics, and freedom all include manifoldness, definiteness, differentiation, and limitation. To be something is not to be something else. To be here and now in the process of becoming is not to be there and then. . . . To be something is to be finite.[50]

But man's experience of his finitude, his knowledge that his being is threatened by nonbeing, depends upon the fact that he has a power of self-transcendence which is essentially unlimited. "Man's finitude implies the question of the 'infinite'; for man could not look upon himself as finite if he were not in some way beyond it."[51] Man is not, like the animals, completely immersed in the temporal flux; he can look out over his finite being as a whole from the point of view of a potential infinity and thereby imaginatively transcend his finitude. He can imagine infinity, not, to be sure, in concrete terms, but as an abstract possibility. This he can do because his finite individuality has the potentiality of universal participation, his finite vitality is in union with an essentially limitless intentionality, and his finite freedom is set within an embracing destiny. Though infinity thus stands in polarity with finitude, it is not a constitutive element of man's being, as are the elements of the three polarities previously discussed, nor something actually realized. It is a directing concept, impelling the human mind to experience its own unlimited potentialities; and it can be defined only negatively, as the dynamic and free self-transcendence of finite being.

Man alone among all other beings directly experiences his finitude, the fact that his being is threatened by nonbeing. He is consciously aware, through looking out over his finite being as a whole, that he is moving towards death. By the very fact that he can imagine infinity he becomes sharply aware of his own finitude. This self-awareness of the finite self as finite is, Tillich, declares,[52] *anxiety*.

For Tillich, as for many other Existentialists, man's anxiety or *Angst* is a fundamental quality of his being. It is the "inward" expression of his "outward" finitude and is, therefore, just as much as finitude, an ontological quality.[53] Anxiety, though often merely latent and not consciously experienced, is as omnipresent as finitude itself. Following Kierkegaard[54] and Heidegger,[55] Tillich sharply distinguishes anxiety from fear.[56] Fear is a special psychological state produced by and dependent on a special object, while anxiety is a universal constituent of man's being which is dependent on the omnipresent threat of nonbeing implicit in human finitude. The "object" of anxiety—if it may be said to have one—is "nothingness," but since this is not an object that may be acted upon, anxiety is not, as is fear, conquerable by action. This essential anxiety which is inseparable from human finitude is distinguished by Tillich not only from fear but also from neurotic or compulsory forms of anxiety.[57] The latter, which also have no special object or cause, can be removed by psychotherapy through the healing of inner conflicts, but ontological anxiety is beyond the power of psychotherapy to remove since it is occasioned by the unchangeable structure of human finitude.

V. The Categories as Forms of Human Finitude and Anxiety

The reality, as well as the nature, of human finitude and of the anxiety which is its concomitant is illustrated by Tillich in his discussion of the categories of time, space, causality and substance.[58] This discussion forms one of the most valuable and original parts of his doctrine of man.

Tillich regards the categories as the forms in which finitude necessarily manifests itself. He rejects the notion that they are merely logical ideas which are used to determine discourse but are not directly related to reality. The categories are considered by Tillich to be ontological forms which determine content; as such, he holds,[59] they are present in everything. Since everything that is, is a mixture of being and nonbeing, the categories are related to both and express both. From an external point of view, i.e., in relation to the world of external objects, the categories express the union of being and nonbeing in which all things, including man, participate; from an internal point of view, i.e., in relation to the self, they express the union of anxiety and that courage which fights against, and seeks to overcome, anxiety. They express man's situation both objectively and subjectively, but the latter expression is not to be considered merely psychological. Following the self-world correlation, Tillich believes that it is just as ontological as the former.

In the case of each of the four major categories which he analyzes, Tillich shows that there is a balance between its positive and negative implications, that is, its qualities of expressing both being and nonbeing, both courage and anxiety. This makes it impossible to determine the ultimate significance of the given category by ontological analysis. An existential decision, he seems to believe, is here necessary, and, in our chapter on his theological answer to the questions of being and existence,[60] we shall see how Tillich, in contradistinction to Heidegger and the other so-called "atheistic" Existentialists, decides in favor of the ultimacy of the positive side of each category.

In the case of time, which Tillich regards as the central category of finitude, the negative element is expressed by the transitoriness of all things and the impossibility of fixing the present within the never-stopping temporal flux. Time moves "from a past that is no more towards a future that is not yet through a present which is nothing more than the moving boundary line between past and future."[61] But if the present has no reality, then being is overcome by nonbeing, for to be means to be present. On the other hand, time has also a positive character. It is an undeniable fact that the temporal process is creative, producing novelty and moving in an irreversible direction. Thus, neither the positive nor the negative side can be exclusively maintained. Those who emphasize the negativity of time must recognize that the movement from past to future and the identification of these temporal modes as such is possible only if there is an actual bridge between them, namely, a real present. And those, on the other side, who emphasize the positive character of time must recognize the fact that, though time *is* undoubtedly creative, it nevertheless sweeps away what it has created and the further fact that "creative evolution is accompanied in every moment by destructive disintegration."[62]

The tension, from an objective point of view, between the positive and negative sides of time, its relation to being and nonbeing, is experienced inwardly, in man's self-awareness, as the tension between the anxiety of transitoriness and the courage of a self-affirming present. The transitoriness of time is experienced most acutely by man in the anxiety of having to die, of having inevitably to move from being to nonbeing. In this anxiety, which is always at least potentially present and which colors all of human existence, nonbeing is experienced from within. The anxiety of transitoriness and having to die, Tillich insists, is part of the necessary structure of man's *essential* being, not the result of the distortion of this structure *in existence* through sin and estrangement. Using the language of Christian theology, Tillich declares that this anxiety, being a necessary concomitant of finitude, is actual in "Adam before the Fall," i.e., in man's essential nature, as well as in "the Christ," i.e., in man's new and healed reality.[63] But the universal and essential anxiety of man concerning the movement of all temporal existence, including his own, from being to nonbeing is in tension with, and balanced by, a courage which, through its affirmation of the significance of the present and through its defense of this present against man's vision of an infinite past and an infinite future from which he is excluded, affirms temporality and gives him the power to resist the annihilating character of time. Though the courage which resists nonbeing is present in all beings, it is most markedly effective in man, according to Tillich.[64] Being able to anticipate his own end and to imagine both an infinite past and an infinite future which are not his, man is the most anxious of all beings; but in resisting his anxiety he is also at the same time the most courageous. His courage is as ontologically real as his anxiety, but the question of the ultimate foundation of this ontological courage cannot be answered by philosophical analysis. It must be given by revelation.

An analysis similar to that of the category of time is provided by Tillich for the category of space. Space, he holds, is implied by the reality of the present as a mode of time. "Time creates the present through its union with space. In this union time comes to a standstill because there is something on which to stand."[65] Since to be means to have a space, every being seeks to provide and maintain a place for itself. For man this means not only a physical location—a home, a city, a country—but also a "social space"—a vocation, a sphere of influence, belonging to various groups, a definite place in the historical life of his period. The striving for space is an ontological necessity, and insofar as it is met, being is affirmed and the positive character of the category of space must be recognized. But, on the negative side, it must also be recognized that the possession by any finite being of some definite space is always limited. Man, in his finitude, is not only "a pilgrim on earth," having no necessary or abiding relationship to any space which he may have provided for himself, but he must also, as he is aware, finally lose every space and, thereby, being itself. A flight into "spaceless" time is impossible for man. In losing his space he loses, at the same time, that which makes temporal presence possible.[66]

Corresponding to this balance between the negative and positive sides of spatiality as an objective category is the balance between anxiety and courage in the self-awareness of spatial, that is to say, all finite, beings. Man's anxiety about space is expressed in his feelings of insecurity and of concern about the future. It is also expressed in his attempts to provide a secure physical space for himself and to create social and political systems for the maintenance of general security. But though anxiety may be temporarily repressed by these means, it cannot be finally overcome, for man realizes that death necessarily means for him loss of all space. Knowing this, man nevertheless courageously affirms his present and the space which is its pre-condition. His anxiety about not having a permanent place is balanced by his courageous affirmation of the space that *is* his as long as he has being. Such courageous affirmation, according to Tillich, is universal and shared by all beings. "Everything affirms the space which it has within the universe. As long as it lives, it successfully resists the anxiety of not-having-a-place."[67] But the question of the basis on which this courage is founded can again be answered, according to Tillich, only by revelation.

The third category which Tillich analyzes, causality, is also shown to be, like time and space, an ambiguous expression of being as well as nonbeing, courage as well as anxiety. The positive character of causality lies in its pointing to the power from which things proceed and by which they are sustained. As Tillich puts it, "If something is causally explained, its reality is affirmed, and the power of its resistance against nonbeing is understood."[68] This positive meaning of causality is balanced by a negative meaning which is nothing more than its reverse side, for to show that a thing or event is caused by something else is to show that it does not have its own power of coming into being. The negative character of causality points to what

Heidegger has called the *Geworfenheit,* the "thrownness," of finite things, their contingency and lack of aseity.

> Causality expresses by implication the inability of anything to rest on itself. Everything is driven beyond itself to its cause, and the cause is driven beyond itself to its cause, and so on indefinitely. Causality powerfully expresses the abyss of nonbeing in everything.[69]

The infinite regress involved in the search for the ultimate cause of the finite and contingent phenomena of the universe is not avoided, according to Tillich,[70] by traditional theism, for in relation to a God who is conceived as a highest being, the question may still be asked, What is *his* cause? Causality, when its negative meaning is grasped, points less to such a God than to the danger, in which all finite beings stand, of falling into nonbeing.

The objective fact indicated by the negative interpretation of causality, namely, that no finite being is absolute or self-caused, is reflected subjectively, in man's self-awareness, as anxiety about the non-necessitation of his being. The human being, in becoming aware that he is causally determined, thereby also knows that he is threatened by nonbeing. "The same contingency which has thrown man into existence may push him out of it."[71] But man's anxiety about his contingency and dependence is balanced by a courage which accepts these negativities and which, in spite of them, achieves a kind of self-reliance. That man possesses such courage, enabling him to ignore his causal dependence and to rest in himself, is attested by the very continuation of his life itself, which, without it, would be impossible. But the question which Tillich poses—"How can a being who is dependent on the causal nexus and its contingencies accept this dependence and, at the same time, attribute to himself a necessity and self-reliance which contradict this dependence?"[72]—remains to be solved, he urges, by the idea of God in revelation.

Substance is the fourth category of finitude which Tillich analyzes. Substance in general, in his understanding of it, "points to something underlying the flux of appearance, something which is relatively static and self-contained."[73] In relation to man, the positive character of substantiality is revealed in human self-identity, in the persistence of a certain structure through which the ever changing processes of his life (in traditional terminology, the accidents of this substance) are actualized. It is from the substance to which they belong that the accidents receive their ontological power, according to Tillich. But man's substantiality or self-identity is not something that endures separately and apart from his accidents, as the Platonic doctrine of the soul, for example, would hold. Tillich insists that "the substance is nothing beyond the accidents in which it expresses itself."[74] Because the substance is thus dependent upon its accidents, and *vice versa,* the positive element in both is balanced by a negative element.

Subjectively the negative element of the category of substance is experienced as anxiety concerning not only the final loss of self-identity or substantiality involved in death, but also the preliminary losses involved in the continuous changes of life.[75] The anxiety which individuals and societies feel in times of personal or social change is really anxiety about the threat of nonbeing implied in this change, and the preoccupation of human beings with the idea of an immortal substance of the soul[76] really reflects their profound anxiety in anticipating the final loss of their self-identity and, indeed, of their whole being through death.

But the anxiety produced by the negative element of substantiality is balanced by a courage which "accepts the threat of losing individual substance and the substance of being generally."[77] Man, knowing that the ultimate loss of the substance of these things is inevitable, nevertheless affirms, and attributes substantiality to, finite realities such as a creative work, a love relation, a concrete situation, himself. How such an affirmative courage is possible, despite man's awareness of the inevitablity of the loss of his substance, is a question, Tillich holds, which, like the question of the possibility of the courage involved on the positive side of the three other categories, can be answered only by the doctrine of God given through revelation.

VI. The Anxiety Involved in the Tension of the Ontological Elements

Tillich's analysis of the categories shows how essential anxiety concerning the threat of nonbeing in the sense of annihilation is produced in man by his finitude. But another type of anxiety, he maintains,[78] arises in human beings through their apprehension of the possibility that the opposite elements in each of the three ontological polarities[79] may become dissociated from each other and the balance between them lost. Their balance makes man what he essentially is. But in finite beings the balance may be disrupted; the polarity may become tension.[80] Man is anxiously aware of this possibility. Since in each of the polarities the opposite elements are limited as well as sustained by each other, man knows that, in losing one or the other element, he may lose his essential ontological structure. This anxiety concerning the possibility that the tension between the elements may lead to an actual break and that the ontological structure may thereby be destroyed is the "anxiety of existential disruption"; it is anxiety concerning man's possible estrangement from his "true" or "essential" self.

Tillich explains how this possibility may be actualized in relation to each of the polarities. In the individualization-participation polarity, excessive emphasis on finite individuality and self-relatedness produces the threat of "a loneliness in which world and communion are lost."[81] Excessive emphasis on participation, on the other hand, produces the threat of "a complete collectivization, a loss of individuality and subjectivity whereby the self loses its self-relatedness and is transformed into a mere part of an embracing whole."[82] Man, according to Tillich, oscillates between individualization and participation, loneliness and collectivization, anxiously aware that in either extreme he loses his essential being. Both solitude and social belongingness are aspects of man's essential being; but when the balance between them is broken and one is emphasized at the expense of the other, essential solitude becomes existential loneliness and essential belongingness becomes existential self-surrender to the collective.

In the dynamics-form polarity essential balance is again transformed by finitude into tension, and man becomes anxious about a possible break between the elements. When the essential polar balance has been changed into actual tension the drive of dynamics towards form produces a danger that dynamics may be lost through the rigidity of the very forms which it has itself created. On the other hand, an insistent emphasis on dynamics can break through structured patterns, but the results may be a chaos in which not only form but eventually dynamics as well is lost. In man the tension between dynamics and form manifests itself in his anxiety, on the one hand, that the cultural forms and institutions produced by the drive of his vitality in conjoint operation with his intentionality may threaten his vital power by the very fact of incorporating it in themselves, and, on the other, that vitality in its drive to break through form may separate itself from intentionality and produce a destructive and chaotic formlessness in which not only intentionality but vitality also is ultimately lost.[83]

The essential polar balance between freedom and destiny is similarly changed by finitude into a tension which produces in man anxiety about the possible breaking of this tension and the consequent loss of his essential ontological structure. Anxiously aware that the necessities implied in his destiny may destroy his freedom, man may seek to salvage his freedom by arbitrarily defying his destiny. On the other hand, his anxiety that the contingencies implied in his freedom may cause him to lose his destiny can lead man to attempt to save his destiny by surrendering the freedom which threatens it. No matter which of these two attempts is made, the balance is destroyed and both freedom and destiny are ultimately lost. Man's anxiety about the possible loss of the balance between freedom and destiny in his ontological structure is reflected, Tillich suggests,[84] both in his embarrassment about the decisions that are demanded of him by his freedom and in his fear of an unreserved acceptance of his destiny. Man knows that essentially his free decisions should proceed from a knowledge and will that are in complete unity with his destiny, and that only so are both freedom and destiny to be preserved; but he realizes in his anxiety that, as Tillich puts it, "he lacks the complete cognitive and active unity with his destiny which should be the foundation of his decisions."[85] Similarly, man is afraid unreservedly to accept his destiny because he is anxiously aware that his decision to do so may result in an acceptance of no more than a part of his destiny, that he may fall "under a special determination which is not identical with his real destiny."[86]

The finitude of man, Tillich thus shows, lays him open not only to anxiety about the threat of nonbeing in the sense of death and annihilation but to another kind of anxiety which is the expression of his awareness that it is possible for him to lose his balanced ontological structure and, with it, his true or essential self. However, the actual loss of this structure, Tillich insists,[87] is not a matter of necessity. The "fall" from essence to existence, i.e., the transformation of essential finitude into existential disruption and of essential anxiety into existential despair, occurs in all men, that is, is a matter of universal destiny, but it is mediated by man's finite freedom. How this fall takes place and the characteristics of the disrupted human existence which is its result are topics which we shall consider in our next chapter. First, however, we must consider briefly what Tillich has to say about the various types of anxiety and the nature of man in his book *The Courage To Be.*

VII. THE THREE TYPES OF ANXIETY DISTINGUISHED IN *The Courage To Be*

In *The Courage To Be* Tillich undertakes an ontological analysis of human courage, understood as man's self-affirmation in the face of the threats posed by nonbeing. Here[88] he declares that though, in itself, nonbeing has no quality and no difference of qualities, it acquires these in relation to the being upon which it is dependent even while threatening it. "The character of the negation of being is determined by that in being which is negated."[89] The fact that it is thus possible to distinguish qualities of nonbeing makes it possible to distinguish various forms, or types, of anxiety, for anxiety is the awareness of nonbeing.

Nonbeing, Tillich maintains,[90] threatens man's being in three directions, giving rise to three basic types of anxiety. These, unlike the special forms of neurotic or psychotic anxiety, are existential, in the sense of belonging to human existence as such. Furthermore, though they are distinguishable, they are not mutually exclusive; each is immanent in the other two types.

Nonbeing, first and foremost, threatens man's "ontic" self-affirmation, defined by Tillich as "the basic self-affirmation of a being in its simple existence,"[91] and thereby produces the first and most universal type of anxiety—that of fate and death. This is the type of anxiety which Tillich describes in his *Systematic Theology* through his analysis of the categories. In it man is aware that the inevitable biological extinction towards which he is moving necessarily implies his eventual complete loss of self. Within this awareness of the absolute threat to his being posed by death man is also aware of the relative threat to it posed by fate. Fate is "the rule of contingency"[92] in man's being, contingency not in the sense of causal indeterminacy but in the sense that the determining causes of man's existence are brute facts without any ultimate logical necessity about them. The concrete anxieties arising from man's apprehension that he is dominated by fate, or that the conditions of his being, i.e., the specific temporal, spatial, and causal context into which he finds himself thrown, are non-necessitated—have, according to Tillich, "a certain independence and, ordinarily, a more immediate impact than the anxiety of death."[93] Nevertheless, it is the latter anxiety which stands behind them, overshadows them, and gives them their ultimate seriousness.

Secondly, nonbeing threatens man's spiritual self-affirmation, producing the relative anxiety of emptiness and the absolute anxiety of meaninglessness. "Spiritual self-affirmation," Tillich declares, "occurs in every moment in which man lives creatively in the various spheres of meaning."[94] When man lives spontaneously, in action and reaction, with the meanings embodied in the contents of his cultural life, he affirms himself through them as one who receives and transforms reality creatively. In participating in the contents of his cultural or spiritual life and loving them, he loves himself.

According to Tillich, spiritual self-affirmation requires a center in an ultimate concern, or "a meaning which gives meaning to all meanings."[95] But man's spiritual center, his conviction that there is an ultimate meaning to his existence, is always threatened by nonbeing. This threat is implied in man's finitude and actualized in his estrangement. When man's spiritual center is actually lost, he succumbs to the anxiety of meaninglessness. This is the form of anxiety aroused by the absolute threat of nonbeing to man's spiritual self-affirmation. But nonbeing also threatens man's spiritual self-affirmation relatively, in the form of a possible loss of a sense of meaning in the special contents of an individual's spiritual life. When a cherished belief breaks down, when one is cut off from creative participation in a sphere of culture, when something formerly valued and passionately affirmed becomes an object of indifference or aversion, the relative threat of nonbeing to the individual's spiritual self-affirmation is experienced and the relative anxiety of emptiness is aroused. In this anxiety the person may turn away from all concrete contents and search for an ultimate meaning, only to discover, according to Tillich, "that it was precisely the loss of a spiritual center which took away the meaning from the special contents of the spiritual life."[96] Thus the absolute anxiety of meaninglessness lies in the background of the relative anxiety of emptiness.

To escape the anxiety implicit in the experiece of total doubt and meaninglessness, the individual may decide to surrender his freedom to ask and answer questions for himself, submitting to some authoritarian system under which all questioning and doubt is silenced. But such submission is purchased at the price of fanatical self-assertiveness. "Fanaticism is the correlate to spiritual self-surrender: it shows the anxiety which it was supposed to conquer by attacking with disproportionate violence those who disagree and who demonstrate by their disagreement elements in the spiritual life of the fanatic which he must suppress in himself."[97]

The third direction in which nonbeing threatens man, Tillich maintains, is in his moral self-affirmation. Here the threat is experienced relatively as the anxiety of guilt and absolutely as the anxiety of condemnation. Man feels responsible for his being —ontic as well as spiritual—which he recognizes as not only given to him but also demanded of him. He knows that in his finite freedom to make decisions "he is asked to make of himself what he is supposed to become, to fulfill his destiny."[98] But he knows also that he can act against the ethical norms, however defined, which lead to fulfillment; he can contradict his essential nature and lose his destiny. Under the conditions of existence this possibility becomes a reality. Moral perfection, according to Tillich, is an impossibility for man.

> Even in what he considers his best deed nonbeing is present and prevents it from being perfect. A profound ambiguity between good and evil permeates everything he does, because it permeates his personal being as such. Nonbeing is mixed with being in his moral self-affirmation as it is in his spiritual and ontic self-affirmation.[99]

The sense of guilt which ensues is inescapable. "It is present," Tillich writes, "in every moment of moral self-awareness and can drive us to complete self-rejection, to the feeling of being condemned—not to an external punishment but to the despair of having lost our destiny."[100] Attempts to escape this anxiety or despair—whether they take the form of anomism, the rejection of all moral norms and demands, or of a rigorous legalism— are finally ineffective. It is the anxiety of guilt and condemnation, Tillich adds, following the dictum of Paul that "sin is the sting of death," which lends added weight to the anxiety of death; and the anxiety of fate and death awakens and increases the anxiety of guilt and condemnation. "The two forms of anxiety provoke and augment each other."[101]

All three forms of anxiety, according to Tillich, drive to the situation of despair in which they are fulfilled. Despair is the boundary situation, the situation in which the individual can find no further hope but feels nonbeing to be absolutely victorious. All of human life, says Tillich, may "be interpreted as a continuous attempt to avoid despair. And this attempt is mostly successful."[102] But the boundary situation of despair, though it may be exemplified only infrequently in any given human life, casts valuable light on human existence as a whole and determines its interpretation. Furthermore, despair, for Tillich, is not the last word. He believes, as we shall see,[103] that even in the face of the most radical threat of nonbeing, courage—the "courage of despair"—is possible and the supremacy of being over nonbeing may be experienced and affirmed by man.

VIII. Criticism and Evaluation

The analysis of the structure of man's being which Tillich has elaborated is certainly an impressive achievement. Though he is heavily indebted to the Existentialists, particularly Heidegger, for this analysis, Tillich differs from most of the Existentialists in that, instead of concentrating largely on the uprootedness and lostness of human existence, he emphasizes also the essential structures of being which remain at least partially effective even in the most disrupted and estranged forms of existence. In this respect he is more in the classical philosophical tradition than in the Existentialist.

Tillich, following Heidegger, who holds that *Dasein* (human "being there") is the key to *Sein* (being), claims that his description of the structure of man's being can be applied by analogy to all of being and is, therefore, not merely an anthropological analysis but also an ontological one. That this is so is surely open to question. It is a far-fetched use of analogy, indeed, that Tillich makes in positing[104] an essential similarity between the roles of freedom and destiny in human behavior and the roles of spontaneity and natural law in the behavior of subatomic particles. Nor do the other polarities which Tillich distinguishes in man's being appear genuinely susceptible to generalization and application to subhuman being. However, we are not required here to decide the question whether this anthropology may also be ontology. For our purposes we shall consider it only as anthropology, and we shall be concerned with evaluating and criticizing it as much.

Tillich speaks of the ontological concepts which he sets forth as *a priori*. They are, he tells us,[105] the necessary "conditions" of experience and are "presupposed" in it. But this use of idealistic and, more specifically, Kantian, terminology is somewhat misleading. These concepts, according to Tillich, are not brought *to* experience by the mind. They are discovered *in* experience, in the self's interaction with its world. Tillich is here an epistemological realist, and his use of idealistic terms can only confuse the reader as to his real position.

To begin, as Tillich does, with the self-world correlation as the fundamental fact in man's being is surely the most promising approach to the problem. He thus succeeds in avoiding, as he claims, the pitfalls both of a reductive naturalism and a deductive idealism, as well as the insuperable difficulties of a dualism of the Cartesian type. Furthermore, he recognizes and does justice thereby to the basic incongruity which seems to lie at the heart of human personality, namely, that man is both an item in the flux of nature, dependent upon it and conditioned by it, and a unique being who, by virtue primarily of his possession of reason and the power of language, is capable of transcending the natural flux in which other beings seem to be totally immersed.

Tillich's analysis of the three polarities which, according to him, constitute the basic ontological structure, is a very valuable one. These certainly do not exhaust the polarities in man's being which an ontological analysis might distinguish, but they are clearly of fundamental importance and Tillich's description of them is a most enlightening one.

It is noteworthy that, in his discussion of the interdependence of personality and communion in the first polarity, Tillich follows Buber's emphasis on the possibility of creative encounter between individuals and rejects, at least by implication, the extreme Sartrean[106] thesis that each individual always tries to annihilate as an independent subject the individual opposite himself and that conflict is, therefore, the only possible pattern of interpersonal relationships. Tillich here, of course, also rejects the Kierkegaardian emphasis on inwardness and isolation as constituting the whole of human personality. For him, being shut-up within oneself and isolated from one's fellows is a mark of man's estrangement and not of his essence.

Tillich's analysis of the elements of the second polarity, dynamics and form, or, in human terms, vitality and intentionality, seems to us an apt description of a very real and basic tension in man's being. So also his discussion of the third set of polar elements, freedom and destiny. By emphasizing the reality of human freedom Tillich, if we are to take his words at face value, reaffirms the dignity of man against the attempts of some extreme forms of naturalism to reduce him to a set of conditioned reflexes, a mere object of social and biological determination. In this emphasis he also restates a fundamental theme of contemporary Existentialism, which has been concerned to protect man's freedom against the threat posed to it by the growing depersonalization and mechanization of modern industrial society. But against the tendency of some of the Existentialists, particularly Sartre, to absolutize man's freedom, Tillich points, by his equal emphasis on the polar element of destiny, to the finitude of freedom, the fact of its limitations and conditions.

The question might be raised, however, whether Tillich, despite his specific avowals, really believes in human freedom. Do not his emphasis, which we shall observe in his description of man's existential state (which he holds to be universally true), on the inevitability of man's so using his freedom as to fall into estrangement, and his acceptance of the Lutheran doctrine of the bondage of the will, actually constitute a denial of human freedom? This is a question which we shall have to look into more particularly later.[107]

We turn our attention now to Tillich's account of man's finitude which, it will be recalled, he defines as the fact that man's being is limited by nonbeing. What Tillich means when he uses the word "nonbeing" is often extremely difficult to determine. It is employed by him in various contexts in at least six different senses. Sometimes he uses it in the restricted sense of logical negation. At times it appears to mean for him, following Plato's *Sophist*, that everything, in its determinateness, is "other than" something else. At other times it appears to mean non-existence, in the sense either of having no reality in space and time or of lacking any determinate character. At still other times, it appears to mean the general possibility of ceasing to be, which, in man, is represented by the fact of his mortality. In *The Courage To Be*,[108] as we have seen, Tillich distinguishes, besides the nonbeing which threatens man's "ontic self-affirmation" in the form of mortality, two other forms of nonbeing, namely, the possibility of falling into a state where one is attacked by a sense of meaninglessness and futility and the possibility of being overcome by a sense of moral guilt. Tillich does not always specify in which sense he uses the word nonbeing, and, indeed, the employment of one term to cover such a wide variety of meanings cannot but lead to confusion.

It is, by and large, with the nonbeing which threatens man in the fact of his mortality that Tillich is concerned in the first volume of his *Systematic Theology*. His analysis here of man's relationship to the categories of time, space, substance and causality is a brilliant interpretation of man's being as "being-toward-death." Man's "encounter with nothingness," in his realization of the fact that he must die, is here held by Tillich to be the source of a basic anxiety which is universally, though not always consciously, present in man and pervasive of his entire being. The anxiety aroused in man by his awareness of his mortality is regarded as a fundamental constituent of his essential being.

In all this Tillich, of course, is following the Existentialist tradition and particularly the two of its representatives to whom he is most indebted, Kierkegaard and Heidegger. It is more the emphasis of Heidegger, who concentrated largely on the anxiety aroused in man by the existential awareness of his moving towards death, than that of Kierkegaard, who stressed equally the anxiety involved in man's realization of his moral freedom,[109] that he here follows. But Tillich does not, to be sure, neglect the anxieties of freedom and guilt.

Where Tillich differs fundamentally from Heidegger is, as we shall see, in maintaining that man's anxiety about death is balanced or even conquered by courage, whether it be the courage derived from faith in an omnipotent God or the "courage to be" of every human being which is not in any specific sense religiously derived. For Heidegger the existential becoming aware of one's "being-toward-death" creates only the possibility of a "resolute" or "authentic" individual existence, as distinguished from a cowardly flight into the anonymity and falsehood of *das Man*. In the resolute acceptance of one's moving toward death, however, according to Heidegger, anxiety is in no way mitigated.

The basic question, of course, is whether Tillich is justified in following the Existentialist philosophers in taking anxiety to be the individual's immediate experience of his finitude and, even more, whether he is justified in erecting an ontology on this basis. That his entire cosmological view is colored by his acceptance of anxiety as man's fundamental psychic experience is clear. Man's apprehension over his mortality, his dread of the possibility of falling into meaninglessness and moral guilt, determines, for Tillich, the entire interpretation of the cosmos, which he finds "fallen" and "estranged" from "the divine ground."

Tillich appeals particularly to psychoanalysis and depth psychology for support of his contention that anxiety, in the sense of awareness of finitude and the threat of nonbeing, is a basic constituent of man's psychic being.[110] But it is not obvious that such support is really to be found in these sources. Freud, as Harry M. Tiebout, Jr., has shown,[111] can be interpreted as approaching, to some extent, the Existentialist conception of anxiety as the awareness of the threat of nonbeing, but his explicit statements on the matter make it clear that he tended generally to regard anxiety as a defense-reaction to the specific traumatic situations encountered by the individual in the course of his development. Gordon W. Allport, the distinguished American psychologist, has denied the universality of anxiety in man's experience. "Anxiety, though obviously not a universal trait, is a common condition among neurotics and may be said to be the *raison d'être* for the whole theory of psycho-analysis."[112] We are in no position to decide this matter, but it should be emphasized, at any rate, that it is a debatable issue. Tillich may be justified in taking his conception of anxiety as the key to an interpretation of man's being, but it is open to question whether in so doing he is not acting more on the basis of an existential decision as a Christian theologian than on the basis of objective empirical evidence.[113]

CHAPTER FIVE

Man's Estranged Existence

I. Man's Transition from Essence to Existence

MAN AS HE EXISTS is not what he essentially is and ought to be. He is estranged from his true being."[1] So Tillich summarizes the central conviction of his anthropology.

How does the existential estrangement of man from his true or essential being occur? What is the nature of the process by which man passes from the one state to the other? What makes the transition possible in the first place, and what motives drive toward it? These are the questions which first engage our attention in the present chapter.

Before examining Tillich's answers to these questions, we must consider briefly his understanding of the general philosophical distinction between essence and existence. The distinction itself is one that he finds pervading the whole tradition of Western ontological thought. Plato, he points out, hypostatized essence and existence into two realms; Aristotle combined them in the polar relation of potentiality and actuality; the later Schelling, Kierkegaard and Heidegger contrasted them with each other; Spinoza and Hegel derived existence from essence; and Dewey and Sartre derived essence from existence.[2] In making the essence-existence distinction, philosophy, Tillich holds,[3] has taken cognizance of a real split or duality in being which everywhere manifests itself. "Whenever the ideal is held against the real, truth against error, good against evil, a distortion of essential being is presupposed and is judged by essential being."[4]

In the common meanings which philosophy has come to attach to the terms essence and existence, there is, however, Tillich observes, a fundamental ambiguity. In the term essence this ambiguity consists "in the oscillation of the meaning between an empirical and a valuating sense."[5] Essence, in the empirical or logical sense, means the "universal" or "nature" in which a thing participates. In the valuational sense it means the "true and undistorted nature" from which a thing has "fallen." This ambiguity in the meaning of essence, which Tillich sees as persisting in philosophy ever since Plato, derives, he believes, from the ambiguous character of existence. The first meaning, essence as *ousia*, reflects the fact that any existent thing receives its power of being the definite thing that it is from its essence; the second meaning, the valuational, derives from the fact that the existent thing, although it is—as existing—more than it is in the state of mere potentiality, always reflects its essence imperfectly and in a distorted manner.

According to Tillich, philosophy has not been alone[6] in recognizing that duality in being which it expresses through its distinction between essence and existence. Christian theology, in drawing the distinction between the "created" and "actual" worlds, reflects, he suggests, its own experience and vision of the same duality. In its claim that the actual world as it exists is the creation of God, this theology asserts the positive character of existence, that is, its goodness as deriving from the essential structure of reality in which it participates; in its contention at the same time that the actual world has "fallen away" from its created goodness, it points to just that split which philosophy denotes in its distinction between essence and existence.

With regard to man, the classical Christian doctrine is that he is created good but falls into sinfulness.[7] This doctrine, Tillich believes, is profoundly true. He insists,[8] however, that man's fall or transition from created goodness to sinfulness must not be conceived, as it often has been in traditional Christian theology, in temporal or historical terms. Human history as a whole did not pass, and individuals as such do not pass, at a specifiable moment from essential goodness to sinfulness or existential distortion. Within any historical situation and within all men throughout all history the split between essential nature and actual existence is already given.

If it be not interpreted literally as the story of an event that happened once upon a time, the biblical myth of the Fall, according to Tillich,[9] has a universal anthropological significance and accurately symbolizes the basic reality of the human situation, namely that man in his actual existence is estranged from his true or essential being. To emphasize this understanding of the meaning of the myth Tillich translates the fall from created goodness to sinfulness as "the transition from essence to existence,"[10] and proceeds, largely through an interpretation of the myth, to provide an explanation of this transition.

Before outlining the explanation that Tillich gives, we must, however, point out that he is not unmindful of the objections that could be raised, and are in fact raised, by philosophies such as idealism and naturalism against accepting the Christian myth of the Fall as a symbol which expresses the real situation of man. Tillich is aware of the idealistic doctrine that the Fall ought not to be understood as symbolizing anything more than the difference between the ideal and the real, as well as the idealistic faith that there is a progressive movement toward the actual fulfillment of the ideal on the part of the real in the future or even a fulfillment of the ideal in principle in the present. He is also aware of the challenge to his own interpretation of the Fall as expressive of a radical split between man's essence and existence in the tendency of naturalism to take man's existence for granted without asking any questions about its negativities, and in its denial that such concepts as "estrangement," "man against himself," and "the human predicament" are properly applicable to man's life. He is cognizant, also, of the further challenge to the idea of the Fall in that mixture of idealism and naturalism which characterizes both ancient and modern forms of Stoicism. Nevertheless, he insists that these supposedly "philosophical" and neutral views of man have no more intrinsic claim to acceptance than does an avowedly theological view such as his own. In holding that "there is no human predicament," the naturalist or idealist, Tillich maintains, is not stating an objective fact but making an existential decision about a matter of ultimate concern. In so doing he is really operating, though not consciously so, as a theologian, and his existential decision is no more entitled to regard than that of the professed theologian who has decided that man's existence *is* estranged from his essence. Indeed, the professed theologian's decision, he suggests, is much closer to the facts in that it more clearly recognizes the demonic implications of history and the self-contradicting power of human freedom.[11]

According to Tillich, it is just this aspect of man's freedom, his power to contradict himself and his essential nature, that makes possible the transition from essence to existence. "Man is free even from his freedom; that is, he can surrender his humanity."[12] But the freedom of self-contradiction is, like every other quality of human freedom, limited by destiny, with which freedom in general always stands in polarity. This means, for Tillich, that finite freedom produces the human transition from essence to existence not individually and accidentally but within the framework of a universal destiny. Sin is the result neither of individual moral choice alone nor of necessity alone. Decision and destiny are both involved here.

Freedom provides the possibility for the human transition from essence to existence. But what motives drive men so to exercise their freedom that the transition actually occurs? An answer to this question, Tillich declares, presupposes some image of the state of essential being, or, in terms of the biblical myth, "Adam's state before the Fall." The state of essential being, however, is not an actual stage of human development. It must be understood as a state of potentiality, without actualization in any place or time.[13] It cannot be known or described directly. It may, however, be symbolized, Tillich suggests,[14] either theologically as the state of "being hidden in the ground of the divine life" or psychologically as "the state of dreaming innocence."

It is in terms of the psychological symbol that Tillich actually develops his analysis.[15] The state of dreaming, he believes, is particularly appropriate for symbolizing the non-actualized, non-spatial and non-temporal character of the state of essential being. "Dreaming," he writes

> is a state of mind which is real and non-real at the same time —just as is potentiality. Dreaming anticipates the actual, just as everything actual is somehow present in the potential. In the moment of awakening, the images of the dream disappear as images and return as encountered realities. Certainly, reality is different from the images of the dream, but not totally different. For the actual is present in the potential in terms of anticipation. For these reasons the metaphor "dreaming" is adequate in describing the state of essential being.[16]

The word "innocence" expresses the same basic point as the word "dreaming," namely, that the state of essential being is one of non-actualized potentiality. But innocence has, in addition, several specific connotations, all of which are helpful in contributing to an understanding of man's state of essential being. The word connotes lack of experience, lack of personal responsibility, and lack of moral guilt. When innocence is lost, all three of these things are acquired, as is illustrated in the sexual development of human beings. Tillich regards the typical pattern in the growth of human sexual consciousness as offering a useful analogy to the transition of man from his created or essential state to his sinful or existential condition. In the early state of sexual innocence, which is the analogue to the essential or created state of man, sexual potentialities are present, but they are unactualized; and the child, up to a point, is almost completely unconscious of them. But an "awakening" from this dreamlike state inevitably occurs; and if the sexual potentialities are then actualized—as they are in most human beings—experience, responsibility and guilt are acquired and dreaming innocence is lost.

The "awakening" from dreaming innocence, Tillich holds, is inevitable, for "the state of dreaming innocence drives beyond itself."[17] This is so because this state is not one of stable perfection but rather of uncontested and undecided potentiality. As such, it is a state which is charged with the possibility of tension and disruption, and the fundamental expression of the fact that it is so charged is man's anxious awareness of his

finite freedom. In the state of dreaming innocence, Tillich
maintains,[18] man's freedom and destiny are in harmony, but
neither of them is actualized nor is their unity actualized; both
of these elements, as well as their unity, are still only essential
or potential. When, however, man becomes aware of his finite
freedom—and the universality of anxiety, its fundamental symptom or concomitant, indicates that this awareness always occurs
—he is driven by this "aroused freedom," as Tillich calls it,
towards efforts to actualize it. In terms of the biblical myth,
Adam's "desire to sin," the existence of which is indicated by the
fact that in the myth the issuance to him of a prohibition against
eating from the tree of knowledge had been deemed necessary by
God, is the expression of this "aroused freedom."[19] But when freedom is aroused, that is, becomes conscious of itself and tends to
become actual, a reaction occurs, produced by the essential unity
of freedom and destiny characterizing the state of dreaming
innocence, which wishes to preserve itself. Man is thus placed in
a state of temptation in which he is, as Tillich puts it, "caught
between the desire to actualize his freedom and the demand
to preserve his dreaming innocence."[20]

This state of temptation, Tillich contends, is reflected in the
anxiety involved in man's awareness of his finite freedom, for
this anxiety is of a twofold nature. Man is simultaneously anxious, on the one hand, about losing himself by actualizing himself
and his potentialities, and, on the other, about losing himself
by *not* actualizing himself and his potentialities. "He stands,"
Tillich declares, "between the preservation of his dreaming innocence without experiencing the actuality of being and the loss
of his innocence through knowledge, power and guilt."[21] In
this situation of anxiety or temptation[22] man generally decides
for self-actualization, thus ending his dreaming innocence. Here
again Tillich cites human sexual development as providing a useful analogy to the transition from innocence to the state of sin
and guilt, as he conceives this transition. The typical adolescent,
he reminds us, wavers between the anxiety of losing himself by
actualizing his sexual potentialities or losing himself by not
actualizing them, but ultimately decides for actualization.

The transition from essence to existence is a universal quality of finite being in general, according to Tillich, and its specific manifestation in human life is the transition of every person from dreaming innocence to actualization and guilt. This human transition from essence to existence which is to be understood, Tillich repeatedly reminds us, not as an event of the past but as something that occurs in all three modes of time, must also be recognized, he maintains, as the result not of individual moral freedom alone but of universal tragic destiny as well. For Tillich, freedom, as we have already observed, is one of the basic elements in man's ontological structure, but it is never absolute and unconditioned; it is always limited by that element with which it stands in polarity, namely, destiny. The inseparability, in general, of freedom and destiny is especially manifested in the transition from essence to existence.

> The individual act of existential estrangement is not the isolated act of an isolated individual; it is an act of freedom which is imbedded, nevertheless, in the universal destiny of existence. In every individual act the estranged or fallen character of being actualizes itself. Every ethical decision is an act both of individual freedom and of universal destiny.[23]

Against the Pelagian view that estrangement from created goodness is the result only of individual moral decision and therefore may or may not occur in any given person, Tillich insists that strong biological, psychological and sociological forces affect every individual decision and make estrangement a matter of universal destiny. In a sense, nature as well as man must be regarded as implicated in the Fall.[24] A recognition of the inseparability of man and nature, and of their mutual participation in each other, demands a rejection of the idealistic doctrine of an innocent nature as distinguished from guilty man.

In support of his contention that the personal decisions producing man's estrangement from his essential being occur within a context of natural and social forces from which they cannot be separated, and which give them the character of destiny as well as freedom, Tillich points to several considerations.[25] He cites, first, the fact that there is no absolute discontinuity between animal bondage and human freedom in the development of man and that it is impossible to determine at just what point in the evolutionary process animal nature is replaced by what we now regard as human nature. He points, secondly, to the fact that legal and moral thought have found it impossible to determine precisely the limits of responsibility in the human individual and have had to acknowledge that such things as lack of maturity, fatigue, intoxication, and physical and mental illness serve to condition the act of personal decision and the freedom expressed in it. Thirdly, he refers to the emphasis of psychoanalysis and depth psychology on the determining power of the unconscious over man's conscious decisions and on the strong influence of unrecognized motives, in the form of bodily and psychic strivings, on what seem to be wholly free and rationally chosen acts. He alludes, lastly, to the influence on the individual's personal decision of his social environment, both its consciously received elements and those of its real but unacknowledged strivings which are referred to in the term "the collective unconscious." The recognition of the reality of these natural and social drives and influences, Tillich maintains, effectively refutes the Pelagian idea of moral freedom without supporting the Manichean doctrine of tragic destiny. Both of these extreme positions contain an element of truth, but their error lies in their onesidedness and their failure to recognize that in every act of the human personality freedom and destiny are inseparable.

Tillich wishes to distinguish between the finitude which he holds to be an ontological quality of man's essential or created nature and the state of sin and estrangement which he regards as a characteristic of his existential being, or, to put the matter in traditional theological terminology, between man's Creation and his Fall. Nevertheless, his account of man's transition from essence to existence presupposes, as he himself recognizes, a point of coincidence between Creation and Fall, despite their logical difference. Creation has as its end, in the case of man, the actualization of his finite freedom, but this very actualization is also the beginning of the Fall, since it separates man from the creative ground of the divine life.[26] As Tillich himself puts it, "Actualized creation and estranged existence are identical."[27]

But this recognition of the coincidence at a certain point of Creation and Fall, he maintains,[28] is unavoidable unless one accepts the literal interpretation of the paradise story according to which there was once a "utopia" in which created goodness was really actualized without any admixture of existential estrangement. If the idea of an actual historical stage of essential goodness is rejected, the coincidence of Creation and Fall must be acknowledged, but this, Tillich insists, does not mean there is any logical or rational necessity about the transition from essence to existence, or from created goodness to existential estrangement. This transition is an underived fact, not a matter of structural necessity.

II. The Characteristics of Man's Existential State

We have followed Tillich's account of the process whereby man, as he variously puts it, falls from created goodness into sinfulness, or becomes estranged from his true being, or passes from essence to existence. We turn now to a consideration of his description of the qualities that characterize this fallen or estranged existence.

Classical Christian theology has usually described it summarily as the state of sin. If the word "sin" is still to be used for the characterization of man's existential state, Tillich maintains,[29] certain connotations that have come to be associated with it must be removed. Sin must be understood basically as the state of 'separation[30] from that to which one belongs— God, one's self, one's world—and not as the violation of a moral principle; and sins in the latter sense must be seen as only symptoms or expressions of sin in the former sense.[31] Besides this, the terms "hereditary" or "original,"[32] applied to sin, must not be understood literally. They are to be interpreted, rather, as pointing to the fact that sin is a state in which men become involved as a matter of universal and tragic destiny as well as by reason of their personal freedom and individual choices.[33]

Provided that the element of personal responsibility involved in the transition from essence to existence is not overlooked— and it is this element that is most strongly emphasized in the traditional idea of sin—it is possible and desirable, Tillich suggests,[34] to use the philosophical term "estrangement" rather than the religious term "sin" to describe man's existential predicament. Both point to the same reality, but the term estrangement is particularly valuable because it explicitly emphasizes that alienation of man from God, from other beings, and from his true self which is the basic quality of his existential state.

> Man as he exists is not what he essentially is and ought to be. He is estranged from his true being. The profundity of the term "estrangement" lies in the implication that one belongs essentially to that from which one is estranged. Man is not a stranger to his true being, for he belongs to it. He is judged by it but cannot be completely separated, even if he is hostile to it. Man's hostility to God proves indisputably that he belongs to him.[35]

Man's sinful or estranged state is expressed, according to Tillich,[36] by three major attitudes or qualities which serve as its identifying marks. These are unbelief, *hubris* or self-elevation, and concupiscence. We shall examine briefly his conception of each.

Unbelief, as Tillich defines it, is not the refusal or inability to give assent to certain theological doctrines but rather the expression of the fact that in his existential self-realization man "turns toward himself and his world and loses his essential unity with the ground of his being and his world."[37] Like its opposite, faith, it is an act of the total personality, involving knowledge, will and emotion. This turning away from God and towards the self is expressed in various realms of human life. In the intellectual realm it is manifested in the disruption of man's cognitive participation in God. That this disruption occurs universally among men in the state of existence is evidenced by the fact that in this state men must *ask* for God. As Tillich puts it, "He who asks for God is already estranged from God, though not cut off from him."[38] In the moral realm unbelief means the separation of the human from the divine will, and the universal occurrence of this separation is attested by the fact that men need a law which tells them how to act and which they can choose to obey or disobey. This shows that men are "already estranged from the source of the law which demands obedience."[39] In the realm of emotion, the universal occurrence of unbelief, or turning away from God, is manifested in the fact that man's love for self and his love for God are two distinct loves. "In order to have a self which not only can be loved but can love God," Tillich declares, "one's center must already have left the divine center to which it belongs and in which self-love and love to God are united."[40]

The second mark of man's estrangement, *hubris*, is, according to Tillich,[41] simply the other side of unbelief. Having turned away from the divine center to which he essentially belongs, man makes himself the center of his world.[42] In his *hubris*, or self-elevation, he refuses to acknowledge the fact that he is excluded from that infinity which belongs only to God. This sin, like the sin of unbelief, is committed by man in the totality of his personal being, and no one in the state of existence is exempt from it.

> Every individual . . . falls into moments of *hubris*. All men have the hidden desire to be like God and they act accordingly in their self-evaluation and self-affirmation. No one is willing to acknowledge, in concrete terms, his finitude, his weakness and his errors, his ignorance and his insecurity, his loneliness and his anxiety. And if he is ready to acknowledge them, he makes another instrument of *hubris* out of his readiness. A demonic structure drives man to confuse natural self-affirmation with destructive self-elevation.[43]

It is man's very greatness and dignity, the fact that he has not only self-consciousness or complete centeredness but also the freedom to transcend any given situation, that makes his *hubris* possible. Aware that he is potentially infinite, man will not admit his actual finitude. His *hubris* is expressed, according to Tillich,[44] in many ways: metaphysically, in his identification of the partial truth that he can attain with ultimate truth; morally, in his identification of his limited goodness with absolute goodness; culturally, in his identification of his finite creations with divine creativity. These, as well as all other forms of *hubris*, must always end, Tillich believes,[45] in tragic catastrophe and self-destruction, for man's claims to infinity are ungrounded and contradictory and must ultimately be shattered in the face of the real infinity of God.

Hubris is the result of the fact that man is situated between actual finitude and potential infinity. This position, in which he is aware that as an individual he is separated from the whole which is potentially his, further engenders in him, according to Tillich, the desire to draw the whole of reality into himself. This desire on the part of man to overcome the "poverty" of his separated state and to become united with the whole by drawing it into himself is what is meant by the sin of "concupiscence" in classical Protestant theology. Concupiscence, Tillich insists, is not to be identified, as it has been by some theologians, with the striving for sexual pleasure alone, but refers rather to "all aspects of man's relation to himself and to his world . . . to physical hunger as well as to sex, to knowledge as well as to power, to material wealth as well as to spiritual values."[46] It is the unlimited character of the strivings for these things that makes them symptoms of man's estrangement. Related to a definite and limited content, they are expressions of man's essential *eros* and are not demonic or self-destructive.

Tillich sees in Freud's theory of the libido and in Nietszche's doctrine of "the will to power" two valuable and enlightening conceptual expressions of that state of estrangement which traditional theology has called concupiscence. But the value of both Freud's and Nietszche's analyses for an understanding of the human situation is limited, Tillich holds,[47] by the fact that they are adequate descriptions of man's existential state of estrangement only and not of his essential being.

The basic criticism to be made of Freud's theory of the libido, Tillich maintains,[48] is that it does not distinguish between libido as concupiscence and libido as love. According to Tillich,[49] Freud's contention that man is in the grip of unlimited desire deriving from his sexual makeup, and that libidinous elements enter into even his highest spiritual activities and experiences, is justified, as is his claim that the endlessness of this desire and the impossibility of satisfying it lead to the longing to escape from its pain through death. But where Freud went astray was in his failure to see that the libido *need* not be concupiscent, that is, endless and insatiable. It is so for man in the state of existential estrangement, but here it has been distorted. "In man's essential relation to himself and his world," Tillich declares, "libido . . . is not the infinite desire to draw the universe into one's particular existence, but it is an element of love united with the other qualities of love—*eros, philia,* and *agape.*"[50] The libido which is an expression of love is directed to a specific object. It desires union with the being who is its object and not, as does the distorted or concupiscent libido, merely its own pleasure through that being. It was because of his own puritanical attitude toward sex that Freud, according to Tillich,[51] did not recognize that for man in his essential or created nature libido is not infinite desire for pleasure but rather the definite desire to be united with the object of one's love for its own sake.

Nietzsche's concept of "the will to power" is regarded by Tillich as another important source of insight into the nature of concupiscence, but in the form in which Nietzsche generally proclaimed it, it must also be understood as applicable only to man's existential state. Basically "the will to power" symbolizes, according to Tillich,[52] that natural self-affirmation and dynamic self-realization which man shares with everything that has the power of being. Self-affirmation as such, united with *eros* and confined within proper limits, belongs to man's essential or created nature and is not a characteristic of estrangement. But Nietzsche, following Schopenhauer, generally held the will to power to be an infinite, never-satisfied drive which, by very reason of its endlessness and insatiability, produces in man the desire to come to rest by negating it. When the will to power is thus unlimited, not directed to any definite object and not subject to any norms or principles, it is no longer an expression of created goodness but rather a demonic and destructive drive. It is that form of estrangement which is properly called concupiscence.

Sin or estrangement, of which unbelief, *hubris,* and concupiscence are the basic expressions, is, according to Tillich, "a universal fact before it becomes an individual act."[53] What he means by this is that the sins of the individual, i.e., those acts for which he is personally responsible and comes to feel a sense of personal guilt, are dependent, despite the fact that they are the results of free choice, on the universal destiny of estrangement. Man's freedom, Tillich holds, "is inbedded in the universal destiny of estrangement in such a way that in every free act the destiny of estrangement is involved and, vice versa, that the destiny of estrangement is actualized by all free acts."[54] Sin as fact and sin as act are therefore inseparable; and he who feels himself guilty of an act of estrangement, while he is aware that the act is dependent on his own special destiny as well as mankind's universal destiny, must nevertheless accept full responsibility for it. None of the explanations of estrangement given by the various philosophies of determinism—neither the physical theory of a mechanistic determinism, nor the biological theory of the decadence of the power of life, nor the psychological theory of the compulsory force of the unconscious— can account, according to Tillich, "for the feeling of personal responsibility that man has for his acts in the state of estrangement."[55]

III. Man's Existential Self-Destruction and Despair

In connection with his analysis of the categories in the preceding chapter, we have seen[56] how Tillich concludes that man, by reason of his finitude, or the fact that his being is limited by nonbeing, must necessarily be the victim of anxiety. Even in his essential being, when the polarities constitutive of his ontological structure remain undisrupted, man suffers from the anxiety[57] which is the accompaniment or expression of his awareness that he is finite and threatened by nonbeing in the sense of annihilation. He suffers also from that form of anxiety which Tillich calls the "anxiety of existential disruption" and which arises out of his apprehension that it is possible for him to lose his ontological structure and, with it, his true or essential being. In the state of existence, i.e., of sin or estrangement, this possibility becomes an actuality. Man's essential being is in fact lost, and his anxiety is replaced by the deeper ailment of despair. How this occurs is described by Tillich in his discussion of the nature of evil, understood as the consequence of the state of sin or estrangement.

According to Tillich, each of the basic expressions of man's existential or estranged state—unbelief, *hubris*, and concupiscence —contradicts man's essential being and drives the polar elements of this being into conflict with each other. The destruction which ensues, he declares, "is not the work of special divine or demonic interferences, but is the consequence of the structure of estrangement itself."[58] The estranged state is held by Tillich to contain within itself "structures of destruction"[59] which "aim" at chaos. These structures of destruction constitute what is commonly called "evil."[60]

The basic structure of destruction, or evil, is the disruption of the self-world polarity, which, as we have seen,[61] is held by Tillich to be the fundamental ontological fact, exemplified in every finite being to some degree but fulfilled only in man, who alone has a completely centered self and a structured world to which he simultaneously sustains the relationship of belongingness and separateness. Under the conditions of existential estrangement man can, and often does, lose himself and thereby also his world, for the loss of one necessarily brings about the loss of the other. Self-loss is "the loss of one's determining center" or "the distintegration of the centered self by disruptive drives which cannot be brought into unity."[62] This disintegration is exemplified, Tillich points out, in moral conflicts and psychopathological disruptions in which the individual comes to feel that both he and his world are falling to pieces. In extreme situations the world tends to become unreal for the individual and he is left with only the awareness of his own empty self which, inasmuch as it now lacks all content, tends to become increasingly disintegrated. *Hubris* and concupiscence are productive, according to Tillich, of just such a tendency to disintegration of the self.

> The attempt of the finite self to be the center of everything gradually has the effect of its ceasing to be anything. Both self and world are threatened. Man becomes a limited self, in dependence on a limited environment. He has lost his world; he has only his environment.[63]

It is only in the state of existential estrangement from his essential nature that man becomes what certain sociological theories hold him to be, a being who is determined by his environment rather than one who transcends every given environment by creating his own world.

The loss of self and the loss of world which necessarily accompanies the loss of self constitute the first and most fundamental evil in man's estranged state. Other subsidiary evils result from the separation of the elements of the major ontological polarities. These polarities, as we have noted above,[64] are freedom and destiny, dynamics and form, and individualization and participation.

In man's essential ontological structure, freedom and destiny, Tillich maintains, "lie within each other, distinct but not separated, in tension but not in conflict."[65] Both are rooted in the ground of being, which is their source and the ground of their polar unity. But when freedom is aroused and the decision for self-actualization is taken—and this, it will be recalled, is held by Tillich to take place universally among men—freedom begins to separate itself from the destiny to which it belongs and tends to become arbitrariness or willfulness. Man's *hubris* and concupiscence, Tillich contends, break the essential relation of his freedom to the definite contents provided by his destiny and cause it to relate itself to an indefinite variety of objects.

> When man makes himself the center of the universe, freedom loses its definiteness. Indefinitely and arbitrarily, freedom turns to objects, persons, and things which are completely contingent upon the choosing subject and which therefore can be replaced by others of equal contingency and ultimate unrelatedness . . . if no essential relation between a free agent and his objects exist, no choice is objectively preferable to any other; no commitment to a cause or person is meaningful. No dominant purpose can be established. The indications coming from one's destiny remain unnoticed or are disregarded.[66]

Tillich admits that this description of the distortion of freedom into arbitrariness is applicable only to individuals in extreme situations, but he insists that it indicates a real danger to which all men are subject in their estranged state.

Since the elements of each polarity are interdependent, the distortion of freedom into arbitrariness is accompanied by a corresponding distortion of destiny into mechanical necessity. Internal and external compulsions come to condition the acts and choices of the individual whose freedom has become separated from his destiny. The deciding center in such an individual tends to become weakened or altogether lost, and centered decision is replaced by contingent motives or by determination through partial and conflicting aspects of the self.

It is as descriptions of man's estranged state that the traditional theories of indeterminism as well as determinism have their validity, according to Tillich.[67] Both theories are false as far as man in his essential state is concerned, but they do reflect the existential predicament of man. Man's behavior in the state of estrangement is in fact the result both of contingent motives, as the theory of indeterminism holds, and of conditioning by external forces, as the theory of determinism holds.

Dynamics and form, the elements of the second major ontological polarity, are also disrupted in man's estranged state. In man's essential nature the specifically human expression of dynamics, vitality, is united with the specifically human expression of form, intentionality. The drive of man's vitality towards self-transcendence is here directed, through intentionality, to specific and meaningful objects or contents. But when man becomes estranged from his essential nature intentionality ceases to direct vitality.

> Under the control of *hubris* and concupiscence, man is driven in all directions without any definite aim and content. His dynamics are distorted into a formless urge for self-transcendence. It is not the new form which attracts the self-transcendence of the person; the dynamics has become an aim in itself.[68]

The evil involved in this distortion of dynamics through its separation from form is that man can no longer be genuinely creative in such a situation. In his endless and insatiable quest for the new he sacrifices the possibility of creating anything real, for nothing real can be created without form.

Dynamics separated from form leads to chaos and emptiness

in man's personal and social life. This provokes a reaction in which dynamics is suppressed and form becomes dominant. The manifestation of this situation is a rigid and uncreative legalism. But both chaos and legalism are self-destructive; each necessarily provokes a flight to the other. The reason for this is that neither dynamics nor form can permanently maintain itself in separation from its polar opposite. When one side of the polarity is lost or suppressed, the other must also disappear. Man's oscillation in his existential state between oppressive legalism and empty chaos is the basic symptom of the disruption of their polar unity. A further reflection of the disruption, Tillich holds,[69] is the conflict in philosophical anthropology between dynamic doctrines of man, such as that which holds man to be essentially unlimited libido or unlimited will to power, and formal doctrines, such as the rationalistic and idealistic interpretations which reduce man's true being to a set of logical, moral, and aesthetic forms. Neither type of doctrine, according to Tillich, is true of man's essential state, in which dynamics and form are united, but both are expressions of his estranged state, in which these polar elements are disrupted.

The essential unity of the third set of polar elements in man's ontological structure, individualization and participation, is also disrupted as a consequence of estrangement. In the estranged state, according to Tillich, "man is shut within himself and cut off from participation."[70] The loneliness[71] of this situation is intolerable and provokes, in reaction, the desire to submerge oneself in a collective. The interdependence of the loneliness of the individual and his wish to become absorbed into a collective may be especially exemplified in our own historical era; it is not, however, Tillich insists, the creation merely of contemporary sociological conditions, but rather a universal expression of man's estrangement.

Other reflections of the separation of individualization and participation in the state of estrangement are found by Tillich in the idealistic conception of man, according to which he is nothing more than "a cognitive subject (ens cogitans), who perceives, analyzes, and controls reality,"[72] and in that mode of knowing in which the subject approaches its objects without *eros* or emotional participation in them.[73] Such a mode of knowing, Tillich holds, may be apropriate at certain levels, but if it determines the cognitive approach as a whole, including the approach to man, it is a symptom of estrangement and a source of evil. When man is approached by way of controlling knowledge, he tends to be reduced to a thoroughly calculable object, similar to all other objects and wholly explainable in terms either of physiological and chemical structures or of psychological mechanism; and the step from such a theoretical understanding of man to a practical dealing with him as a mere object is a very short one.

Estrangement, then, transforms the possibility of the disruption of the polar elements of his ontological structure, of which man is anxiously aware even in his essential state, into an actuality. Beyond this, Tillich maintains,[74] it also transforms the anxiety about nonbeing which grasps man in his essential state into a "horror of death." The change, according to him, is due to the element of guilt, for in the state of estrangement, "the loss of one's potential eternity is experienced as something for which one is responsible in spite of its universal tragic actuality."[75] When associated with his consciousness of his own sin and guilt, death becomes for man not only an end which he awaits with anxiety but an evil, a structure of destruction, which he regards with horror and despair.

The state of estrangement, according to Tillich,[76] also transforms the anxiety which man experiences in connection with the categorical forms of finitude, namely, time, space, causality and substance. In the essential state the anxiety which they produce is balanced by courage and can even be overcome by courage, if the predominance of being-itself, or the ultimate power of being, over nonbeing is experienced. But in the state of estrangement the relationship of man to the ultimate power of being is lost; now it is nonbeing which is predominant in man's experience, and his response to the categories is no longer anxiety balanced or overcome by courage but rather, at first, resistance, and then, when resistance fails as it inevitably must, despair.

Tillich shows how this happens, first, in man's relationship to the category of time. In his existential state man is estranged from the ultimate power of being and from the sense of participation in the "eternal now" which the presence of this power conveys. Therefore, he experiences time "as mere transitoriness without actual presence" or "as a demonic power, destroying what it has created."[77] The resistance that he offers to this transitoriness and the threat of ultimate nonbeing implied in it assumes different forms.

> Man tries to prolong the small stretch of time given to him; he tries to fill the moment with as many transitory things as possible; he tries to create for himself a memory in a future which is not his; he imagines a continuation of his life after the end of his time and an endlessness without eternity.[78]

But man is defeated in all these forms of resistance, and the consequence of his defeat is a despair in which he comes to look upon time as an evil, a structure of destruction.

Spatiality, under the conditions of existence, is experienced by man as complete uprootedness. Estranged from the presence of the ultimate power of being and debarred from the experience of the immovable ground of the "eternal here" which this presence produces, man comes to feel that there is no place—whether in the physical, sociological or psychological sense—to which he necessarily belongs and which belongs to him. His attempts to make some definite space absolutely his own, or to capture for himself as many spaces as possible, are forms of resistance against spatial contingency which must necessarily fail, and a consequence of his failure, according to Tillich,[79] is that he is thrown into a despair in which he knows that he must ultimately be uprooted from all space.

Despair, Tillich concludes,[80] is also the inevitable result of man's attempts in the state of existence to resist the threat of nonbeing implicit in the categories of causality and substance. Estranged from the ultimate power of being which is the ground of all accidental change, man comes to feel that he is the victim of total necessitation and that he may completely lose his self.

identity. The futility of his efforts, in reaction, to make himself an absolute cause and to give himself an absolute substance cannot but lead to despair.

The state of estrangement, according to Tillich,[81] also has destructive effects on man's rational or cognitive life. Even in his essential state, man experiences doubt and its accompanying anxiety, for he knows that in his finitude he is excluded from the whole which constitutes the true. Essential doubt assumes many forms: the methodological doubt of science; the insecurity of the individual about himself, stemming from his awareness that contingency characterizes not only his personal choices, decisions and emotions, but the very fact of his being at all; the uncertainty about one's world which is necessarily produced by the uncertainty about one's self; the questioning of the ultimate meaning of both. All these forms of doubt, insecurity and uncertainty are present in the state of essential finitude but not destructively so, for here, Tillich declares, they are "accepted in the power of the dimension of the eternal."[82]

> In this dimension there is an ultimate security or certainty which does not cancel out the preliminary insecurities and uncertainties of finitude (including the anxiety of their awareness). Rather it takes them into itself with the courage to accept one's finitude.[83]

But when, in the state of estrangement, man is cut off from the dimension of the ultimate, doubt and insecurity become absolute and man is driven to despair not only about the possibility of reaching any truth but about his very being as such. His attempts to escape from this despair take numerous forms. He may make absolute claims for what he irrationally chooses to regard as certainties and securities, and defend these with all the more fanaticism the more he is aware of the threat that they will break down. Or he may be thrown into restlessness, emptiness, and the experience of meaningless. Or he may react with an attitude of cynical indifference to all questions of meaning and truth. Whatever his reaction, the state of estrangement transforms man's essential doubt and insecurity into a structure of existential destruction, or evil.

We have observed Tillich repeatedly to maintain that the state into which man is driven by the evils of his existential estrangement is that of despair. This state, he tells us,

> is the final index of man's predicament; it is the boundary line beyond which man cannot go. In despair, not in death, man has come to the end of his possibilities. The word itself means "without hope" and expresses the feeling of a situation from which there is "no exit" (Sartre). . . . Despair is the state of inescapable conflict. It is the conflict, on the one hand, between what one potentially is and therefore ought to be and, on the other hand, what one actually is in the combination of freedom and destiny. The pain of despair is the agony of being responsible for one's existence and of being unable to recover it. One is shut up in one's self and in the conflict with one's self. One cannot escape, because one cannot escape from one's self.[84]

A common reaction to the experience of despair, Tillich points out, is the desire to get rid of one's self through suicide. But suicide cannot be considered an escape from despair because "the element of guilt in despair points to the dimension of the ultimate"[85] and suicide cannot release man from this dimension. Man knows that the problem of salvation from his guilt trancends the level of temporality and can be solved only by the reestablishment of his participation in the eternal.[86]

But man, according to Tillich, cannot by himself achieve reunion with the eternal or God. All of his attempts at self-salvation must necessarily fail. Only the actual appearance of a New Being in whom there is no split between essence and existence can "overcome" man's estrangement and the evil and despair which are its consequences. Tillich's conception of the New Being and how it heals man's disrupted existence are, however, basically theological matters which must be left for discussion in the next chapter. There we shall examine those aspects of his doctrine of God and the Christ which he believes offer solutions to the problems raised in the analysis of man's essential ontological structure and his existential estrangement from his essential being.

IV. CRITICISM AND EVALUATION

It is obvious, even upon a superficial reading, that Tillich's account of the nature of human existence is basically little more than an attempt to restate, with the aid of philosophical terminology and of selected corroboratory insights from the disciplines of depth psychology and sociology, several major doctrines of classical Christian theology. His analysis of man's transition from essence to existence is, in effect, a restatement of the Christian doctrine of the Fall; his account of the qualities that characterize man's existential state is a reformulation of the Christian doctrine of sin; and his description of man's existential self-destruction and despair is a reworking of the Christian doctrine of evil.

The fact that, both in its elements and its totality, Tillich's portrayal of human existence derives so largely from the Christian theological tradition does not, of course, invalidate its claim to truth. But it does show, as we have already suggested,[87] that the method of correlation which Tillich professes is not the method which he actually follows. The description of the nature of human existence, according to the method of correlation, should be a detached and objective philopohical analysis in which the theologian's existential commitments to his religious tradition may be permitted to focus his vision but certainly ought not to be as massively determinative of the final outcome as they here obviously are.

Apparently it is Tillich's belief, however, that his own interpretations of the Christian doctrines of the Fall, sin and evil provide insights into the nature of human existence whose truth should be apparent even to those outside the theological circle of Christianity and without existential commitment to it.

Considering his philosophical translation of the doctrine of the Fall as the "transition from essence to existence," we note first that Tillich uses the word "essence" not only in the two major senses which he finds exemplified in the philosophical tradition, namely, as "the nature of a thing" or its "universal" and as the ideal "from which a thing has fallen,"[88] but in a third sense, namely, as the undifferentiated unity of being in the

divine ground before creation.[89] Thus man's essential being is
described by Tillich as the state of being "hidden in the ground
of the divine life";[90] and, as a result, man's existential being
seems to be, for him, not only the state in which man contradicts his own essence as "finite freedom" but his very individuality, his existence as a separate self or personality.

Creation and Fall, though distinguished, coincide. For Tillich,
"actualized creation and estranged existence are identical."[91]
For man to pass beyond the state of essentiality or potentiality
which is described alternatively as "dreaming innocence" and
"hiddenness in the divine ground" and to emerge as an individual
personality or a separate self is for him to have become, by that
very fact, sinful and estranged; for, as Tillich puts it, "in order
to have a self which can not only be loved but can love God,
one's center must already have left the divine center to which
it belongs and in which self-love and love of God are united."[92]

Despite Tillich's emphatic denial[93] of the charge that he has
identified finitude as such with evil, or selfhood as such with
estrangement, it is difficult to reconcile this denial with his explicit statements. Before commenting on the general validity
of his doctrine on this matter, it may not be amiss to point out
that it is open to question whether he is here faithful to the
biblical mythology which he professes to be interpreting or
even, for that matter, to the dominant tradition of Christian
thought. In defending his contention that the end of Creation,
which is the actualization of personal existence, and the beginning of the Fall, coincide, he declares, "Those theologians who
are not willing to interpret the biblical creation story and the
story of the fall as reports about two actual events should draw
the consequence and posit the mystery where it belongs—in the
unity of freedom and destiny in the ground of being."[94] But it
is quite obvious and undeniable that the stories of creation and
fall *are* two different stories in the Bible; and even if creation
and fall are interpreted, as they are by Tillich, as non-temporal
events, their common non-temporality does not make them
identical. And, surely, Christian tradition, in speaking of the
"innocency" of "Adam before the fall," has understood this
innocency in historical terms, whereas for Tillich, dreaming

innocence is non-actualized and non-temporal—a state of mere potentiality.

In his *Propositions,* mimeographed for private circulation, Tillich writes, "The myth of 'the transcendent fall' describes the transition (from essence to existence) as a universal event in ontological terms. The myth of 'the immanent fall' describes the transition as an individual event in psychological terms." And in his *Systematic Theology*[95] he ascribes the same general significance to the Platonic myth of the transcendent fall of the soul as to the biblical myth of the fall of Adam. But there is no myth of a transcendent fall in the Bible; the fall, or disobedience,[96] of Adam is here clearly regarded as an actual historical event, and it has been interpreted as such in the dominant strain of Christian theological thought. As Reinhold Niebuhr writes, "The idea of a transcendent fall always appears in Christian theology, from Origen on, whenever ontological speculations lead to the conclusion that evil is involved in finiteness as such."[97] Tillich himself decries the doctrine of the suprelapsarian Calvinists as seemingly "demonic,"[98] but it is difficult to resist the conclusion that he has himself made the fall from created goodness an ontological fate or necessity; and one wonders whether his own doctrine is any less "demonic."

Whether Tillich's account of man's fall, or transition from essence to existence, is in agreement with the major trend of classical Christian thinking on the subject is not for us to decide. We may say that, so far as we can see, he is here considerably closer to Hinduism than to Christianity. As Professor Bernard Loomer, in interpreting Tillich's doctrine, has pointed out, "To renounce his sin, it would seem that man would have to give up his actuality and return to being a potentiality within the undifferentiated unity of God. . . . Eschatological fulfillment would involve the obliteration of individual beings."[99] The more important question, however, is whether Tillich's account is a valid description of the reality of the human condition. In defense of his view that the fall is unavoidable, Tillich states that it is derived "from a realistic observation of man, his heart, and his history"[100] and appeals to philosophy.

> . . . I think that theology should take seriously the fact that some of the greatest philosophers (Plato, Origen, Kant, Schelling), in spite of their belief in the power of reason, have been driven to the myth of the transcendent fall. It is not "speculation" (today a disparaging word) but their impression of the radical and universal nature of evil which drove them to conceive of a myth in which both human freedom and the tragic nature of existence are asserted—though not explained—in terms of structural necessity.[101]

But is evil as "radical and universal" in man as Tillich and these philosophers think? Certainly the optimism about man of nineteenth-century idealism and liberal Christian theology now seems somewhat shallow and unrealistic. But is not an unrelieved concentration on the evil in human nature equally untrue to the facts? Is there no spontaneous goodness in man, even if moral perfection is beyond his attainment? And should not this goodness be given due recognition, as it has been—most notably—in the Jewish tradition? Tillich seems to have succumbed to the general tendency of Christian theologians to "load the question" on this matter, to pretend that the only alternative to a foolish and unjustified optimism about man's goodness is a belief in his radical sinfulness. Obviously these alternatives do not exhaust the possibilities.

Tillich seems to believe that once man actualizes his potentiality of existence and becomes an individual self, he must necessarily center his life in himself; that is to say, he makes no clear distinction between selfhood and selfishness. But certainly these are very different states, and the one does not imply the other. Man may use his selfhood to make of himself an absolute center in *hubris* and concupiscence, but he may also choose to relate himself in love and cooperation to his fellow man.

That men may and do fall into sinfulness is obvious, and that not only, as Tillich holds, by their free and conscious decisions but also as a result of all the biological and social influences which he includes under the heading of destiny. But Tillich seems to believe that it is impossible for man not to fall into sinfulness; the fall, for him, is unavoidable.[102] What, then, happens to the freedom which he ascribes to man and which he regards as involved in the fall? Surely, to say that man is free in a certain situation means that he might choose otherwise than he actually does. But Tillich does not appear to believe that man has any alternative other than to fall into estrangement. Indeed, man, for him, does not even *become* sinful at any specifiable time. All men everywhere and at all times are already in existential estrangement and under the compulsions of the "bondage of the will." It is only essential man who seems to have any alternative, and even here his further freedom disappears as soon as he has made his decision to actualize his individuality and to "separate" himself from "the divine ground." And essential man, it will be remembered, is, for Tillich, only a state of potentiality, not an actual existent.

Tillich speaks of man's fall as a "mystery,"[103] and, indeed, his own account of the process contains many mystifying elements. We are not convinced that his philosophical translation of the myth of man's fall as the "transition from essence to existence" is very successful or enlightening. We are tempted to ask Tillich how essential man, being only a potentiality, can choose or act; and what warrant, beyond his own decision to do so, he has for defining man's essential being as the state in which he is still not separated from the undifferentiated unity of being in the divine ground, with the consequence that selfhood becomes identical with estrangement and the fall becomes a necessary consequence of individualization. Above all, we are not convinced that Tillich, in making the fall an ontological necessity rather than a moral possibility, has done justice to the full reality of the human situation and given sufficient recognition to man's power to make the right, as well as the wrong, choices. In developing his description of man's existence, which he holds to be a faithful picture of the human condition, Tillich seems to us to have removed most of the dignity and goodness which he ascribes to man in his analysis of the structure of man's being.

Though we cannot follow Tillich either in his account of the fall or in his contention that his description of man's sinful state is an accurate picture of the general human situation, we

may acknowledge the significance of the analysis which he gives
of unbelief, concupiscence, and *hubris,* as the marks of human
estrangement. His description of the basic role of *hubris* in the
human predicament is particularly valuable. We cannot but
wonder, however, whether he might not have done well to draw
a sharper distinction between man's unjustified self-elevation and
his legitimate desire to exercise his creative powers and to ascribe
significance to their results.

A comment is also in order here on Tillich's contention that
unbelief in the moral realm means the separation of the human
and divine wills and that the witness of this separation is the
fact that men need a law which tells them how to act and which
they can choose to obey or disobey. Tillich is here reflecting the
antinomianism of St. Paul who, in his polemic against so-called
"Jewish legalism," held that the law is the major sign of man's
estrangement from God. But that man's need for law, which is
admitted even by the most extreme Christian antinomianists, is
a symptom of estrangement is surely open to serious question.
Cannot the law be an aspect of the "good" creation? Indeed, it
has been so regarded in classical Judaism, which looks upon the
law as a means of uniting man with God and as a gift of God's
grace to man.

An important question also arises concerning the relationship
between Tillich's account of human estrangement and particularly of the self-destructive conflicts and contradictions which
he holds to be its consequences, on the one hand, and the
psychoanalysts' description of the neurotic and psychotic personality, on the other. Harry M. Tiebout, Jr., has written an
informative paper whose well-documented thesis is that there
are "marked similarities between Freud's analysis of human
estrangement, as manifested in neurosis and other pathological
conditions, and Tillich's analysis of sin."[104] Tillich himself has
gone even further and admitted[105] that some of the conflicts
and compulsions he describes are fully exemplified only in
psychopathic personalities. Now, while it may be true that
all human beings are neurotic to a degree, one cannot help
asking whether a description of the neurotic state—a description
which, indeed, goes even further and borrows elements from

psychopathology—should be considered of universal applicability and a generally faithful rendering of the human condition.

One more observation we may be allowed. Tillich makes much of the "horror of death" that he believes grips man in the state of existential estrangement. Surely, this horror, if it exists, is in no small measure the result of conditioning by Christian doctrine which has, ever since Paul, tended to associate death with guilt. But is the association a necessary one? Judaism does not generally look upon death with horror. The Buddha also, after his enlightenment, is said to have transcended all anxiety, and the legends of his death stand in marked contrast to those of Jesus' anxious and horrified anticipation of his death in the Gospels. It may be said, of course, that Jesus was awaiting the awful death of a convict on the cross, but, according to Jewish legend, when Rabbi Akiba faced his Roman executioners who tore his limbs apart and seared his flesh with fire he did not despair but rejoiced rather that he could now serve his God with "all his might," that is, through the surrender of life itself.

Too much, we believe, is made by Tillich—following the classical Christian tradition—of the unnaturalness of death. Why should death be regarded as unnatural and, furthermore, as a punishment for sin? Tillich cannot say that he is merely following the doctrine implied in the story of Adam's punishment in the Book of Genesis, for he feels quite free to disregard or reinterpret those aspects of biblical mythology which do not suit him. It may well be that unexpiated guilt will cause a man to look upon his impending death with horror, but surely there are and have been men who could die completely at peace with themselves and with God. Tillich might look upon the story as unbelievably shallow, but he might nevertheless ponder the significance of the probably legendary tale concerning Thoreau who, when asked by a relative on his death-bed "Henry, have you made your peace with God?" is supposed to have replied, "I have never quarreled with Him."

CHAPTER SIX

The Source of Man's Courage and of the Healing of His Estrangement: God and the Christ

I. INTRODUCTION

TWO BASIC QUESTIONS emerge from Tillich's description of the ontological structure in which he holds man and all other beings in nature to participate. The first and more general one, which proceeds from the assumption that the ontological structure is not ultimate and underived, is the question, In what is this structure grounded and what is the nature of its ground? The second relates specifically to man and the finitude of his being as revealed with particular sharpness in Tillich's analysis of the categories. It is the question, What is the source of the courage which serves as a balance to man's essential anxiety about the threat of nonbeing implicit in his finitude and which enables him to take this anxiety upon himself? The answers to both questions, Tillich believes, are to be found in the doctrine of God. In this chapter we shall examine these answers in their major outlines. No attempt will be made to deal in detail with all the ramifications of Tillich's rich and complex treatment of the idea of God. Our attention will be focused on those aspects which are most directly relevant to the explanation (1) of the ground of the ontological structure in which man and all other finite beings participate and (2) of man's courage to be and to resist the threat of nonbeing.

The fundamental question with which Tillich concludes his analysis of man's existence is the nature of the power whereby man's existential estrangement from his essential being can be conquered and whereby he can be saved from the evils and the despair which are the consequences of this estrangement. The answer to this question, Tillich maintains, is to be found in the doctrine of Jesus as the Christ, who is the final manifestation and bearer of the New Being, by participation in which man's old and estranged being can be healed. In the pages that follow we shall also examine this answer, confining ourselves to those basic aspects of Tillich's Christology which relate specifically to the New Being overcoming the split between man's created or essential being and his sinful or estranged existence.

Both the doctrines of God and of the Christ are, for Tillich, the products of revelation. In terms of his method of correlation they are theological, as distinguished from the questions which he regards them as answering and which he believes to be philosophical, or more precisely, philosophically formulated. We examine them here because, without them, Tillich anthropology cannot be fully understood or evaluated; for, as he himself has indicated,[1] his philosophical analysis of the nature of man's being and of his existence is dependent to a considerable degree on these theological doctrines. Furthermore, they are worth examining in a philosophical context because for Tillich, it will be recalled,[2] the products of revelation, i.e., "saved" or "ecstatic" reason, are not supernatural truths. Nor are they irrational or, indeed, in any way antithetical to ordinary reason. It is his claim in fact that the *logos* manifested in the Christian revelation is identical with the universal *logos* and that in principle the content of this revelation might be given by ontological reason in its essence.[3]

II. GOD

According to Tillich, man cannot through ordinary reason arrive at knowledge of God. The classical philosophical arguments for the existence of God, which are the substance of all natural or rational theologies, are unable to *prove* anything. What they claim to establish, namely, the existence of God, is self-contradictory even, for God is not an existent being.[4] He is, we shall see Tillich maintain, *being-itself*, the creative ground of essence and existence and beyond both. The significance of the arguments is found by Tillich to lie in a direction other than the answers they give. They are meaningful, he believes, only because of the fact that they express, at least by implication, those aspects of man's finitude which make the question of God possible and necessary.

Basically the ontological argument shows only, according to Tillich,[5] that in man's awareness of his finitude is included also an awareness of a potential infinity which essentially belongs to him but from which he is in fact excluded. It points to the presence of an infinite or unconditional element in the structure of reason, an element which appears in its theoretical functions as what Augustine called *verum ipsum*, the true-itself as the norm of all approximations to truth, and in its practical functions as what Kant called *bonum ipsum*, the good-itself as the norm of all approximations to goodness. But the experience of this infinite or unconditional element in reason does not establish the existence of an infinite or unconditional being within reality, whether this being is envisaged as a divine guarantor of truth or as a divine giver of moral laws and guarantor of the coordination between morality and happiness. *Verum ipsum* and *bonum ipsum* are rather, Tillich declares, "manifestations of *esse ipsum*, being-itself, as the ground and abyss of everything that is."[6] What Tillich, then, is saying about the ontological argument is that, rather than being a proof for the existence of God, it is an indication that man has an awareness of God which precedes his asking the question of God.

While the ontological argument points to the presence of the unconditional in man's reason which makes the asking of the question of God *possible* for man, the cosmological and teleological arguments, according to Tillich,[7] point to the threat of non-being to man's being which makes the asking of this question on his part *necessary*. The cosmological argument proceeds from man's awareness of the categorical structure of finitude in which his being and all other beings are involved and which subjects him to the danger of annihilation. The asnwers at which it arrives, God as first cause or necessary substance, do not solve the problem of explaining how categorical finitude is overcome or, in regard to man, how the non-being by which he feels threatened is conquered by being or how his anxiety is conquered by courage. Since cause and substance are still categories of finitude even when preceded by the adjectives "first" and "necessary," the answers of the cosmological argument only serve, according to Tillich, as "symbols which express the question implied in finite being, the question of that which transcends finitude and categories, the question of being-itself embracing and conquering non-being, the question of God."[8]

The teleological argument is based, Tillich holds, not on the threat of nonbeing in the sense of annihilation, as is the cosmological, but on the threat of nonbeing in the sense of the loss of that unity of the polar elements in the ontological structure of finite being which gives this being its *telos* or meaningful character. Anxiety about meaninglessness, Tillich declares, "is the characteristically human form of ontological anxiety . . . the form . . . which only a being can have in whose nature freedom and destiny are united."[9] It is as an expression of man's anxiety about the loss of this and the other polar unities which give meaning to his being that the teleological argument serves. It does not logically establish the existence of an infinite and unthreatened ground of meaning, but rather drives man to the question of such a ground.

Philosophy, in the form of the classical rational arguments for the existence of God, Tillich thus concludes, cannot answer the question of God for man. It can only raise it for him and prepare him for the answer of revelation. This is so because philosophy, as such, can do no more than describe and analyze the structure of finite being. It cannot go beyond this structure to its unconditional and inexhaustible depth. This depth is uncovered only in revelation, in which the unconditional and infinite is made manifest through the transparency of some finite object, event, or person.

Before proceeding to elaborate the answer of revelation to the question of God, Tillich gives a definition of the meaning of the "idea" of God as he understands it and as he also finds it exemplified in a phenomenological survey of mankind's religions. "'God' is the answer to the question implied in man's finitude; *he is the name for that which concerns man ultimately.*"[10] The quality of holiness which is usually ascribed to God is just this quality of ultimate concern. "Only that which is holy can give man ultimate concern, and only that which gives man ultimate concern has the quality of holiness."[11] Rudolf Otto's description of the mystery of the holy as *tremendum et fascinans* is, according to Tillich's interpretation of it, an expression of "the experience of 'the ultimate' in the double sense of that which is the abyss and that which is the ground of man's being."[12] In surveying the history of religion, that is, the history of the forms in which the realm of the holy has been discovered by man, Tillich finds one outstanding fact of central importance, namely, that man can be ultimately concerned only about that which is simultaneously both concrete and absolute, capable of being encountered in direct experience and yet transcending everything that is finite and conditioned.[13] It is this tension between the demand for concreteness and the demand for absolute transcendence and ultimacy in the idea of God that, according to Tillich, has largely determined the religious history of mankind and is reflected in the various types of theism that have emerged in it. This tension, he holds, explains the development from polytheism to dualism and finally to monotheism in its various forms.[14] It has also determined, according to him, the classic types of philosophy, which he takes to be fundamentally only theoretical transformations of the various religious doctrines of God.[15]

Having defined the "idea" of God and summarized its history, Tillich proceeds to describe the "actuality" of God. Revelation, or reason which has become "ecstatic" and transcended its ordinary structure through a simultaneous experience of the shock of nonbeing and of the power of being overcoming it,[16] yields the basic understanding that the actuality of God is being-itself, or, what amounts to the same thing, that he is the infinite ground or power of being in everything and above everything whereby it resists and conquers nonbeing. Once God is understood as the ground of being, it follows, according to Tillich, that he is the ground of the ontological structure in which man and all other finite beings participate, while at the same time transcending this structure. "Since God is the ground of being," Tillich writes, "he is the ground of the structure of being. He is not subject to this structure; the structure is grounded in him."[17]

God as being-itself is, then, the answer yielded by revelation or ecstatic reason, according to Tillich, to man's question about the ultimate ground of his own ontological structure and that of all other finite beings. But what can be known about God? What, if any, specific, positive assertions can be made about him? That God is being-itself is, according to Tillich,[18] the only non-symbolic or literal statement about him that theology, in its attempt to formulate cognitively the deliverance of revelation, can make. Everything else that is said about God is only a symbolic statement deriving from an interpretation of the structure of finite being, its elements and categories, and the application of this interpretation analogically to the infinite.

It is the *analogia entis*, Tillich declares, that "gives us our only justification of speaking at all about God."[19] The fact that God, in one sense, *is* the structure of being,[20] makes possible positive assertions about him on the basis of man's knowledge of this structure as he encounters it in his own experience. But the further fact that God, as the ground and depth of the structure of being, transcends it and is not subject to or conditioned by it, makes all such assertions analogical or symbolic. For a symbol is something which both participates in the reality to which it points and is transcended by this reality, and whose proper meaning is therefore simultaneously affirmed and negated.[21] Symbols, deriving as they do from the material of finite reality, cannot be understood as applying literally to that which transcends the finite infinitely. "To say anything about God in the literal sense of the words used means to say something false about Him. The symbolic in relation to God is not less true than the literal, but it is the only true way of speaking about God."[22]

Symbolic knowledge of God, then, is attainable through the structure of being. The elements of this structure, Tillich expressly asserts,[23] supply the materials for symbolizing the divine life. But this does not mean, he insists, that a doctrine of God can be derived philosophically from an ontological system.

> The character of the divine life is made manifest in revelation. Theology can only explain and systematize the existential knowledge of revelation in theoretical terms, interpreting the symbolic significance of the ontological elements and categories.[24]

We shall consider here a few of the statements about God or being-itself that Tillich believes may be made by theology in its attempt to explain the "existential knowledge of revelation" through a symbolic interpretation of the ontological structure and its elements.

Revelation, at least that documented in the Bible, particularly the Old Testament, speaks of God as "living." What, in ontological terms, does the attribution of life to God or to being-itself mean? Ontologically speaking, life, according to Tillich, is "the process in which potential being becomes actual being" or "the actualization of the structural elements of being in their unity and their tension."[25] These structural elements, Tillich believes, simultaneously separate and reunite in every life-process.[26] Insofar as God is the ground of life, he may be said to be himself living, but only symbolically so, for in God there is no distinction between potentiality and actuality. What the symbol of "living" applied to God must be understood as meaning, according to Tillich, is, negatively, that he is neither "a pure identity of being as being" nor that there is in him "a definite separation of being from being," and, positively, that "he is the eternal process in which separation is posited and is overcome by reunion."[27] So understood, God may also be symbolized as love.

In symbolizing the nature of the divine life through the ontological elements, man, according to Tillich, gives predominant emphasis to the elements belonging to the self or subject side of the basic ontological structure, i.e., individualization, dynamics, and freedom. This is only natural, for it is man's being as a self that determines his existential relationship to God, which is the source of all symbolization. Man cannot help envisaging that which is his ultimate concern in analogy to what he himself is—namely, personal, dynamic and free. But in God as being-itself or the ultimate ground of the structure of being, Tillich maintains, "every ontological element includes its polar opposite completely, without tension and without the threat of dissolution;"[28] and, he adds, "the religious mind—theologically speaking, man in the correlation of revelation—always realizes implicitly, if not explicitly, that the other side of the polarities is completely present in the side he uses as symbolic material."[29]

In the case of the symbolic assertions about the nature of the divine life derived from the ontological polarity of individualization and participation, the symbol of God as "personal" or "the absolute individual" must be balanced, Tillich insists,[30] by the symbol of God as "the absolute participant." The symbol of God as "personal" must, furthermore, not be interpreted to mean that God is *a* person in the sense of being a self, for selfhood implies "separation from and contrast to everything which is not self,"[31] and God as being-itself is separate from nothing. To symbolize God as personal is to say only that, as the ground of everything personal and the source of the ontological power of personality, he is not less than personal.[32] And the symbol of God as "the universal participant" must be taken to mean not that he participates in everything spatially or temporally, but only that, as the creative source of everything, he is somehow present to it. Both "personality" and "omnipresence" may be attributed symbolically or analogically to God because "both individualization and participation are rooted in the ground of the divine life and . . . God is equally 'near' to each of them while transcending them both."[33]

The elements of the second ontological polarity, dynamics and form, are also grounded in the divine life, where they are balanced by each other without conflict and without threat of disruption. It was the mistakenly exclusive emphasis on the second of these elements that, according to Tillich, produced the classical symbol of God as *actus purus,* "the pure form in which everything potential is actual, and which is the eternal self-intuition of the divine fullness (*pleroma*)."[34] This symbol, Tillich believes, must be rejected, for "the God who is *actus purus* is not the living God."[35] The concepts—Tillich cites as examples the *Urgrund* or the "nature in God" of Böhme, the "first potency" of Schelling, the "will" of Schopenhauer, the "given in God" of Brightman, the *meonic* freedom" of Berdyaev, and the "contingent" of Hartshorne—developed by those philosophers who have emphasized the presence of a dynamic element in the divine life are regarded with favor by him.[36] But, he argues, these concepts must not be understood literally—for then they would make God limited and finite—but rather as pointing symbolically to "the negative element in the ground of being which is overcome as negative in the process of being itself."[37] Furthermore, they must not be interpreted as establishing the idea of a "becoming" God. There is self-transcendence in God, but, Tillich declares, God's "self-transcendence never is in tension with his self-preservation, so that he always remains God."[38] When God is understood as being-itself and the symbol "living" is applied to him, self-transcendence and self-preservation, or dynamics and form, are both included, but to speak of God as "becoming" disrupts the balance between these elements in God and limits him in a way that undercuts his divinity. Tillich appears to regard the attributes of "will" and "intellect" ascribed to God in medieval theology and derived from the polarity of vitality and intentionality in man's ontological structure as useful symbols for the elements, respectively, of dynamics and form. But the controversy over which is primary and which subordinate in God is meaningless. Both must be included and given parity in the symbolization of the divine life, for this life is the ground both of dynamics and form.

The divine life further includes in undisrupted balance the ontological elements of freedom and destiny, of which it is again the ultimate ground. The doctrine of classical theology concerning the *aseity* of God, his being self-caused or self-derived, asserts the unconditional freedom of God and denies that there is anything prior to him or alongside him which can limit him. It also means that nothing is given in God which is not at the same time affirmed by his freedom. Understood symbolically and in terms of the existential correlation of man and God, as it must be, the freedom of God means, according to Tillich, "that that which is man's ultimate concern is in no way dependent on man or any finite being or any finite concern."[39] If destiny is attributed to God, as it may be, this element of the ontological structure must also be understood symbolically, for there is no power above God which determines his destiny. He is his own destiny, and in him freedom and destiny are one. The ideas of structural necessity in God and of God "being his own law" may be useful as interpretations, according to Tillich,[40] but they lack the connotative power of the symbol of destiny, which points both to the infinite mystery of being-itself, which precedes any structure or law, and to the participation of God in becoming and history.

Each of the symbols derived from the ontological elements contributes something to the understanding of the divine life, but "the most embracing, direct, and unrestricted symbol" for this life, Tillich declares,[41] is the symbol of God as "Spirit." Spirit, as he defines it, is "the unity of the ontological elements and the *telos* of life."[42] To say that God is Spirit is to say that in him all the ontological elements are present in undisrupted balance and that he is the ultimate unity of both power and meaning.

The symbolization of God as personal, dynamic and free gives expression to the power side of the divine life, that which has been called its abyss or depth. The side of meaning or structure in the divine life—what has been called the divine *logos*, or the mirror of the divine depth, or the principle of God's self-objectification—is symbolized through the attribution to God of participation, form and destiny. Both the divine abyss and the divine *logos* are contained and united in the symbol of God as Spirit. The ultimate basis of the trinitarian idea of God is to be found, Tillich maintains in concluding his discussion of the symbol of God as Spirit,[43] in the recognition that the two divine principles of abyss and *logos* are actualized and fulfilled by the third principle of Spirit which, as the unity of the other two, represents in a sense the whole of the divine life.

What Tillich takes to be the answer of revelation to the first of the two basic questions which emerge from his philosophical analysis of being and with which we are concerned in this chapter may now be briefly summarized: God as being-itself is the ground of the ontological structure of man and all other finite beings, without being himself subject to this structure.

Nothing more can be asserted of God in a literal or direct way than that he is being-itself. But the fact that finite being participates in being-itself, and that God is not only the ground of the ontological structure but, in a sense, *is* this structure itself, makes it possible for man in the situation of revelation to gain some symbolic knowledge of the nature of the divine life through an interpretation, on the basis of the *analogia entis,* of the structural elements of finite being. The knowledge so gained may be summarized in the symbolic assertion that God is Spirit, by which is meant that he unites and actualizes in his life all the ontological elements, but in such a way that the polar tension and the consequent liability to disruption which characterize them in the structure of finite being is overcome.

The second major question which arises out of Tillich's ontological analysis, namely, the question whence man derives the courage to overcome the anxiety accompanying the threat of nonbeing implicit in his finitude, finds its solution, he believes, in an understanding of the creative activity of God and the symbols which point to it. The doctrine of creation, as given by revelation, Tillich asserts,[44] is not "the story of an event which took place 'once upon a time'" but rather "the basic description of the relation between God and the world" and "answers the question implied in man's finitude and in finitude generally."

The divine creativity, we must first of all notice, is, for Tillich, identical with the divine life. God creates because he is God, and it is meaningless to ask whether creation is a contingent or necessary act on his part. It comes from both God's freedom and destiny, which, in him, are one. "Since the divine life is essentially creative," Tillich adds,

> all three modes of time must be used in symbolizing it. God *has* created the world, he *is* creative in the present moment, and he *will* creatively fulfill his *telos.* Therefore, we must speak of originating creation, sustaining creation, and directing creation.[45]

The concept of God's *originating* creativity means for Tillich that everything that is derives its power of being from the creative ground of the divine life. Originating creation has been characterized by classical Christian theology, he points out, as *creatio ex nihilo.* This formula means first, in Tillich's understanding of it, that there is nothing "given" to God "which influences him in his creativity or which resists his creative *telos*"[46] and that there is therefore nothing in the essential nature of things which necessarily imposes a tragic character on existence. But the *nihil* out of which the creatures are said to come emphasizes also, according to Tillich,[47] that creatureliness, which is the character of all finite beings, carries within itself "the heritage of nonbeing."[48] This heritage is, of course, balanced by the heritage of being through the participation of the creature in being-itself.

God's *sustaining* creativity is explained by Tillich[49] as the continuous preservation of those structures of reality which endure amidst change and which provide the basis for being and action. What Tillich means by such structures is, it would seem, what are ordinarily called "the laws of nature." As against deism, Tillich maintains that God is immanent in the world as its permanent creative ground. But God, he insists, is also transcendent to the world through the divine freedom which stands over against the finite freedom of man. Man's freedom, in turn, makes the world transcendent to God.

The *directing* creativity of God is Tillich's translation of the traditional idea of providence.[50] This aspect of the divine creativity is to be understood as the direction of all things by God to their *telos* or fulfillment. The faith that such direction actually takes place is, Tillich declares, faith in spite of appearances to the contrary, "in spite of the darkness of fate and of the meaninglessness of existence."[51] The conception of providence as divine interference in the conditions of individual life or of world history must be rejected; there is no such interference.

> Providence is a quality of every constellation of conditions, a quality which "drives" or "lures" toward fulfillment. Providence is "the divine condition" which is present in every group of finite conditions and in the totality of finite conditions. It is not an additional factor, a miraculous physical or mental interference in terms of supranaturalism. It is the quality of inner directedness present in every situation.[52]

In the divine creativity in all its forms the power of being, resisting and conquering nonbeing, is present.[53] As creative in and through everything in every moment, God is appropriately symbolized, Tillich holds,[54] as almighty or omnipotent, and the classical symbol of the divine omnipotence provides the basic answer to the question implied in finitude, the question of the source whence man derives the courage to overcome the anxiety of his finitude.

> Faith in the almighty God is the answer to the quest for a courage which is sufficient to conquer the anxiety of finitude. Ultimate courage is based upon participation in the ultimate power of being. When the invocation "Almighty God" is seriously pronounced, a victory over the threat of nonbeing is experienced, and an ultimate, courageous affirmation of existence is expressed. Neither finitude nor anxiety disappears, but they are taken into infinity and courage.[55]

Omnipotence is for Tillich the inclusive or general symbol for the divine power in its relation to the creature.[56] Since what this power essentially does is overcome the negativities involved in the categories of finitude, the meaning of the symbol of omnipotence is largely definable through these. In relation to the categories, however, the general symbol of omnipotence may be divided, Tillich believes,[57] into a number of more restricted and special symbols. With respect to time, omnipotence is, for him, the divine eternity; with respect to space, it is the divine omnipresence; with respect to causality and substance, it is God as the creative and abysmal ground of being. Aside from its relation to the categories, the symbol of omnipotence is also related to the subject-object structure of being, and here it becomes the divine omniscience. We must consider briefly Tillich's interpretation of the meaning of each of these special symbols which collectively constitute the general symbol of omnipotence.

To say that God is eternal does not mean that the divine life is either timeless or endless in time. It means rather that this life includes in a "transcendent unity" the "dissected moments of existential time."[58] The only analogy to the divine eternity found in human life, Tillich maintains,[59] is the experience of a present which unites a remembered past and an anticipated future. On the basis of this analogy, the divine eternity may be symbolized as an eternal present (*nunc eternum*). "But this *nunc eternum*," he adds, "is not simultaneity or the negation of an independent meaning of past and future."[60] Both past and future are real for God, but they are not independent of him. God as creator creates the future and in so doing also recreates the past, for the potentialities of the past which are actualized in the future determine not only the character of the future but also that of the past. As Tillich himself puts it,

> From the point of view of eternity, both past and future are open. The creativity which leads into the future also transforms the past. If eternity is conceived in terms of creativity, the eternal includes past and future without absorbing their special character as modes of time.[61]

Both the nonbeing which Tillich has shown to threaten man in temporality and its accompanying anxiety are held to be overcome by man's participation, through faith, in the eternity of the divine life.

> Faith in the eternal God is the basis for a courage which conquers the negativities of the temporal process. Neither the anxiety of the past nor that of the future remains. The anxiety of the past is conquered by the freedom of God toward the past and its potentialities. The anxiety of the future is conquered by the dependence of the new on the unity of the divine life. The dissected moments of time are united in eternity. Here, and not in a doctrine of the human soul, is rooted the certainty of man's participation in eternal life. The hope of eternal life is based not on a substantial quality of man's soul but on his participation in the eternity of the divine life.[62]

Omnipresence symbolizes God's relation to space. Tillich rejects the view that God as Spirit may be related to time but not to space. God is not body, to be sure, but as Spirit he includes the ontological elements of vitality and personality which have a bodily basis. This means that the divine life must be regarded as participating in bodily existence. "God creates extension in the ground of his life, in which everything spatial is rooted."[63] Omnipresence is, for Tillich, the symbol for God's

"creative participation in the spatial existence of his creatures."[64] But God's participation in extension or spatiality does
not mean his subjection to it.[65] Participating in spatial existence,
God nevertheless transcends it. It is faith in the omnipresent
God, Tillich concludes,[66] which gives man the courage to overcome the anxiety of not having a permanent place that is his
own and to accept the contingencies of his spatial existence.

The categories of substance and causality, Tillich points
out,[67] have been used by man to express the relation of being-
itself or the power of being to the finite beings who participate
in it. Neither category, as such, is adequate for this purpose. But
when God is called the *prima causa* or the *ultima substantia*
the categories of causality and substance are transcended as
categories and become symbols. When this is done

> the difference between substance and causality disappears, for
> if God is the cause of the entire series of causes and effects, he
> is the substance underlying the whole process of becoming.
> But this "underlying" does not have the character of a substance
> which underlies its accidents and is completely expressed by
> them. It is an underlying in which substance and accidents
> preserve their freedom. In other words, it is substance not as a
> category but as a symbol. And, if taken symbolically, there is
> no difference between *prima causa* and *ultima substantia*. Both
> mean what can be called in a more directly symbolic term, "the
> creative and abysmal ground of being."[68]

What Tillich conceives God as the creative and abysmal
ground of being to do has already been indicated in our
summary above of his conception of the threefold nature of the
divine creativity as originating, sustaining and directing. Here
we are concerned only to add that, according to him, faith in
the God so symbolized provides man with the courage to overcome the anxiety connected with his awareness of the threat of
nonbeing implicit in his subjection to the categories of causality
and substance. For when God is understood as the creative and
abysmal ground of all being he is, as creative, the cause of the
entire series of causes and effects and, as ground, the substance
which underlies the whole process of becoming but which, in its
abysmal nature, transcends all its accidents. The term "creative,"

Tillich asserts,[69] contains and transcends causality, while the term "ground" contains and transcends substance. The divine life includes these categories, but in such a way that the threat of nonbeing which is inherent in them as they characterize the life of finite beings is conquered.

The final special symbol regarded by Tillich as contributing to the meaning of the general symbol of the divine omnipotence, namely, omniscience, is directly related, as we have already indicated, not to one of the categories but to the subject-object structure of reality. In a sense, however, it is only a qualification of the symbol of omnipresence, expressing the spiritual character of the divine participation in everything. What the symbol of omniscience must be interpreted to mean is not "the faculty of a highest being who is supposed to know all objects, past, present and future, and, beyond this, everything that might have happened if what has happened had not happened"[70] but rather that, in relation to God,

> Nothing is outside the centered unity of his life; nothing is strange, dark, hidden, isolated, unapproachable. Nothing falls outside the *logos* structure of being. The dynamic element cannot break the unity of the form; the abysmal quality cannot swallow the rational quality of the divine life.[71]

Faith in the omniscient God, Tillich maintains,[72] gives man the courage to overcome the anxiety of what is dark, hidden, or unconscious in his own being through the certainty that all this is present in God's spiritual life. It also gives man the power to take upon himself the doubt about truth and meaning which is the heritage of finitude.[73] The divine omniscience, Tillich writes,

> is the logical (though not always conscious) foundation of the belief in the openness of reality to human knowledge. We *know* because we participate in the divine knowledge. Truth is not absolutely removed from the outreach of our finite minds, since the divine life in which we are rooted embodies all truth.[74]

It is, then, in faith in God symbolized as omnipotent creator that Tillich, in his *Systematic Theology*, finds the source of man's courage to be and to overcome the anxiety of nonbeing. The

content of this faith cannot be given to man by any resources
of his own, but is "spoken" to human existence from beyond it,
according to Tillich.[75] The existential experience of revelation
alone has produced the classical symbols in which Christianity
has expressed its experience of God.

In the final chapter of his book, *The Courage To Be,* Tillich,
however, states what appears to be a quite different approach
to the problem. Here he describes the situation of extreme
doubt in which faith in all specific religious symbols has been
lost and a sense of complete meaninglessness grips the person,
and asserts that even in such a situation the power of being
is experienced. In this situation of despair, faith in the concrete
symbols of a religious tradition can no longer provide any
assurance of meaning or any ultimate courage, but a different
kind of faith, which Tillich calls "absolute" faith and which he
declares "has no special content" and "is undefinable, since
everything defined is dissolved by doubt and meaninglessness,"
supervenes and makes possible "the courage of despair."[76]
This absolute faith is the experience of the power of being as
present even in the face of the most radical manifestation of
nonbeing.[77] It is the awareness that the experience of nonbeing
is ultimately dependent on the experience of being and that
the experience of doubt and meaninglessness is dependent on
the experience of meaning. The act of despair about the meaning of life itself presupposes being and meaning; absolute faith
apprehends and affirms these and, in so doing, provides the
courage of despair.

Tillich declares here that "the courage to be in all its forms
has, *by itself*, revelatory character."[78] There is no mention in this
book of revelation in the sense in which he defines it in his
Systematic Theology as involving "miracle," "ecstasy," and the
transcendence of the subject-object structure of experience, and
little reference to any symbols deriving from a specifically religious revelation. Instead, man's invincible self-affirmation, his
courage to resist even the most radical threats to his being, is
regarded as itself the means of attaining truth about God or
being-itself. For the absolute faith which apprehends and affirms being in the experience of nonbeing, while without special

content, does have a content, according to Tillich, and this is the "God above God."[79] Only at the very end of *The Courage To Be* does Tillich mention the Cross and the Church, but these seem to be brought in adventitiously and in no way affect his basic contention that "absolute faith" in "the God above God" is unmediated by any religious symbol. Though he here ends by declaring that it is "the Church under the Cross which alone can give men a courage which takes doubt and meaninglessness into itself,"[80] this is hardly consistent with the entire drift of his previous discussion.

Though Tillich does not say very much about him, the "God above God" of *The Courage To Be* seems to be identical with the God expounded in his *Systematic Theology*. Both transcend the God of ordinary theism, who is *a* being alongside other beings. Both are defined as being-itself, resisting and conquering nonbeing. But the God of the *Systematic Theology* is, in Tillich's view, the answer given by the Christian revelation to the questions implicit in man's finitude, and the life of this God is here regarded as describable in terms of certain symbols which are the product of this revelation. It is through faith in the God apprehended by means of these symbols that man conquers the anxiety of nonbeing and attains the courage to be. The "God above God" of *The Courage To Be*, on the other hand, is held by Tillich to be directly experiencable by man in the boundary situation of meaninglessness and despair; and the absolute faith in which one is grasped by him and which gives one the ultimate form of the courage to be, the courage to overcome despair, is declared to be possible even when all the traditional symbols of Christianity as well as of other religions have lost their power and to yield no symbols itself. Thus Tillich, in this work, appears to achieve a direct answer to the question of human finitude and anxiety by means of an ontological analysis of man's courage, without reference to any theological or specifically religious symbols.

Whether Tillich's approach in *The Courage To Be* does not emphatically contradict his professed method of correlating philosophy and theology as outlined in his *Systematic Theology* is a question on which we shall have something to say in the concluding section of this chapter. Now we must turn to his doctrine of the Christ, in which he finds the answer to the question concerning the means whereby man's existential estrangement may be overcome.

III. THE CHRIST

According to Tillich,[81] man in the state of existential estrangement cannot, by his most strenuous efforts, restore the harmony between himself and God or between himself and his essential being. Destiny keeps him in estrangement. All his attempts to overcome it must fail because they arise from within the state of estrangement and reflect the contradictions and conflicts of this state. The impossibility of controlling the compulsions of existential estrangement is the truth behind the idea of the "bondage of the will."[82] New action, beyond these compulsions, is possible only in the power of a New Being through which union with God has already been re-established.

In the light of the principle that being precedes action, Tillich reviews the various forms of self-salvation which men have attempted in the course of history and concludes that all of them have failed in their object.[83] The legalistic, ascetic, mystical, sacramental, doctrinal and emotional ways of self-salvation exemplified in the history of religion all have their value, he maintains,[84] but none of them has proved fully and unambiguously capable of reuniting man with God and of healing the disruptions and conflicts of man's existential state.

In pursuing the ways of self-salvation and seeing them fail, men have come universally to recognize the need for a New Being. In every religion and even in every autonomous culture there has been, Tillich believes, an expectation of a new and saving reality which would replace the old and estranged reality. "The quest for the New Being," he writes, "is universal because the human predicament and its ambiguous conquest are universal."[85] The character of the quest changes from religion to religion and from culture to culture, but two major types may be distinguished, namely, a non-historical[86] type in which the New Being is sought above and beyond history and is ex-

pected only to invade history vertically from above, and a historical[87] type in which the New Being is understood as the aim of
history and expected to appear in a horizontal direction within
the historical process. The claim of Christianity to universality,
Tillich declares, is based on its belief that "the different forms
in which the quest for the New Being has been made are fulfilled in Jesus as the Christ."[88] Christianity emphasizes the
appearance of the New Being within the historical process in
the form of the personal life of Jesus, but the term "Christ" or
"Messiah" which it borrowed from Judaism to symbolize this
life includes both a transcendent, or trans-historical, character
and historical functions. In its conception of the New Being
appearing in Jesus as the Christ, Christianity, Tillich holds,[89]
unites the horizontal direction of the historical type of expectation of the New Being deriving predominantly from the Old
Testament with the vertical direction of the non-historical type
deriving predominantly from Hellenism.

The fundamental and paradoxical[90] affirmation of the Christian message, according to Tillich, is that "in *one* personal life
essential manhood has appeared under the conditions of existence
without being conquered by them."[91] In maintaining a permanent unity with God despite his participation in all the
conditions and consequences of existential estrangement, Jesus
is the actualization of essential manhood or essential God-
manhood.[92] His being is the final manifestation of the New
Being, or the re-established unity between God and man; and
he is the Christ or Messiah, in the sense of being the ultimate
bearer to men of that New Being for which they have universally longed and through participation in which their own
estranged existence can be transformed.

We cannot here enter into Tillich's extended discussion and
evaluation of the "search for the historical Jesus" pursued in
the last two hundred years. It must suffice to note that, according
to him,[93] critical historical study can neither establish nor
destroy the foundation of the Christian faith. This foundation is
the *picture* of Jesus as the Christ in the New Testament.[94]
Tillich admits that historical research cannot verify any aspect

of this picture or arrive at a factual description of the "real" Jesus who is supposed to be its subject. Beyond this picture, which was constructed by those who had already received Jesus as the Christ and which shows everywhere their interpretation of him as such, there are no other sources upon which the historian can draw. The methodological skepticism of historical research may cast doubt upon every detail of the life portrayed in the biblical picture, even that the name of its bearer was Jesus of Nazareth. But it cannot, Tillich insists,[95] overthrow what is guaranteed by the experience of faith, namely, that this picture has a transforming effect upon those who are grasped by it and that the power of the New Being is expressed in and through it. Nor can it shake the conviction that such a picture is not the product of human imagination but is based, rather, on a real life. Only an actual encounter with a real life on the part of the first witnesses to it, Tillich argues, could have created a picture with such power.

> A picture imagined by the same contemporaries of Jesus would have expressed their untransformed existence and their quest for a New Being. But it would not have been the New Being itself. That is tested by its transforming power.[96]

Tillich, then, maintains that Jesus as the Christ is both a historical fact and a subject of believing reception, and that Christianity must assert both sides of this event on which it is based. Christian theology must emphasize first the actuality of the personal life referred to by the name Jesus.

> If theology ignores the fact to which the name of Jesus of Nazareth points, it ignores the basic Christian assertion that Essential God-Manhood has appeared within existence and subjected itself to the conditions of existence without being conquered by them. If there were no personal life in which existential estrangement had been overcome, the New Being would have remained a quest and an expectation and would not be a reality in time and space. Only if existence is conquered in one point—a personal life, representing existence as a whole—is it conquered in principle, which means "in beginning and in power."[97]

But the other side, the believing reception of Jesus *as* the Christ, that is, as the ultimate bearer and final manifestation of the New Being in time and space, by the disciples and all the subsequent generations of faithful Christians, must be equally emphasized, Tillich holds.[98] Without such reception he would not have been the Christ, for he would have created no church or community in which the message of the New Being is proclaimed and its transforming power experienced and transmitted.[99]

We must now turn our attention to those aspects of the New Testament picture of Jesus as the Christ which, according to Tillich, bear out his character as essential manhood participating in all the negativities of existence and yet remaining unconquered by them. Before doing this, however, it is important to note that, for Tillich, "Jesus as the Christ is the bearer of the New Being in the totality of his being, not in any special expressions of it."[100] Tillich insists that "neither his words, deeds, or sufferings nor what is called his 'inner life' make him the Christ."[101] All these are only expressions of the New Being which is his being and which, as such, precedes and transcends all its expressions.

The New Being in Jesus as the Christ "is new in so far as it is the undistorted manifestation of essential being within and under the conditions of existence."[102] More specifically, Tillich writes,

> It is new in two respects: it is new in contrast to the merely potential character of essential being, and it is new over against the estranged character of existential being. It is actual, conquering the estrangement of actual existence.[103]

In order to conquer the estrangement of actual existence, Jesus as the Christ had to participate completely in this existence, and such participation is emphasized, Tillich holds, in the biblical picture of his life. This picture stresses, first of all, the finitude of Jesus.[104] In it he is portrayed as having to die and as sharply experiencing the anxiety connected with the awareness of this fact. In it he is also portrayed as subject to homelessness or lack of a definite place in the world; to want; to bodily, social and mental insecurity; to loneliness and separation from others; to uncertainty and outright error in his intellectual conceptions and beliefs; to doubt about himself and his work; and to the feeling that he has been abandoned by God. All of these details confirm his total involvement in the negativities of human existence which stem from its finitude.

Jesus is also pictured, according to Tillich,[105] as participating in the tragic aspect of human existence and as becoming involved in the ambiguity of tragic guilt. By making the Pharisees and the leaders of his people guilty in his tragic[106] conflict with them, he himself becomes guilty.[107] Tragic guilt also accrues to Jesus in his relationship to Judas, insofar as he becomes responsible for the guilt of the one who contributes to his death.

Beyond this, the biblical picture, Tillich maintains,[108] also emphasizes the reality and seriousness of the temptations which Jesus encountered. As finite freedom, Jesus confronted possibility, and possibility "is itself temptation."[109] But if the seriousness of temptation presupposes, as we have seen Tillich to hold,[110] an antecedent desire for that which tempts, is there not already estrangement even before the decision to give way or not to give way to temptation? And does this not mean that, if the temptations of Jesus were serious and there was actual desire on his part, he was estranged from God, just as are all other human beings? No, answers Tillich, for there is a difference between the desire of the finite for reunion with everything, which is a part of man's natural self-transcendence, and distorted concupiscence, "which does not want reunion with anything but the exploitation of everything through power and pleasure."[111] Desire in itself is justified, if its objects are desired in unity with God and not outside or alongside him. Such was the desire of Jesus, a desire which existed within his state of unity with God. But for Jesus to attain the objects of his desire in the way urged by Satan in the New Testament story would have meant the transformation of this desire into concupiscence; and this, Jesus, in the power of his unbroken unity with God, resisted. Had he given way, he would have surrendered his messianic quality.

Jesus' rejection of his temptations, according to Tillich, was not a matter of contingency. Had it been such, "the salvation of mankind would be dependent on the contingent decision of an individual man."[112] Jesus' decision not to succumb to his temptations was an act of his finite freedom. But the freedom of Jesus, like that of all human beings, was imbedded within his destiny. His decision was a free choice on his part but it was also the result of his destiny as determined by the directing creativity, or providence, of God. Just as the fall of man is not contingent upon the wrong decision of Adam, so man's salvation is not contingent upon the right decision of Jesus. In both cases the directing creativity of God is at work.

> Man's destiny is determined by the divine creativity, but through man's self-determination, that is, through his finite freedom. In this respect the "history of salvation" and the "history of the Savior" are ultimately determined in the same way as history is generally and as the history of every individual man. This refers also to the state of estrangement in which mankind finds itself. Nobody can seriously defend the absurd idea that the universal cause of the human predicament was contingent upon the wrong decision of an individual man. In the same way the appearance of the Christ is at the same time freedom and destiny and is determined by God's directing creativity. There is no undetermined contingency in the negative and the positive situation of mankind, but there is the unity of freedom and destiny under God's directing creativity.[113]

The Christ-character of Jesus, that is, his character as the New Being or as the one who—despite his being only finite freedom and despite his involvement in all the negativities of the human predicament—does not lose his essential unity with God, is borne out in the biblical picture not only by his victory over concupiscence as stressed in the story of his rejection of the temptations in the desert, but also, according to Tillich, by his victory over the two other marks of human estrangement, unbelief and *hubris*.

> There are no traces of unbelief, namely, the removal of his personal center from the divine center which is the subject of his infinite concern. Even in the extreme situation of despair about his messianic work, he cries to his God who has forsaken him.[114]

In the same way the Biblical picture shows no trace of *hubris* or self-elevation in spite of his awareness of his messianic vocation. In the critical moment in which Peter first calls him the Christ, he combines the acceptance of this title with the acceptance of his violent death, including the warning to his disciples not to make his messianic function public. This is equally emphasized in Paul's christological hymn, Philippians, chapter 2, where he combines the divine form of the transcendent Christ with the acceptance of the form of a servant. The Fourth Gospel provides the theological foundation for this in the passage ascribed to Jesus: "He who believes in me does not believe in me, but in Him who has sent me."[115]

In every point, Tillich insists, the biblical picture of Jesus as the Christ contradicts the marks of estrangement as he has elaborated them in his analysis of man's existential predicament.[116]

The New Being, then, as it is manifest in the life of Jesus as the Christ conquers concupiscence, unbelief, and *hubris*. But it does not remove the general negativities of human existence, finitude and anxiety. Jesus as the Christ, according to Tillich, is portrayed in the biblical picture as accepting these and yet transcending them in the power of his unity with God.

The anxiety about having to die is not removed; it is taken into participation in the "will of God," i.e., in his directing creativity.[117]

His homelessness and insecurity with respect to a physical, social and mental place are not diminished but rather increased to the last moment. Yet they are accepted in the power of a participation in a "transcendent place," which in actuality is no place but the eternal ground of every place and of every moment of time.[118]

His loneliness and his frustrated attempts to be received by those to whom he came do not suddenly end in a final success; they are taken into the divine acceptance of that which rejects God, into the vertical line of the uniting love which is effective where the horizontal line from being to being is barred. Out of his unity with God he has unity with those who are separated from him and from one another by finite self-relatedness and existential self-seclusion.[119]

Both error and doubt equally are not removed but are taken into participation in the divine life and thus indirectly into the divine omniscience.[120]

Because Jesus maintains an unbroken unity with God, Tillich appears to believe, his anxiety and the other negativities inherent in the finitude to which he is subject lose the ultimately destructive character which is theirs for man in the state of estrangement.[121]

The New Testament picture of Jesus as the Christ, or the bearer of the New Being, emphasizes, then, two basic characteristics; his subjection to the conditions of existential estrangement and his victory over them. This dual relationship to existence is further expressed and confirmed, according to Tillich, by the two central symbols in which the New Testament expresses its understanding of the universal significance of the event Jesus as the Christ, namely, the Cross, symbolizing his subjection to existence, and the Resurrection, symbolizing his ultimate victory over it.

The story of the Cross, Tillich asserts, "is the myth of the bearer of the new eon who suffers the death of a convict and slave under the powers of that old eon which he is to conquer."[122] Behind the myth or symbol, however, lies a factual reality, for "without the factual element, the Christ would not have participated in existence and consequently not have been the Christ."[123] But it is not possible nor, for faith, necessary to determine the exact nature of the historical reality underlying the often contradictory and legendary reports of the Crucifixion story in the New Testament. What is essential for faith is the belief in the actual subjection of Jesus to the destructive consequences of existential estrangement which is symbolized in the story.

The only factual element in it having the immediate certainty of faith is the surrender of him who is called the Christ to the ultimate consequence of existence, namely, death under the conditions of estrangement. Everything else is a matter of historical probability, elaborated out of legendary interpretation.[124]

Tillich believes that an actual historical event also underlies the myth of the Resurrection but admits that there is a qualitative difference between this event and the event underlying the Crucifixion stories.

> While the stories of the Cross probably point to an event that took place in the full light of historical observation, the stories of the Resurrection spread a veil of deep mystery over the event. The one is a highly probable fact; the other a mysterious experience of a few.[125]

Reviewing the various theories which have been developed in the attempt to make the event of the Resurrection probable, Tillich finds all of them inadequate.[126] His own theory, which he calls the "restitution theory," lays emphasis on the negativity which is symbolized as having been overcome in the Resurrection stories. This negativity is the disappearance from present experience, through death, "of him whose being was the New Being . . . and his consequent transition into the past except for the limits of memory."[127] According to Tillich's theory, the power of Jesus' being impressed itself so sharply on his disciples as the power of the New Being that, after his death, they underwent an ecstatic experience in which "the concrete picture of Jesus of Nazareth became indissolubly united with the reality of the New Being."[128] They then experienced him as one whom death was not able to push into the past but who is spiritually present wherever the New Being is present. This experience of the disciples, Tillich holds, is duplicated in "all those who in every period experience his living presence here and now,"[129] and is the event which was interpreted in the New Testament through the symbol of Resurrection. But though Tillich maintains that his theory is adequate to the facts, he admits that it is only a probable one and does not have the certainty of faith. "Faith can give certainty," he writes, "only to the victory of the Christ over the ultimate consequence of the existential estrangement to which he subjected himself."[130] This certainty of faith is immediate because faith itself rests upon it. In the experience of being grasped by the power of the New Being as manifested in Jesus as the Christ, the experience which—according to Tillich—*is* faith, one is certain of "one's own victory over the death of existential estrangement" and this certainty "creates the certainty of the Resurrection of the Christ as event and symbol."[131]

Tillich regards many other elements in the biblical picture as subsidiary symbols which corroborate the central symbols of the Cross and the Resurrection. Stories such as those dealing with Jesus' lowly birth in Bethlehem, his flight to Egypt, the early threat to his life by the political powers, his agony at Gethsemane, all confirm his subjection to existence.

> Whether these expressions are mythical, legendary, historical, or mixtures of all of them, they as well as the Cross for which they are supporting symbols, are not important in themselves in the context of the Biblical picture. They are important in their power to show the subjection of him who is the bearer of the New Being to the destructive structures of the old being.[132]

Confirming the symbol of the Resurrection, Tillich maintains, are such things as the myth of the virgin birth[133] of Jesus; the stories of his transfiguration, of his conversation with Moses and Elijah, and of his miracles; and the symbols of his Ascension into heaven, of his "sitting at the right hand of God," of his Second Coming, and of his ultimate Judgment of the world. All these are significant not in their literal sense but only in showing, each in a special form, the victory of the final bearer of the New Being over existence.[134] Some of these symbols, Tillich believes, may no longer be living, in the sense of possessing the power to evoke faith. But even if this is so, the message of the New Being as manifest in the Christ is in no way affected, for "the New Being is not dependent on the special symbols in which it is expressed. It has the power to be free from every form in which it appears."[135]

Tillich rejects the dominant conception of classical Christological thought derived from the decision of the Council of Chalcedon according to which Jesus as the Christ is the personal unity of two full and perfect natures, a divine and human. The word "nature," he holds,[136] cannot be applied to Jesus in the same sense as to other human beings, for though, like all men, he has only finite freedom, unlike them, he resists existential estrangement; and it cannot be applied to God at all, for, as eternally creative, God transcends every nature or essence. Rather than being the unity of a divine and human nature Jesus as the Christ is the unique individual in whom "the eternal unity of God and man has become historical reality."[137] Tillich seems here to be following the doctrine of Hegel, who interpreted the Christ as the supreme appearance "in the sensuous form appropriate to history" of the unity of man with God.[138]

It is in the light of this understanding of the character of Jesus as the Christ, Tillich believes,[139] that the idea of the Incarnation is to be understood. This idea must not be interpreted as meaning literally that "God has become man" but rather that "God is manifest in a personal life-process as a saving participant in the human predicament." The Johannine statement about the *Logos* becoming flesh is also not to be understood, according to Tillich, as signifying an actual metamorphosis or transmutation but rather as the self-manifestation of God in the personal life of Jesus.[140]

As essential manhood or God-manhood, Jesus as the Christ, according to Tillich,[141] is properly called the Mediator, inasmuch as he represents God to man or makes the ultimate concrete for man. He represents God to man, "for essential man, by his very nature represents God" or "the original image of God embodied in man."[142] As the Mediator, however, he is also the Savior, the one in whose face man may not only "see the face of God" but the one also in whom they may "experience the reconciling will of God."[143]

We shall consider presently how, according to Tillich, the New Being, or the re-established unity of God and man in Jesus as the Christ, saves men, and the threefold character of the salvation that is made possible through him. First, however, the nature of "salvation" in general and the special relation of Jesus as the Christ to it, as they are understood by Tillich, must be made clear.

Salvation, says Tillich, is to be interpreted as "healing," in the sense of "reuniting that which is estranged, giving a center to what is split, overcoming the split between God and man, man and his world, man and himself."[144] It is the healing of the conflicts and disruptions of the state of existential estrangement, or the old being, through the power of the New Being. Such healing occurs, according to Tillich,[145] throughout history and is not restricted to the appearance of Jesus as the Christ. It occurs wherever there is revelation, understood as "the ecstatic manifestation of the Ground of Being in events, persons, and things."[146]

> Such manifestations have shaking, transforming and healing power. They are saving events in which the power of the New Being is present. It is present in a preparatory way, fragmentarily, and is open to demonic distortion. But it is present and heals where it is seriously accepted. On these healing forces the life of mankind always depends; they prevent the self-destructive structures of existence from plunging mankind into complete annihilation. This is true of individuals as well as of groups and is the basis for a positive evaluation of the religions and cultures of mankind.[147]

Since, according to Tillich, revelatory events occur both before and after the appearance of Jesus as the Christ, who is not the sole revelation but rather the final revelation, it follows that salvation or the power of the New Being is not present in him alone but is effective throughout all of history. Jesus as the Christ is, then, for Tillich, not the only bearer of the New Being but rather its final manifestation, in the sense of being "the ultimate criterion of every healing and saving process."[148] In him "the healing quality is complete and unlimited,"[149] although even those who encounter him are only fragmentarily healed.

For those who are grasped by the New Being in Jesus as the Christ, salvation or healing, according to Tillich,[150] assumes a threefold character. It is Regeneration, Justification, and Sanctification.[151] These are not three different events, but rather different aspects of the one saving event. In describing the character of salvation through them, Tillich declares that he is not here primarily concerned with the humanly receptive side of salvation, the psychological and spiritual processes through which the power of the New Being lays hold of those who are grasped by it,[152] but with the objective side, the activity of the New Being itself and its relation to those who encounter it.

Regeneration, the first aspect of salvation, is, objectively, the New Being itself, and, subjectively, the individual's rebirth or the transformation of his life through participation in the power of the new reality as it is manifest in the Christ.[153] The characteristics of the regenerated state are the opposite of those of the state of estrangement—faith instead of unbelief, surrender instead of *hubris,* love instead of concupiscence. Man's subjective participation in this state, according to Tillich, is always fragmentary and ambiguous. But even such participation is possible only because the regenerated state, or the New Being, is an objective reality which precedes it.

> Regeneration is a state of things universally. It is the new state of things, the new eon, which the Christ brought; the individual "enters it," and in so doing he himself participates in it and is reborn through participation. The objective reality of the New Being precedes subjective participation in it. The message of conversion is, first, the message of a new reality to which one is asked to turn; in the light of it, one is to move away from the old reality, the state of existential estrangement in which one has lived.[154]

Regeneration, or the state of having been drawn into the new reality manifest in Jesus as the Christ, Tillich declares, makes possible the experience of faith, "the state of being grasped by the divine presence."[155] In the state of faith, salvation is experienced in a second aspect, as Justification. Justification, like Regeneration, is first an objective event and then a subjective reception. Objectively, it is "the eternal act of God by which he accepts as not estranged those who are indeed estranged from him by guilt and the act by which he takes them into the unity with him which is manifest in the New Being in Christ."[156] This act of acceptance by God, Tillich holds,[157] is in no way dependent upon man's attempts to make himself acceptable. Man is accepted in the state of his unacceptability; he is, in the paradoxical Lutheran formula, *simul peccator, simul justus.* Only the message of the forgiving and justifying act of God who accepts men despite their estrangement and unacceptability can save the individual from despair about his guilt, for "it enables man to look away from himself and his state of estrangement and self-destruction to the justifying act of God."[158] All attempts at self-salvation must fail; "he who looks at himself and tries to measure his relation to God by his achievements," Tillich asserts, "increases his estrangement and the anxiety of guilt and despair."[159] But the objective and eternal justifying act of God must also be received subjectively by man; man must accept that he is accepted. And this, according to Tillich, he can do, under the knowledge of his own guilt, only through the grace of God mediated through faith, which is itself made possible through his first having been drawn into the power of the New Being in Christ.[160]

The third aspect of salvation, Sanctification, is distinguished from the first two, Tillich asserts, "as a process is distinguished from the event in which it is initiated."[161] Regeneration and Justification both describe the same divine act or event, the conquest of man's estrangement and his reunion with God, the former emphasizing the reality of this reunion and the latter its paradoxical character. Sanctification is the process in which salvation actually works itself out in history. It is "the process in which the power of the New Being transforms personality and community, inside and outside the Church."[162] Just how the divine Spirit, who is declared by Tillich to be "the actuality of the New Being,"[163] effects his sanctifying work on individuals and the church, and on both the religious and secular realms, is not here discussed, but Tillich promises to describe the process in the yet to be published concluding parts of his *Systematic Theology*.

Insofar as Tillich's answer to the question, What is the nature of the power whereby man's existential estrangement from his essential being can be conquered and whereby he can be saved from the evils and despair which are its consequences, is complete in the already published sections of his system, it may be summarized as follows: Existential estrangement *has* been overcome in one personal life, namely, that portrayed in the biblical picture of Jesus. Here was a life which actualized the potentialities of essential manhood, or man as he should be. Though Jesus was, like all men, thrown into existence in space and time, he did not, as do other men universally, employ his finite freedom in such a way as to become separated from God, or the divine ground of being and meaning. Participating in all the negativities implicit in creaturely existence and finitude, Jesus nevertheless maintained an unbroken unity with God. In so doing, he became the representative of "fulfilled" or "realized" eschatology, the ultimate bearer of that New Being for which men everywhere have longed and which is the actualized re-union of man with God or of man in existence with his essential being. By participating, through faith, in the power of this New Being, man finds his life transformed. The marks of his estrangement begin to give way to their opposites, and its consequences begin to lose their character as unredeemed evils. Man now accepts his finitude and the negativities inherent in it without rebellion. As a result, hope, instead of despair, becomes his final attitude.

IV. CRITICISM AND EVALUATION

It is no part of our intention here to offer detailed criticism of even the most important of these aspects of Tillich's doctrine of God and the Christ that we selected for discussion in our exposition. Adequate criticism would require a full volume or more. We must here restrict ourselves to a few general comments and questions.

It should be noted first that Tillich rejects all notions of a supernatural God or a transcendent world. Not only can the transcendent not be known, according to Tillich, but there *is* no transcendent realm beyond the world we know. God is not an existent being, but rather a quality which man may discern in all beings in his encounters with them. God is a depth within particular beings, a depth which is "presupposed" in man's experience of these beings and which becomes manifest to him in the revelatory situation as the object of his ultimate concern. Beyond this, God as being-itself is also the "ground" of man's ontological structure, as well as that of all other beings. God is further held by Tillich to be the power within all beings whereby they resist nonbeing. This power seems to be identical with the Spinozist notion of a *conatus in suo esse perseverandi* in all things. But if this identification is correct, what, it may be asked, can the "power of being" be except an inward drive in all individual beings?

The basic and only non-symbolic statement about God that can be made, according to Tillich,[164] is that he is being-itself. This truth about God, though discoverable only by virtue of an implicitly "ecstatic" or revelatory awareness in man, is presumably an ontological statement about ultimate reality, and not a theological concept. Theology begins only when man, as a consequence of explicitly revelatory experience, becomes aware of the divine depth in finite events, objects, or persons and symbolizes this depth through them; the function of theology is to explain the resultant symbols. J. H. Randall, Jr., however, has denied the ontological character of the concept of being-itself. "Being-itself," he writes, is "a concept at which ontological analysis can never arrive. Ontology can find only the 'being' which is common to all particular and determinate beings. 'Being-itself,' in any other sense, seems to be a religious myth or symbol."[165] We are not so sure as Randall that being-itself, as Tillich defines it, is not a valid ontological concept, but it seems fairly clear to us that it is not a purely religious symbol, either. It appears rather to be the result of a strange mixture, on Tillich's part, of independent philosophical speculation and an attempt to justify certain inherited or traditional religious conceptions.

This same mixture, we believe, is evident in Tillich's exposition of the nature of the life of God as being-itself, or as the ground of the ontological structure of man and all other finite beings. Tillich explicitly denies that knowledge of the divine life can be derived philosophically from an ontological system. "The character of the divine life," he insists, "is made manifest in revelation. Theology can only explain and systematize the existential knowledge of revelation in theoretical terms, interpreting the symbolic significance of the ontological elements and categories."[166] It seems to us, however, that Tillich's theoretical interpretation of the divine life is very far removed from the existential knowledge of the God given in the biblical revelation. One may doubt, indeed, that Tillich and the Bible are even talking about the same God. The God who is described by Tillich as "being-itself" seems to have very little in common with the God of Abraham, Isaac and Jacob or the God of Jesus and Paul. One wonders even whether Tillich is not guilty of a gross abuse of language in calling his "being-itself" God until one recalls how thoroughly ambiguous has been the meaning of the word God in the philosophical and theological tradition. In any case, it seems certain that Tillich's description of the divine life *is* largely dependent upon his ontology,[167] and that with a different ontology he would have a different conception of God. Tillich's doctrine of God, in short, appears to us to be not an explication of the God of the Judaeo-Christian tradition, but rather a philosophical doctrine that uses most of the traditional terms but reinterprets them through the use of a radical symbolic method.

There is no doubt that Tillich's doctrine of God is a highly impressive and ingenious achievement, one that takes account of many facets of human experience and many elements of the religious tradition and that seeks to do justice to these. Whether it is also a philosophically valid doctrine, in the sense, at least, of being coherent and non-self-contradictory, is a question that we cannot enter upon here. Suffice it to say that it seems to us to bristle with logical difficulties and ambiguities that do not on the surface appear susceptible of harmonization. For a detailed and brilliant criticism the reader is referred to the article "Tillich's Doctrine of God"[168] by Charles Hartshorne, who criticizes Tillich not only from his own "dipolar" or "panentheistic" point of view but also exhibits with great acumen the logical difficulties involved in Tillich's doctrine and the problems inherent in his symbolic approach.

Tillich's doctrine of God does, however, seem to be relevant to the basic problem which it is supposed to solve. It *is* an answer, as Professor Bernard Loomer has pointed out, to the "incompleteness, the brokenness, and the despair of man in the existentialist sense" in terms of "the completeness, the wholeness, and the unity of God in the classical sense."[169] Though Tillich's doctrine of God is not wholly classical insofar as he denies the reality of a transcendent God and regards him only as a depth within particular beings, and insofar as he also attempts to include some of the insights of modern process theology, his "being-itself" does, in the final analysis, seem to have the same qualities of aseity, self-sufficiency and majesty that are attributed to the God of the classical philosophical and theological tradition. Tillich's discussion of the symbol of the omnipotence of God in his *Systematic Theology* and his account of "the God above God" in *The Courage To Be* do give an answer of a sort to the Existentialist analysis of man's condition and to the question of the source of man's courage to be. The discussion in the latter book particularly may provide, for those who have lost all conviction of significance in the traditional religious symbols and ideas, some possibility of regaining a religious orientation to life.

The question may be raised, however, whether Tillich's God is religiously "available" in any further and stronger sense. Insofar as Tillich moves away from the traditional conception of God as pure Being or as "the naked absolute," and insofar as he holds that the divine life in some sense involves the finite creatures and that what is positive in the temporal process is included in it, he incorporates into his doctrine those features of process theology, as exemplified particularly in Whitehead's conception of the Consequent Nature of God, which have made this theology of genuine religious significance. But it seems to us a serious weakness on Tillich's part that he concentrates so heavily on God as the ground of being to the relative neglect of God as the ground of meaning and value. To be sure, meaning and value are not ultimately to be separated from being, but we believe that Tillich does not sufficiently stress that in God which enables man not only to go on living but to go on living with a sense of significance and purpose. Above all, the question of the "personality" of God seems to us not to have been adequately dealt with. Tillich is surely right when he says, "The personal encounter with God and the reunion with him are the heart of all true religion";[170] but it is difficult to see that his conception of God as transpersonal or superpersonal makes any direct personal encounter possible.

What Tillich professes to be most concerned to avoid in his theology is any objectification of God, any positing of the divine as a transcendent objective existent. But has he succeeded in avoiding objectification in his doctrine of God as "being-itself"? Might he not have done better to have gone back to the Mosaic conception of God in the Book of Exodus? Moses sets forth no objective conception of God. His God cannot be pictorially or even verbally represented, nor is there any myth given by Moses which reveals anything of the nature of the divine life. God, for Moses, is—in Buber's terminology—not an It but a Thou. He is not an object of man's vision or even of his thought. He is a dynamic power, addressing man, summoning him, challenging him. God as moral challenge, not as objective existent, is the essence of the Mosaic conception of the divine.

We have already alluded to the difficulty involved in understanding how there can be any personal encounter on the part of man with Tillich's God. It is this difficulty, presumably, that the doctrine of the Christ is to remove. If we may be permitted the observation, it seems to us that in great measure classical Christian thought in general, after having so defined God as to make direct encounter and reunion with him impossible, has sought to remedy this situation in its Christological conceptions. So also for Tillich, who holds that Jesus as the Christ is the mediator between God and man and the power whereby man's estrangement from God may be overcome. But the question might be raised whether the relationship between man and God is properly to be so defined that mediation and the overcoming of estrangement by the Christ are necessary. Here Judaism, for instance, would submit a strong dissent. Man's separation from God, it would urge, is by no means as radical and complete, nor are his own efforts[171] at bringing about a reunion with God as futile, as much of traditional Christian thought has held.

For Tillich, Jesus as the Christ is not the Mediator or the Incarnation in the traditional sense. He is the New Being, the bridge between essence and existence. This interpretation of him determines Tillich's entire theological system, which is admittedly based on the norm of the New Being.[172] Whether such an interpretation is historically justifiable is open to question. N. F. S. Ferré denies it.

The interpretation of Christ, *without historical justification*, becomes controlled by the relation of essence to existence. This historical Jesus, consequently, in Tillich's thought, merely becomes transparent to the Christ by refusing to make anything finite, infinite, and thus transmitted to us through a concrete life the synthesis of essence and existence, not in such a way that essence ever *became* existence . . . but in such a way that existence became perfectly transparent for essence, revealing for us the unique, non-recurring *Kairos*.[173]

Tillich, of course, insists that Jesus was a historical person. But he has not, we submit, taken the problems involved in his historicity seriously enough. When he holds that historical investigation is in no way relevant to the ultimate truth of the revelation in Jesus as the Christ, he is surely overstating the matter. If it is not the historical Jesus, but the *picture* of Jesus as the Christ in the New Testament that is of decisive importance, Jesus may well be an ideal category rather than a reality. But this Tillich will not allow. Obviously something more needs to be said on the subject of the historical Jesus than he has said.

As far as Tillich's "picture" of Jesus as the Christ is concerned, we cannot help feeling that it is a picture constructed through a very selective and highly personal reading of the New Testament sources. Tillich's description of Jesus' participation in the finitude and ambiguities of life is a very moving one, but has he not omitted from his picture many elements of the New Testament account which do not fit into his conception of a life which "maintains its essential unity with God"? Are there, indeed, "no traces of unbelief,"[174] in the sense of removal of his personal center from the divine center, and "no traces of *hubris* or self-elevation"[175] in the biblical picture of the life of Jesus? Is there no rebellion on Jesus' part against the negativities of finitude in which he participates, and against his death? Certainly, an objective and complete reading of the New Testament would result in affirmative answers to these questions.

Tillich may be right in his fundamental contention that the picture of Jesus as the Christ has transforming power over those who are grasped by it, and that the existential estrangement of these persons is at least fragmentarily overcome by their participation, through faith, in it. But does this qualify Jesus as *the* Messiah, *the* New Being, in the sense of being "the ultimate criterion of every healing and saving process"[176] and the one in whom "the healing process is complete and unlimited"?[177] Surely, this is nothing more than an existential commitment of a Christian theologian. Those uncommitted to the Christian revelation as Tillich defines it might find equal saving power in the contemplation of the life and death of a Socrates, a Rabbi Akiba, or a Mahatma Gandhi—to mention only a few.

We are not inclined to quarrel with Tillich's suggestion, in his discussion of the idea of Justification through faith in Jesus as the Christ, that this idea has the same basic import as the stress of modern psychotherapy on the fundamental importance of self-acceptance in the integration and fulfillment of personality. But we cannot help raising the question whether the "acceptance of being accepted" is not, as Tillich himself occasionally seems to suggest,[178] possible apart from faith in Jesus as the Christ. Man needs to accept himself and to accept without rebellion the negativities and ambiguities that inhere necessarily in his finitude and mortality, but surely such acceptance and the avoidance of complete despair are possible without specifically Christian faith.

We cannot, however, conclude these brief and inadequate remarks without expressing a feeling of appreciation for Tillich's Christology, which has not only succeeded in presenting a conception of the Christ that is meaningful and relevant to modern man, but has also avoided the divinization of Jesus and the logical and theological absurdities that are characteristic of so much traditional Christological thought. Whether or not Tillich's interpretation of Jesus is historically justifiable, and whether or not he has taken sufficiently into account what Jesus has meant in the history of Christianity, there is no doubt that his Christology is at least comprehensible. And for this Christian theologians may well be grateful.

Notes and References

Notes for Chapter One

1. "Autobiographical Reflections," in *The Theology of Paul Tillich*, edited by C. W. Kegley, and R. W. Bretall, p. 5.
2. "On the Boundary: An Autobiographical Sketch," in Tillich, *The Interpretation of History*, p. 7.
3. *The Theology of Paul Tillich*, p. 8.
4. *The Interpretation of History*, p. 4.
5. *The Theology of Paul Tillich*, p. 8.
6. *Loc. cit.*
7. *The Interpretation of History*, p. 6.
8. *The Theology of Paul Tillich*, p. 9.
9. *Ibid.*, p. 10.
10. *The Interpretation of History*, p. 35.
11. *Ibid.*, p. 40.
12. Below, p. 27.
13. *The Interpretation of History*, p. 32.
14. *Loc. cit.*
15. *Ibid.*, pp. 34-35.
16. *Ibid.*, p. 33.
17. *Loc. cit.*
18. See below, pp. 160-61.
19. *The Interpretation of History*, pp. 57-58.
20. *The Theology of Paul Tillich*, p. 13.
21. *The Interpretation of History*, p. 63.
22. *Ibid.*, pp. 63-64.
23. *Ibid.*, p. 65.
24. *The Theology of Paul Tillich*, p. 13.
25. *Loc. cit.*
26. Below, pp. 60ff.
27. *The Interpretation of History*, p. 17.
28. Above, p. 18.
29. *The Theology of Paul Tillich*, p. 14.
30. *The Interpretation of History*, pp. 40-41.
31. Quoted in Walter M. Horton's essay "Tillich's Role in Contemporary Theology" in *The Theology of Paul Tillich*, p. 32.

Notes for Chapter Two

1. Thus far two volumes of this work have been published, the first appearing in 1950 and the second in 1957. Tillich has promised a third and concluding volume in the near future.

2. *Systematic Theology*, I, 18.

3. *Ibid.*, p. 20. Cf. ". . . philosophy . . . tries to understand being itself and the categories and structures which are common to all kinds of beings." "Philosophy and Theology," in *The Protestant Era*, p. 86. "Philosophy is that cognitive endeavor in which the question of being is asked." *Biblical Religion and the Search for Ultimate Reality*, p. 5. ". . . ontology asks the simple and infinitely difficult question: What does it mean *to be?* What are the structures, common to everything that is, to everything that participates in being?" *Love, Power, and Justice*, p. 19.

4. *Systematic Theology*, I, 23.

5. *Love, Power, and Justice*, p. 24. Italics mine. See below pp. 59-60 for a full discussion of Tillich's conception of the method of experiential verification as applied to philosophical principles.

6. ". . . whatever the relation of God, world, and man may be, it lies in the frame of being; and any interpretation of the meaning and structure of being unavoidably has consequences for the interpretation of God, man, and the world in their interrelations." "Philosophy and Theology," in *The Protestant Era*, p. 86. Cf. *Dynamics of Faith*, pp. 90-91.

7. *Systematic Theology*, I, 22. (Italics mine.)

8. *Ibid.*, pp. 22-23. Cf. *Dynamics of Faith*, p. 91.

9. According to Tillich, the "two formal criteria" of every theology are that only those statements are theological which deal with their object "insofar as it can become a matter of ultimate concern for us" (*Systematic Theology*, I, 12) and "insofar as it can become a matter of being or not-being for us." (*Ibid.*, p. 14.)

10. *Ibid.*, p. 23.

11. *Ibid.*, p. 24.

12. *Ibid.*, p. 26.

13. *Ibid.*, pp. 24-25. Cf. *Dynamics of Faith*, pp. 91-93.

14. *Systematic Theology*, I, 26.

15. *Ibid.*, pp. 59ff.

16. Tillich, as we shall see, strongly emphasizes that the language of revelation and theology is fundamentally and inescapably symbolic. Cf. *Dynamics of Faith*, pp. 90-91.

17. *Systematic Theology*, I, 64.

18. In his apprehension, perhaps, of the theological objection to making revelation so anthropocentric a phenomenon as to be

merely a set of answers to human questions, Tillich has suggested that even the questions are formulated under the impact of God's answers. But the unity of man's questions and God's answers thereby implied belongs, he insist, only to man's essential being, not his existential state. *Systematic Theology*, I, 61.

19. *Ibid.*, p. 74.

20. *Ibid.*, pp. 64-65.

21. *Ibid.*, pp. 63-64.

22. *Systematic Theology*, I, 28. For Tillich, as we shall see (below, p. 160), the New Being is paradoxical in the sense of transcending all ordinary human expectations and possibilities, but it is not irrational or logically contradictory.

23. See below, p. 64 for a discussion of this point.

24. We say "later" because in his early work, particularly his *Epistle to the Romans* (1918), Barth developed his dogmatic theology in a dialectic with the existentialist philosophy of Kierkegaard.

25. Below, Chapter VI.

26. *Systematic Theology*, I, 61.

27. *Op. cit.*, p. 147.

28. *Ibid.*, p. 149.

29. "Religionsphilosophie," in *Lehrbuch der Philosophie* (ed. M. Dessoir, 1925), p. 774. Note also Tillich's characterization, in his earlier period, of even such an apparently atheistic philosophy as Heidegger's, as "theonomous." *The Interpretation of History*, p. 40.

30. *Op. cit.*, p. 86.

31. *Ibid.*, p. 88.

32. *Ibid.*, p. 89.

33. In *The Review of Metaphysics*, X, 57-63.

34. *Loc. cit.*, p. 61.

35. Above, p. 27.

36. Below, pp. 81-82.

37. Above, p. 28.

38. In her essay, "Epistemology and the Idea of Revelation," in Kegley and Bretall (eds.) *The Theology of Paul Tillich*, pp. 201-2.

39. Above, p. 28.

40. When Tillich speaks of "philosophy" as "asking" questions about human existence, he largely identifies philosophy in this context with Heidegger's anthropology. Tillich may be right in his assumption that this anthropology is the best contemporary interpretation of human existence, but to identify it with philosophy in general and largely to ignore all other philosophical doctrines of man, regarding the questions that these raise about man as irrelevant, is surely to treat them in a cavalier and unjustified fashion.

41. *Op. cit.*, pp. 155ff.

42. *Ibid.*, pp. 178-79. (Italics mine.)

43. *Ibid.*, p. 156.

44. "Reply to Interpretation and Criticism" in Kegley and Bretall (eds.), *The Theology of Paul Tillich.*

45. See above, p. 31.

46. *Systematic Theology*, I, 61.

47. *The Interpretation of History*, pp. 40-41.

Notes for Chapter Three

1. *Systematic Theology*, I, 74-75, 154-55. This transition is not understood by Tillich as an actual historical event. Man's reason, he holds, has always been what it now is. Actual reason is reason in existence, and the concept of reason in essence is an ideal or normative one.

2. See above, pp. 29-30.

3. For the meaning of this term, see below, pp. 61-62.

4. *Systematic Theology*, I, 72-74.

5. *Ibid.*, p. 72.

6. Technical reason as Tillich describes it here seems to be roughly equivalent to what Aristotle in the *Nicomachean Ethics* calls "deliberative reason."

7. *Systematic Theology*, I, 53-56. Here Tillich points out that "semantic rationality," which is promoted by technical reason, is indispensable to theological discussion.

8. *Ibid.*, p. 72.

9. *Loc. cit.* Cf. *Dynamics of Faith*, pp. 6-7, 75-76. What Tillich calls ontological reason seems to correspond generally to what Greek and Medieval philosophy called *Nous* or *intellectus* and to what German idealism called *Vernunft.*

10. *Systematic Theology*, I, 73.

11. *Loc. cit.*

12. *Ibid.*, p. 74.

13. *Ibid.*, pp. 77-78.

14. *Ibid.*, p. 75.

15. "Theological considerations do not demand a decision between them, and do not favor any one decision. Theology only presupposes that meaning is rooted in reality itself, and that the world can be recognized because its structures and laws have the essential character of being intelligible." Tillich, "Reply to Interpretation and Criticism" in Kegley and Bretall (eds.), *The Theology of Paul Tillich*, p. 333.

16. *Systematic Theology*, I, 171-72.

17. Below, pp. 83ff.

18. *Systematic Theology*, I, 76. Traditional philosophical terminology has, of course, generally noted the distinction as that between theory and practice.

19. *Loc. cit.*

20. *Loc. cit.* Tillich's language here is rather mystifying, but the mystery will be partly lifted when we consider (below, p. 42) that the so-called legal and communal functions, in which shaping or reactive reason expresses itself, form such things as political communities and friendships, which are regarded by Tillich as living structures with the power of being.

21. *Systematic Theology*, I, 92.

22. *Loc. cit.*

23. Tillich, as we shall see, regards myth and cult as important pointers to essential reason under the conditions of existence. We shall observe that they reflect for him not only the unity of essential reason here under consideration, i.e., that between its grasping and shaping activities, but also between its various functions and between what he calls its polarity of structure and depth.

24. *Systematic Theology*, I, 92.

25. *Loc. cit.*

26. *Ibid.*, pp. 76-77.

27. *Loc. cit.*

28. *Loc. cit.* For a discussion of this and the other polarities of reason, see below, pp. 49ff.

29. *Loc. cit.*

30. *Loc. cit.*

31. *Ibid.*, p. 91.

32. *Ibid.*, p. 92.

33. *Ibid.*, p. 77.

34. *Ibid.*, p. 78.

35. *Loc. cit.*

36. Tillich says that "neither nature nor history can create anything that contradicts reason," (*Systematic Theology*, I, 79) but what he obviously means is not that they cannot create such products but that these cannot succeed or endure.

37. *Systematic Theology*, I, 78.

38. *Loc. cit.*

39. *Ibid.*, p. 79.

40. *Loc. cit.*

41. *Systematic Theology*, I, 79-80.

42. "The Ontology of Paul Tillich," in Kegley and Bretall (eds.), *The Theology of Paul Tillich*, p. 143.

43. "Epistemology and the Idea of Revelation," in Kegley and Bretall (eds.), *The Theology of Paul Tillich*, p. 205.

44. *Systematic Theology*, I, 80.

45. Above, p. 41.

46. Above, p. 43.

47. *Systematic Theology*, I, 80-81.

48. Cf. *Dynamics of Faith*, pp. 50-51, where Tillich declares that myth is indispensable to religion and, indeed, to man's spiritual life in general. "One can replace one myth by another, but one cannot remove the myth from man's spiritual life. For the myth is the combination of symbols of our ultimate concern."

49. *Systematic Theology*, I, 81-83.

50. *Loc. cit.*

51. *Loc. cit.* Following Heidegger, Tillich regards Kant's *Critique of Pure Reason* as being an anthropological study, containing a doctrine of human finitude, as much as a piece of epistemology. See Heidegger, *Kant und Das Problem der Metaphysik*, p. 194.

52. Kant, of course, considers time a form of intuition, rather than a category. Tillich uses the word category in a broader sense to include time and space as well as the strictly Kantian categories.

53. The separation, according to Tillich, is always partial, never complete.

54. Above, p. 46.

55. *Systematic Theology*, I, 83-84.

56. *Ibid.*, p. 84.

57. *Loc. cit.*

58. Tillich points out (*loc. cit.*) that non-mythical and non-ritual forms, such as political ideas, may also become heteronomous challenges to the autonomy of reason.

59. Tillich calls that activity of reason in which the unity of structure and depth is maintained by this rather strange name because he believes that it is in God that these are essentially united and that He is the law for both.

60. *Systematic Theology*, I, 85. Theonomous reason, Tillich seems to hold, is identical with the ecstatic reason manifest in the situation of revelation. Cf. *Systematic Theology*, I, 154-55.

61. *Ibid.*, p. 85.

62. *Ibid.*, p. 86.

63. *Ibid.*, p. 86.

64. Tillich also views recent forms of Existentialism as examples of positivistic relativism in philosophy, and notes their marked similarities to pragmatism and to certain forms of European *Lebensphilosophie. Ibid.*, p. 88.

65. *Loc. cit.*

66. *Ibid.*, p. 89.

67. *Loc. cit.*

68. Above, p. 44.

69. *Systematic Theology*, I, 93.

70. Above, p. 41.
71. *Systematic Theology*, I, 93.
72. Above, p. 44.
73. See pp. 56ff. below for a full discussion of what Tillich calls "controlling" and "receiving" knowledge and the distinction between them.
74. Tillich gives detailed and elaborate consideration to the existential conflict in cognition between the requirements of union and detachment. See pp. 56ff. below for a full discussion of this conflict, which derives ultimately from the tension between the polar elements of emotion and form in reason.
75. *Systematic Theology*, I, 90.
77. *Ibid.*, p. 91.
78. *Ibid.*. p. 94.
76. *Loc. cit.*
79. *Loc. cit.*
80. *Ibid.*, p. 98.
81. *Ibid.*, p. 97.
82. *Ibid.*, p. 98.
83. *Loc. cit.*
84. *Loc. cit.*
85. *Loc. cit.*
86. *Loc. cit.*
87. *Ibid.*, p. 102.
88. *Loc. cit.*
89. *Ibid.*, pp. 102-3.
90. *Loc. cit.*
91. *Ibid.*, p. 102.
92. *Loc. cit.*
93. *Loc. cit.*
94. *Ibid.*, p. 103.
95. *Ibid.*, pp. 103-4.
96. *Ibid.*, p. 105.
97. *Ibid.*, p. 104.
98. *Ibid.*, pp. 102, 103, 105.
99. *Ibid.*, p. 105.
100. *Loc. cit.*
101. *Systematic Theology*, I, 106-18. Tillich is deeply indebted for his doctrine of revelation to Rudolf Otto who described revelation in his book, *The Idea of the Holy* (London, Oxford University Press, 1923) as the experience of the *"mysterium tremendum et fascinans."* Tillich, as we shall see, finds the *mysterium tremendum* in the "ontological shock" which accompanies the apprehension of the threat of nonbeing in all things and the *mysterium fascinans* in

the elevating experience of the divine presence, in which the conquest of nonbeing by being becomes manifest.

102. *Systematic Theology*, I, 108-11. Cf. Gabriel Marcel's definition of "mystery," as distinguished from "problem," in his *The Philosophy of Existence* (Chicago, Henry Regnery, 1952).

103. *Systematic Theology*, I, 109.

104. *Loc. cit.*

105. *Ibid.*, p. 110.

106. *Ibid.*, pp. 110, 113.

107. *Ibid.*, p. 110.

108. *Ibid.*, p. 113.

109. *Ibid.*, pp. 111-15. The etymological root of the word "ecstasy," which means "standing outside one's self," points to the self-transcendence of reason in the revelatory experience, according to Tillich.

110. *Ibid.*, p. 112.

111. Cf. *Dynamics of Faith*, pp. 6-7, where Tillich practically identifies revelation and ecstatic reason with faith, and declares, "the ecstatic character of faith does not exclude its rational character although it is not identical with it, and it includes non-rational strivings without being identical with them." Cf. *Op. cit.*, pp. 76-77.

112. *Systematic Theology*, I, 112.

113. *Ibid.*, p. 114.

114. *Loc. cit.*

115. *Ibid.*, pp. 115-18.

116. *Ibid.*, p. 116.

117. This word is borrowed by Tillich from Rudolf Otto's phenomenological description of revelation in *The Idea of the Holy*.

118. *Systematic Theology*, I, 117.

119. *Loc. cit.*

120. *Ibid.*, pp. 118-26.

121. *Ibid.*, p. 124.

122. By "spiritualists" Tillich does not mean occultists but rather such persons as the Enthusiasts of the Reformation period and the early eighteenth century.

123. *Systematic Theology*, I, 125.

124. *Ibid.*, pp. 125-26.

125. Tillich prefers the term "knowledge of revelation" to "revealed knowledge" in order to emphasize that the knowledge given in revelation cannot be separated from the ecstatic revelatory situation in which it is received. *Systematic Theology*, I, 129n.

126. *Loc. cit.*

127. *Loc. cit.* Cf. *Dynamics of Faith*, pp. 78-79, where Tillich rejects the popular concept of revelation as "divine information about divine matters, given to prophets and apostles and dictated by the

divine Spirit to the writers of the Bible, or the Koran, or other sacred books" and insists instead that revelation is "an event in which the ultimate becomes manifest in an ultimate concern, shaking and transforming the given situation in religion and culture."

128. *Systematic Theology*, I, 131.

129. *Loc. cit.*

130. *Loc. cit.*

131. *Loc. cit.*

132. *Ibid.*, pp. 106-8.

133. *Ibid.*, p. 133.

134. *Loc. cit.*

135. *Dynamics of Faith*, pp. 78-80.

136. *Systematic Theology*, I, 133.

137. *Ibid.*, p. 134.

138. *Ibid.*, p. 137. Cf. *Dynamics of Faith*, pp. 97-98. Cf. also Tillich's essay "The Nature of Religious Language," in *Theology of Culture*, pp. 66-67.

139. *Systematic Theology*, I, 147-48.

140. *Ibid.*, p. 148.

141. *Ibid.*, p. 149.

142. *Loc. cit.*

143. *Loc. cit.*

144. *Loc. cit.*

145. *Ibid.*, p. 148.

146. *Ibid.*, p. 150.

147. *Ibid.*, p. 151.

148. *Loc. cit.*

149. *Ibid.*, p. 152.

150. *Ibid.*, pp. 152-53.

151. *Ibid.*, p. 153.

152. *Ibid.*, p. 154.

153. *Loc. cit.* What Tillich refers to here as "the criterion in every act of rational knowledge" is, of course, what he elsewhere calls the depth of reason, understood as God in his nature as Truth-Itself.

154. While what Tillich has done here is comparable to the general protest against technical reason in almost all of the major Existentialist philosophers, it seems that it is with Heidegger, with his concept of *andenkendes Denken* and his discussion of the relationship of *Denken* and *Dichten* that he has the closest affinities. Cf. Heidegger, *Holzwege*, pp. 303ff., and *Was heisst Denken?*

155. *Systematic Theology*, I, 75.

156. *Ibid.*, p. 77.

157. Indeed, it may be considered a language, though, to be sure, not a denotative one.

158. *Systematic Theology*, I, 77.

159. Has he, perhaps, under theological influence, selected only those whose tensions and conflicts he believes revelation, as he defines it, is able to "overcome"?

160. Cf. Tillich's important essay "The Two Types of Philosophy of Religion" in *Theology and Culture*, pp. 10-29, where he describes Augustine's ontological approach to God and the Augustinian doctrine that God is the truth, known immediately and intuitively, which is presupposed in every question and in every doubt and which precedes the cognitive division into subject and object. Here Tillich also states his own formulation of the Augustinian principle which is fundamental to his entire theology: "Man is immediately aware of something unconditional which is the *prius* of the separation and interaction of subject and object, theoretically as well as practically" (p. 22). Tillich often suggests that apprehension of the depth of reason in any rational act or product is identical with apprehension of the unconditional which is implicit in it.

161. In his discussion of the meaning of God's omniscience, Tillich tells us that "the divine omniscience is the logical (though not always conscious) foundation of the belief in the openness of reality to human knowledge. We *know* because we participate in the divine knowledge. Truth is not absolutely removed from the outreach of our finite minds, since the divine life in which we are rooted embodies all truth." *Systematic Theology*, I, 279.

162. Tillich also contends, it will be remembered, that the depth of reason is symbolized in existence by myth and cult.

163. *Systematic Theology*, I, 80.

164. *Ibid.*, p. 117.

165. See below, pp. 77ff.

166. *Systematic Theology*, I, 103.

167. *Ibid.*, p. 105.

168. *Ibid.*, p. 104.

169. *Ibid.*, p. 105.

170. "Autobiographical Reflections," in Kegley and Bretall (eds.), *The Theology of Paul Tillich*, p. 6.

171. See pp. 60-68.

172. *Systematic Theology*, I, 112.

173. "Epistemology and the Idea of Revelation," in Kegley and Bretall (eds.), *The Theology of Paul Tillich*, p. 211.

174. According to him, it is also transcended in the experience of anxiety, for here all objects disappear and the subject encounters only non-being or nothingness.

175. *Systematic Theology*, I, 140-41.

176. *Ibid.*, pp. 154-55.

177. *Ibid.*, p. 133.

178. *Ibid.*, p. 148.

179. The questions whether Tillich's picture of the life of Jesus is not a highly selective one, and whether he has done justice to all the facets of this life as it is presented in the New Testament, are discussed below. See p. 178.

180. *Systematic Theology*, I, 149.

181. See above, p. 47.

182. *Systematic Theology*, I, 147-48. (Italics mine.) Cf. *Ibid.*, p. 110, where Tillich tells us that revelation "expresses itself in symbols and myths which point to the depth of reason and its mystery."

183. *Ibid.*, p. 151.

184. *Ibid.*, p. 57.

185. *Ibid.*, p. 152.

186. This is the major contention of his book *Love, Power, and Justice*.

187. See above, p. 53.

188. See above, p. 81.

188. See above, p. 65.

190. *Systematic Theology*, I, 154.

191. *The Interpretation of History*, pp. 123-75.

192. *Op. cit.*, p. 170.

193. *Loc. cit.*

194. *Ibid.*, p. 171.

195. *Ibid.*, p. 172.

Notes for Chapter Four

1. *Systematic Theology*, I, 168.

2. *Loc. cit.*

3. *Ibid.*, p. 169.

4. *Ibid.*, p. 166.

5. *Ibid.*, p. 167.

6. *Ibid.*, p. 164.

7. Tillich uses the word selfhood rather than ego because he wishes to include in its meaning not only awakened self-consciousness but subconsciousness, the unconscious, and even any reaction to a stimulus which is dependent on a structural whole. This extended meaning makes it possible for him to ascribe self-centeredness in some sense not only to man but to all living beings and even further, by analogy, to all individual *Gestalten* in inorganic nature. The adoption by Tillich of this extended meaning also suggests that, for him, there is no radical dualism between man and nature but that man is continuous with his natural environment. It further reflects the panpsychism which frequently appears in his ontology. *Systematic Theology*, I, 169.

8. *Loc. cit.*

9. *Ibid.*, p. 164.

10. *Systematic Theology*, I, 170. The aggregation of beings opposite man which constitute his world, and to which he simultaneously sustains the relationships of belonging and separateness, is a unified structural whole, according to Tillich, in the sense at least that it is perspectively related to him, no matter how manifold and discontinuous it may be in itself.

11. Tillich, indeed, denies that any being, not only man, is completely conditioned by environment. "The mistake of all theories which explain the behavior of a being in terms of environment alone is that they fail to explain the special character of the environment in terms of the special character of the being which *has* such an environment. Self and environment determine each other." *Systematic Theology*, I, 170. Tillich does admit that though man, in his essence, is related to a world rather than a limited environment, in his actual existence he may come, as a result of estrangement or sin, to lose his world and become a mere object of environmental impact. Cf. *Systematic Theology*, II, 62.

12. *Systematic Theology*, I, 171. Cf. *The Protestant Era*, p. 117, where Tillich says "Confronting a world man becomes a definite self; and, being a definite self, he can confront the world."

13. *Systematic Theology*, I, 171.

14. *Ibid.*, p. 172.

15. *Ibid.*, pp. 172-73.

16. *Ibid.*, pp. 171-74.

17. *Ibid.*, p. 174.

18. Tillich's anthropological ontology, of course, also considers them universal ontological elements, characteristic of all being.

19. *Systematic Theology*, I, 165.

20. *Ibid.*, pp. 175-77.

21. Buber, *I and Thou*.

22. *Systematic Theology*, I, 177. Cf. *Love, Power, and Justice*, p. 78.

23. *Systematic Theology*, I, 176.

24. *Ibid.*, p. 177.

25. *Loc. cit.*

26. *Ibid.*, p. 178.

27. The existence of this dynamism, according to Tillich, is recognized not only in mythology and religion but in philosophy. "It appears in metaphysical speculations as *Urgrund* (Böhme), will (Schopenhauer), will to power (Nietszche), the unconscious (Hartmann, Freud), *élan vital* (Bergson), strife (Scheler, Jung)." *Systematic Theology*, I, 179. "Dynamics," Tillich declares, "is the *me on*, the potentiality of being, which is nonbeing in contrast to things that

have a form, and the power of being in contrast to pure nonbeing."
Loc. cit. This potentiality or power, according to Tillich, cannot be
described literally, but is pointed to symbolically by the philosophical
concepts mentioned above. "If it could be named properly, it would
be a formed being beside others instead of an ontological element in
contrast with the element of pure form." *Loc. cit.*

28. *Systematic Theology*, I, 180.

29. Form, ontologically, is the structure which makes any being
the definite being that it is and which gives reason the power of
grasping and shaping it. "Whatever loses its form loses its being.
Form should not be contrasted with content. The form which makes
a thing what it is, is its content, its *essentia*, its definite power of
being." *Systematic Theology*, I, 178.

30. *Ibid.*, p. 180.

31. *Ibid.*, p. 182.

32. *Loc. cit.*

33. For a discussion of how this occurs, see below pp. 115ff.

34. *Systematic Theology*, I, 183. Elsewhere Tillich declares: "The
concept of freedom . . . precedes the questionable discussion between
determinism and indeterminism about the 'freedom of the will.'
Freedom is the structure of a being (body, psyche, mind) that is
able to know and to act according to universal principles and that
is also able to contradict these principles and to fall under the swing
of self-destructive compulsions." Tillich, "The Nature of Man," *Journal
of Philosophy*, XLIII, (1946), 676.

Tillich also states that his concept of freedom derives from an
existential, rather than an objectifying, understanding of it. "The
existentialist doctrine of freedom shows once more the distinction
of an objectifying and an existential understanding of a concept. In
the traditional discussion between determinism and indeterminism,
the conflict between philosophers is reflected by those who try to
solve the problem of freedom by making freedom an object within
the realm of objects. If this is done, the naturalist has the choice between the element of necessity which determines the movements of objects and the element of contingency which introduces indeterminacy
into their behavior. But neither of these solutions reaches the meaning
of freedom as immediately experienced. Nor does the idealistic concept of freedom. . . . Freedom is the *possibility* (italics mine) of the
existential subject. It is its very "nature". . . . Existence means standing outside the structural necessities of essence. It is neither logically
nor physically nor morally determined by them. It is the freedom of
the non-directed leap. Arguments which tried to show that this leap
was determined by the previous state of the self would not impress
the existentialist, because he would consider it also as a *metabasis eis
allo genos*, namely, the transformation of the existential subject into

an object for the epistemological subject." Tillich, "The Nature and the Significance of Existentialist Thought," *Journal of Philosophy*, LIII (1956), 745-46.

35. The traditional controversy between determinism and indeterminism, Tillich holds, is really a reflection of man's existential estrangement. In man's essence the poles of freedom and destiny are held together in undisrupted tension, but when man is estranged from his essence freedom becomes, as the indeterminist suggests, mere contingency, and destiny becomes, as the determinist holds, mere mechanical necessity. *Systematic Theology*, II, 63-64.

36. *Systematic Theology*, I, 183.

37. *Ibid.*, p. 184.

38. *Loc. cit.*

39. *Ibid.*, p. 185.

40. *Loc. cit.*

41. According to Tillich, the polarity of freedom and destiny is not only the outstanding example of, but also the cognitive entrance to, this more fundamental and universal polarity. *Systematic Theology*, I, 185.

42. And, of course, destiny, in the form of laws of nature.

43. *Systematic Theology*, I, 189. Cf. *Love, Power, and Justice*, pp. 34-39.

44. *Systematic Theology*, I, 187.

45. *Systematic Theology*, I, 187. Tillich distinguishes an objectifying and an existential use of the concept of non-being, referring to his own as of the latter variety. "In the realm of objects, non-being has a definite place, namely, in the relation of the potential to the actual. Non-being is not only a negative judgment, denying a wrong expectation, but it expresses the *modus deficientis* in the case of a justified expectation. Man has the potentiality of seeing; blindness is a *modus deficientis* in man—not in stones. It is non-being in the relation of potentiality to actuality. Yet the existentialist use of non-being goes beyond the problem of deficiency, although it can be derived from it. The example we already have given was finitude. Finitude in itself is not a *modus deficientis*, except in a being which belongs potentially also to the infinite, or, in temporal terms, to the eternal. Finitude includes non-being only insofar as it does not actualize its potential power of being." Tillich, "The Nature and Significance of Existentialist Thought," *Journal of Philosophy*, LIII, 744.

46. *Systematic Theology*, I, 187. By "dialectical" Tillich here appears to mean that nonbeing, which is by definition negative, must at the same time be regarded as somehow positive.

47. *Ibid.*, p. 188. *Me on* is non-being but it is not pure "nothingness," for it has the power of resisting union with the ideas.

48. *Loc. cit.*

49. *Ibid.*, p. 189.

50. *Ibid.*, p. 190.

51. "The Nature of Man," *Journal of Philosophy*, XLIII, 676. Cf. *Dynamics of Faith*, p. 157.

52. *Ibid., Systematic Theology*, I, 191-92. Cf. *The Courage To Be*, pp. 35-36.

53. Tillich sees no reason for giving preference in ontology to concepts taken from "outside" over those taken from "inside." The self-world correlation as the basic articulation of being makes both types relevant and valid. "The self being aware of itself and the self looking at its world (including itself) are equally significant for the description of the ontological structure." *Systematic Theology*, I, 192.

54. Kierkegaard, *The Concept of Dread*, p. 38. Throughout this work the word translated as "dread" is the same as Tillich's "anxiety."

55. Heidegger, *Sein und Zeit*, pp. 186-90.

56. *Systematic Theology*, I, 191. Cf. *The Courage To Be*, pp. 36-39.

57. *Systematic Theology*, I, 191.

58. *Ibid.*, pp. 192-98.

59. *Ibid.*, p. 192.

60. See below, Chapter VI.

61. *Systematic Theology*, I, 193.

62. *Loc. cit.*

63. *Ibid.*, p. 194. Cf. Tillich, "Psychotherapy and a Christian Interpretation of Human Nature," *Review of Religion*, XIII (March, 1949), 265. ". . . disease and death are inescapably connected with finitude. The necessity of dying can be called that germ of disease in man which is dependent on his finitude. But all this does not contradict the essential goodness of human nature."

64. *Systematic Theology*, I, 194.

65. *Loc. cit.*

66. *Ibid.*, p. 195.

67. *Loc. cit.*

68. *Loc. cit.*

69. *Ibid.*, p. 196.

70. *Loc. cit.* Here he follows Kant's discussion of the Antinomies in *The Critique of Pure Reason*.

71. *Systematic Theology*, I, 196.

72. *Ibid.*, p. 197.

73. *Loc. cit.*

74. *Loc. cit.*

75. "Every change," Tillich declares, "reveals the relative non-being of that which changes. The changing reality lacks substantiality, the power of being, the resistance against nonbeing." *Systematic Theology*, I, 197.

76. Tillich dismisses the traditional arguments for the immortality of the soul as invalid and regards them as "attempts to escape the seriousness of the question of substantiality by establishing an endless continuation of what is essentially finite." *Systematic Theology*, I, 198.

77. *Loc. cit.*

78. *Ibid.*, pp. 198-201.

79. These, as we have seen, are individualization and participation, dynamics and form, and freedom and destiny.

80. "Tension," Tillich declares, "refers to the tendency of elements within a unity to draw away from one another, to attempt to move in opposite directions." *Systematic Theology*, I, 198.

81. *Ibid.*, p. 199.

82. *Loc. cit.*

83. *Ibid.*, pp. 199-200.

84. *Loc. cit.*

85. *Ibid.*, p. 200.

86. *Loc. cit.*

87. *Ibid.*, p. 201.

88. *The Courage To Be*, p. 40.

89. *Loc. cit.*

90. *Ibid.*, p. 41.

91. *Ibid.*, p. 42.

92. *Ibid.*, p. 44.

93. *Ibid.*, p. 43.

94. *Ibid.*, p. 46.

95. *Ibid.*, p. 47.

96. *Ibid.*, p. 48.

97. *Ibid.*, pp. 49-50.

98. *Ibid.*, p. 52.

99. *Loc. cit.*

100. *Ibid.*, pp. 52-53.

101. *Ibid.*, p. 54.

102. *Ibid.*, p. 56.

103. Below, p. 157.

104. *Systematic Theology*, I, 185.

105. *Ibid.*, p. 166.

106. See Sartre's *L'Être et le Néant*, p. 431.

107. Below, pp. 137-38.

108. *Op. cit.*, pp. 40-54.

109. See Kierkegaard's *The Concept of Dread*, where he identifies anxiety as "the reality of freedom as possibility anterior to possibility" (p. 38) and as "the dizziness of freedom." (p. 55.)

110. *Systematic Theology*, I, 191. Cf. "The Theological Signifi-

cance of Existentialism and Psychoanalysis," in *Theology of Culture*, pp. 112-26.

111. In his paper "Freud and Existentialism," *Journal of Nervous and Mental Diseases*, 126 (April, 1958), 341-52.

112. Allport, *Personality* (New York: Henry Holt and Company, 1937), p. 182.

113. It is in the Christian writers who have most influenced Tillich—Böhme, Kierkegaard and Schelling—that anxiety is most often interpreted in the way he himself explains it.

Notes for Chapter Five

1. *Systematic Theology*, II, 45.
2. *Ibid.*, I, 165.
3. *Loc. cit.*
4. *Ibid.*, p. 202.
5. *Loc. cit.*
6. *Ibid.*, pp. 203-4.
7. "Psychotherapy and a Christian Interpretation of Human Nature," *Review of Religion*, XIII (March, 1949), 264. Cf. Tillich's essay "The Theological Significance of Existentialism and Psychoanalysis" in *Theology of Culture*, p. 118.
8. *Systematic Theology*, II, 29, 33.
9. *Ibid.*, p. 29. Cf. "Psychotherapy and a Christian Interpretation of Human Nature," *Review of Religion*, XIII (March, 1949), 265, where Tillich, writing of the symbol of "the Fall," declares, "This almost unusable word points to a universal experience of mankind, namely, to man's split within himself, to his separation from and enmity toward other beings, and to the permanent threat of losing the ground and meaning of his life. The "Fall" is not an historical event; it is the permanent and universal transition from innocence to guilt in every human being."
10. *Systematic Theology*, II, 29. Tillich is cognizant of the fact that this philosophical translation does not represent a complete demythologization of the story in the Book of Genesis and does not altogether remove the element of temporality from it. But complete demythologization and the removal of all suggestion of temporality is not possible here, he holds, since man's sinful or estranged existence is not a logical implication or necessary consequence of his created or essential nature, but rather an irreducible fact, a story which must be told, and can be told, only in mythical terms.
11. *Systematic Theology*, II, 29-30.
12. *Ibid.*, p. 32. Cf. Tillich, "The Nature of Man," *Journal of*

Philosophy, XLIII (December, 1946), 676. "Theology, in dealing with man's nature as that of 'finite freedom,' shows that man's freedom drives him into a tragic estrangement from himself, from the other beings, and from the ultimate ground and meaning of his existence."

13. "Psychotherapy and a Christian Interpretation of Human Nature," *Review of Religion*, XIII (March, 1949), 264.

14. *Systematic Theology*, I, 260.

15. *Ibid.*, II, 33-36.

16. *Ibid.*, p. 33.

17. *Ibid.*, p. 34.

18. *Loc. cit.*

19. *Ibid.*, p. 35. The "desire to sin" is called by Tillich "a sin which is not yet sin but which is also no longer innocence." For Tillich, as for Kierkegaard, "sin presupposes itself."

20. *Loc. cit.*

21. *Ibid.*, p. 36. Cf. Tillich, "Psychotherapy and a Christian Interpretation of Human Nature," *Review of Religion*, XIII (March, 1949), 265.

22. The two words are here used synonymously, as referring to the same reality.

23. *Systematic Theology*, II, 38.

24. It should be noted that for Tillich the Fall of nature is not, any more than is the Fall of man, a historical or temporal event. "'Adam before the Fall' and 'nature before the curse' are states of potentiality. They are not actual states. The actual state is that existence in which man finds himself along with the whole universe, and there is no time in which this was otherwise. The notion of a moment *in* time in which man and nature were changed from good to evil is absurd, and it has no foundation in experience or revelation." *Systematic Theology*, II, 40-41.

25. *Ibid.*, pp. 41-42.

26. *Ibid.*, I, 255-56.

27. *Ibid.*, II, 44.

28. *Loc. cit.*

29. *Ibid.*, p. 46.

30. Cf. *The Shaking of the Foundations*, pp. 154-55 where Tillich writes ". . . *sin is separation*. To be in the state of sin is to be in the state of separation. And separation is three-fold. There is separation among individuals, separation of a man from himself, and separation of all men from the Ground of Being."

31. "Psychotherapy and a Christian Interpretation of Human Nature," *Review of Religion*, XIII (March, 1949), 266-67. "In both cases one point must be emphasized; namely, the difference between

tragic guilt and moral failure. Sin is first the former, and only on the basis of 'separation' do moral consequences appear. Sin in the moral sense is a consequence and not the basis of sin in a religious sense."

32. The term "original sin" derives from Augustine. See A. T. Mollegen, "The Fall and Original Sin," *A Handbook of Christian Theology*, p. 132.

33. *Systematic Theology*, II, 46.

34. *Ibid.*, pp. 45-46.

35. *Ibid.*, p. 45.

36. *Ibid.*, p. 47.

37. *Loc. cit.*

38. *Loc. cit.*

39. *Ibid.*, p. 48. Cf. *Love, Power, and Justice*, p. 76. "If man were not estranged from himself, if his essential nature were not distorted in his actual existence, no law would stand against him."

40. *Systematic Theology*, II, 48.

41. *Ibid.*, p. 50.

42. Cf. Augustine, Tractate XXV, 15, *On the Gospel of John*. "Pride is the beginning of all sin; and the beginning of man's pride is the falling away from God."

43. *Systematic Theology*, II, 51.

44. *Loc. cit.*

45. *Loc. cit.*

46. *Ibid.*, p. 52.

47. *Ibid.*, p. 53.

48. *Loc. cit.* Cf. Tillich, *Love, Power, and Justice*, pp. 29-30, 116-17; and "The Theological Significance of Existentialism and Psychoanalysis," in *Theology of Culture*, pp. 118-21.

49. *Systematic Theology*, II, 54. Cf. Tillich, "Psychotherapy and a Christian Interpretation of Human Nature," *Review of Religion*, XIII (1949), 268.

50. *Systematic Theology*, II, 54.

51. *Loc. cit.* Cf. *Love, Power, and Justice*, pp. 29-30.

52. *Systematic Theology*, II, 55. Cf. *Love, Power, and Justice*, p. 36.

53. *Loc. cit.* Cf. Heidegger, *Sein und Zeit*, p. 284. "Being guility is not the result of a guilty act, but conversely, the act is possible only because of an original 'being guilty.'"

54. *Systematic Theology*, II, 55.

55. *Ibid.*, pp. 56-7.

56. Above, pp. 95ff.

57. Tillich calls it "essential" anxiety.

58. *Systematic Theology*, II, 60.

59. Tillich uses this paradoxical term to express his conviction that evil has no positive ontological status in the whole of reality

but that "it is dependent on the structure of that in and upon which it acts destructively." *Loc. cit.*

60. Tillich distinguishes a larger and a narrower sense of the term "evil." The larger sense includes all the negativities of man's existential predicament, both sinfulness or estrangement and the forms of self-destruction which are its consequences. It is the narrower sense—"evil as the structure of self-destruction which is implicit in the nature of universal estrangement"—that Tillich here employs. *Ibid.,* p. 61.

61. Above, pp. 83ff.

62. *Systematic Theology,* II, 61. In his essay on the demonic in *The Interpretation of History,* Tillich argues that "the demonic comes to fulfillment in personality, and personality is the most prominent object of demonic destruction, for personality is the bearer of form in its totality and unconditioned character. Therefore, the contradiction of it, the cleavage of personality, is the highest and most destructive contradiction. Therewith the demonic is disclosed in a new stratum: the personality, the being which has power over itself, is grasped by another power and is thereby divided." *Op. cit.,* 86.

63. *Systematic Theology,* II, 62.

64. Above, pp. 86ff.

65. *Systematic Theology,* II, 62.

66. *Ibid.,* p. 63. Cf. D. E. Roberts, "Tillich's Doctrine of Man," in Kegley and Bretall (eds.), *The Theology of Paul Tillich,* p. 127. "Tillich's observation that sin destroys the unity between freedom and destiny might be translated into psychological language by saying that in neurosis the individual manifests both grandiosity and compulsiveness. His reactions are arbitrary and automatic simultaneously. He yearns for egocentric omnipotence, and he is enslaved to forces (especially unconscious forces within himself) over which he has no control."

67. *Systematic Theology,* II, 63.

68. *Ibid.,* p. 64.

69. *Ibid.,* p. 64-65.

70. *Ibid.,* p. 65.

71. Tillich distinguishes existential loneliness from essential solitude. The latter is the expression of the fact that man is a completely centered self, distinct from the whole of reality opposite himself. While separating man from the remainder of reality, this centeredness enables him to participate in it within limits set only by his finitude. The essential solitude which is the expression of man's centeredness also makes it possible for the individual to have communion with other human beings, for "in solitude man experiences the dimension of the ultimate, the true basis for communion among those who are alone." But in the state of estrangement the individual

is cut off from the dimension of the ultimate, and falls into existential loneliness. In this state his desire for acceptance by, and communion with, other human beings is frustrated. Even if he seeks escape from his intolerable loneliness through surrender to a collective, he still suffers from rejection by the other individuals in the collective, who, like himself, have lost their essential solitude and, with it, their power of communion. *Systematic Theology*, II, 71-72.

72. *Ibid.*, p. 66.

73. This is the cognitive approach which Tillich elsewhere calls "controlling knowledge." See above, pp. 57ff.

74. *Systematic Theology*, II, 67.

75. *Loc. cit.* Cf. H. F. Lovell Cocks, "Death," in *A Handbook of Christian Theology*, pp. 72-73. "The idea of unnaturalness—the abnormality—of death begins to appear. If God created man in His own image in order that man might glorify Him and enjoy Him forever, then death is a contradiction not only of man's hopes and longing for life but also—it seems—of God's gracious purpose in creating him. Man 'thinks he was not made to die.' But it is his consciousness of deserving this dread punishment that makes man fear death and dread its inexorable approach. From the point of view of the Bible, man's fear of death is the sign of a bad conscience."

76. *Systematic Theology*, II, 68-70.

77. *Ibid.*, p. 69.

78. *Loc. cit.*

79. *Loc. cit.*

80. *Ibid.*, pp. 69-70.

81. *Ibid.*, pp. 72-74.

82. *Ibid.*, p. 73.

83. *Loc. cit.*

84. *Ibid.*, p. 75.

85. *Ibid.*, p. 76.

86. Or, as Tillich alternatively puts it, in the ultimate or unconditional. All three terms are employed by him as expressions for God.

87. See above, pp. 33ff.

88. *Systematic Theology*, I, 202-3.

89. *Ibid.*, pp. 255-56.

90. *Ibid.*, p. 260.

91. *Ibid.*, II, 44.

92. *Ibid.*, p. 48.

93. "Reply to Interpretation and Criticism," in Kegley and Bretall (eds.), *The Theology of Paul Tillich*, pp. 342-44.

94. *Systematic Theology*, I, 256. Cf. II, 44. "Creation and Fall coincide insofar as there is no point in time and space in which created goodness was actualized and had existence."

95. *Ibid.*, II, 29-37.

96. The story of Adam in the Book of Genesis does not, of course, contain the word "fall." Adam's specific disobedience of a single command of God which is here recorded has only been interpreted by classical Christian theology as a general fall from innocence into sinfulness. It is not so regarded in Jewish tradition.

97. "Biblical Thought and Ontological Speculation," in Kegley and Bretall (eds.), *The Theology of Paul Tillich*, p. 220.

98. *Systematic Theology*, I, 256.

99. "Tillich's Theology of Correlation," *Journal of Religion*, XXXVI (July, 1956) 156.

100. "Reply to Interpretation and Criticism," in Kegley and Bretall (eds.), *The Theology of Paul Tillich*, p. 343.

101. *Loc. cit.*

102. In response to a question in personal conversation, Tillich has stressed that the fall is "unavoidable" but not "necessary." We must confess, however, that the distinction between these terms is lost upon us.

103. *Systematic Theology*, I, 256.

104. "Tillich and Freud on Sin," *Religion in Life*, XXVIII (1958-59), 223.

105. *Systematic Theology*, II, 61, 63.

Notes for Chapter Six

1. *Systematic Theology*, I, 62-64; II, 126.

2. See above, pp. 64ff.

3. *Systematic Theology*, I, 16-17, 28, 71, 153-54.

4. It is meaningless, Tillich declares, to discuss the existence or non-existence of God. The notion of God contains two elements: "the element of ultimacy, which is a matter of immediate experience and not symbolic in itself, and the element of concreteness, which is taken from our ordinary experience and symbolically applied to God." *Dynamics of Faith*, p. 46. The ultimacy of an ultimate concern is beyond question. The only meaningful question is the adequacy of a concrete symbol to the ultimate reality which is God. It is not meaningful to ask if God "exists" in the sense of being found within the whole of spatio-temporal reality. God does not "exist" in this sense. The "half blasphemous and mythological concept of the 'existence of God'" arose, according to Tillich, out of the paradoxical situation that, though God as being-itself or the power of being is the prius of subject and object and cannot be an object for man as subject, he is "verbally" objectified in our speaking and thinking of him. "The Two Types of Philosophy of Religion," in *Theology of Culture*, p. 25.

5. *Systematic Theology*, I, 206-9.

6. *Ibid.*, p. 207. Cf. Tillich, "The Two Types of Philosophy of Religion," in *Theology of Culture*, pp. 15-16.

7. *Systematic Theology*, I, 208.

8. *Ibid.*, p. 209.

9. *Ibid.*, p. 210.

10. *Ibid.*, p. 211. Italics mine.

11. *Ibid.*, p. 215.

12. *Ibid.*, p. 216.

13. *Ibid.*, p. 211-15.

14. To the forms of monotheism which Tillich distinguishes, in a discussion which we cannot here consider, he gives the names monarchical, mystical, exclusive and trinitarian. *Ibid.*, pp. 225-30.

15. *Ibid.*, pp. 230-35.

16. This double experience is that of the holy as both *tremendum* and *fascinans*. See above, pp. 60ff.

17. *Systematic Theology*, I, 238. Though Tillich holds that God, in one sense, *is* the structure of being, he emphasizes that God is not determined or conditioned by this structure. The unconditional, though present as a quality in all beings, is not exhausted by the structure of being. Tillich also makes the point that God as being-itself is "beyond the subject-object structure of everything that is." "Reply to Interpretation and Criticism," in Kegley and Bretall (eds.), *The Theology of Paul Tillich*, p. 334. He further declares that "in the act of faith (and also, he would say, in the revelatory experi-ence) that which is the source of this act is present beyond the cleavage of subject and object. It is present as both and beyond both." *Dynamics of Faith*, p. 11.

18. *Systematic Theology*, I, 238-39.

19. *Ibid.*, p. 240.

20. Tillich explicitly identifies God with the structure of being in at least two places. *Ibid.*, pp. 238, 239.

21. *Ibid.*, p. 239.

22. *Love, Power, and Justice*, p. 109. For a full discussion of Tillich's theory of the nature and function of symbols, see his essay "The Nature of Religious Language," in *Theology of Culture*, pp. 53-67. Cf. also *Dynamics of Faith*, pp. 41-43.

23. *Systematic Theology*, I, 243.

24. *Loc. cit.*

25. *Ibid.*, p. 241.

26. "In man's experience of love the nature of life becomes manifest. Love is the drive towards the unity of the separated. Re-union presupposes separation of that which belongs essentially together." *Love, Power, and Justice*, p. 25.

27. *Systematic Theology*, I, 242. Cf. *Love, Power, and Justice*,

p. 48. "The power of being is not dead identity but the dynamic process in which it separates itself from itself and returns to itself."

28. *Systematic Theology*, I, 243.

29. *Loc. cit.* Tillich declares that it is the perfect actualization of the categories which is "their negation as polar or qualitatively distinct categories. In this sense the classical doctrine that the divine attributes are identical in God is correct. Moreover, if this is correct, the symbolic character of every attribute is a necessary consequence. The *via eminentiae* . . . needs as its balance the *via negationis*, and the unity of both is the *via symbolica*. If one says that God has personality in an eminent, namely, an absolutely perfect sense, one must add that this very assertion implies the negation of personality in God in the sense of "being a person." Both statements together affirm the symbolic character of the attribute 'personal' for God." "Reply to Interpretation and Criticism," in Kegley and Bretall (eds.), *The Theology of Paul Tillich*, p. 334.

30. *Systematic Theology*, I, 244-45.

31. *Ibid.*, p. 244.

32. See N. F. S. Ferré, "Three Critical Issues in Tillich's Philosophical Theology," *Scottish Journal of Theology*, X (September, 1957), 228.

33. *Systematic Theology*, I, 245.

34. *Ibid.*, p. 246.

35. *Loc. cit.*

36. *Loc. cit.*

37. *Loc. cit.* It is this negative element, Tillich adds, that is "the basis of the negative element in the creature, in which it is not overcome but is effective as a threat and a potential disruption." *Ibid.*, pp. 246-47. Tillich emphasizes that the divine life includes, and overcomes, nonbeing. See *The Courage To Be*, p. 34, where he writes: ". . . being embraces itself and nonbeing. Being has nonbeing 'within' itself as that which is eternally present and eternally overcome in the process of the divine life. The ground of everything that is is not a dead identity without movement and becoming; it is living creatively. Creatively it affirms itself, eternally conquering its own nonbeing."

38. *Systematic Theology*, I, 244.

39. *Ibid.*, p. 248.

40. *Ibid.*, p. 249.

41. *Loc. cit.*

42. *Loc. cit.*

43. *Ibid.*, pp. 250-51.

44. *Ibid.*, p. 252.

45. *Ibid.*, p. 253.

46. *Loc. cit.*

47. *Loc. cit.*

48. It is the element of nonbeing which is present in creatureliness that, Tillich adds, "gives insight into the natural necessity of death and into the potentiality but not necessity of the tragic." *Ibid.*, p. 254.

49. *Ibid.*, pp. 262-63.

50. *Ibid.*, pp. 264-69.

51. *Ibid.*, p. 264.

52. *Ibid.*, p. 267. Cf. Tillich's sermon "Principalities and Powers," in *The New Being*, pp. 50-59, for a further discussion of his conception of providence.

53. *Systematic Theology*, I, 272-73.

54. *Ibid.*, p. 273.

55. *Loc. cit.*

56. *Ibid.*, pp. 272-73. Cf. Tillich's *Love, Power, and Justice*, pp. 110-11, and *Theology of Culture*, pp. 128-29, for further discussion of the meaning of the symbol of omnipotence.

57. *Systematic Theology*, I, 274.

58. *Loc. cit.*

59. *Ibid.*, p. 275.

60. *Loc. cit.*

61. *Ibid.*, p. 276. Cf. Tillich, "Reply to Interpretation and Criticism," in Kegley and Bretall (eds.), *The Theology of Paul Tillich*, p. 340.

62. *Systematic Theology*, I, 276.

63. *Ibid.*, p. 277.

64. *Loc. cit.*

65. *Loc. cit.*

66. *Ibid.*, p. 278.

67. *Ibid.*, p. 237.

68. *Ibid.*, p. 238.

69. *Ibid.*, p. 274.

70. *Ibid.*, p. 278.

71. *Ibid.*, p. 279.

72. *Loc. cit.*

73. *Loc. cit.*

74. *Loc. cit.*

75. *Ibid.*, pp. 64-65.

76. *The Courage To Be*, p. 176.

77. *Ibid.*, p. 177.

78. *Ibid.*, p. 178. Italics mine. It is hard to understand just what the courage "to be" means for Tillich. At times it seems to be equivalent to Heidegger's *Erschlossenheit* or resoluteness. Most often it appears to mean the courage to go on living even under the most desperate of circumstances.

79. *Ibid.*, p. 182.

80. *Ibid.*, p. 188.

81. *Systematic Theology*, II, 78-80.

82. Tillich insists that the Christian doctrine of "the bondage of the will" as developed by Paul, Augustine, and Luther is not a deterministic one which surrenders human freedom and makes man into an object among objects. This doctrine, he declares, "presupposes the freedom of the will. Only what is essentially free can come under existential bondage." *Ibid.*, p. 79.

83. *Ibid.*, pp. 80-86.

84. Indeed, Tillich holds that, as expressions of an awareness of estrangement and the desire for salvation, they are themselves effects of the presence of saving power, or of revelatory experiences, but their tragedy is that they distort what they have received. *Ibid.*, pp. 80, 86.

85. *Ibid.*, p. 86.

86. This type, he maintains, is exemplified in most polytheistic religions, in Brahmanism, in Buddhism, and—preeminently—in Hellenism.

87. The religion of ancient Persia, Judaism, Christianity, Islam, and the humanism of the modern West are cited by Tillich as exemplars of this type.

88. *Systematic Theology*, II, 89.

89. *Loc. cit.*

90. Paradoxical, for Tillich, does not mean irrational or absurd. Nor does it mean rational in any of the ordinary senses. The paradoxical is defined by him as that "which contradicts the *doxa,* the opinion which is based on the whole of ordinary human experience, including the empirical and rational" or that which "transcends all human expectations and possibilities." The paradoxical transcends, but does not destroy, ordinary reason. Ultimately the only paradox of the Christian message, Tillich insists, is that the New Being has appeared under the conditions of existence and conquered them. *Systematic Theology,* I, 56-57; II, 90-92.

91. *Ibid.*, II, 94.

92. This term, Tillich declares, might be used "in order to indicate the divine presence in essential manhood" but is really redundant. *Loc. cit.*

93. *Ibid.*, p. 113.

94. *Ibid.*, p. 115.

95. *Ibid.*, p. 114.

96. *Ibid.*, p. 115.

97. *Ibid.*, p. 98.

98. *Ibid.*, p. 99.

99. Cf. *Theology of Culture*, p. 213. "The Church is the place where the New Being is real, and the place where we can go to introduce the New Being into reality. It is the continuation of the

New Being, even if its organization seems always a betrayal of the New Being."

100. *Systematic Theology*, II, 121.

101. *Loc. cit.*

102. *Ibid.*, p. 119.

103. *Loc. cit.*

104. *Ibid.*, pp. 131-32.

105. *Ibid.*, pp. 132-34.

106. The tragic nature of this conflict lies, according to Tillich, in the fact that the rejection of Jesus on the part of the Jewish leaders was not a matter of their unambiguous religious and moral guilt. The Pharisees were the genuinely pious ones of their times, and they could not, Tillich suggests, have done otherwise than reject Jesus. *Ibid.*, p. 132.

107. Tillich insists that, while it is "an expression of his participation in existential estrangement," this guilt on Jesus' part "did not touch his personal relationship to God" or "produce estrangement" or "split his personal center." *Ibid.*, p. 133.

108. *Ibid.*, pp. 127-31.

109. *Ibid.*, p. 127.

110. In his discussion of the role of "aroused freedom" in man's transition from essence to existence. See above, p. 166.

111. *Systematic Theology*, II, 128.

112. *Ibid.*, p. 129.

113. *Ibid.*, pp. 130-31.

114. *Ibid.*, p. 126.

115. *Loc. cit.*

116. "This," Tillich says, "is not surprising since the analysis was partly dependent on the confrontation of man's existential predicament with the image of the New Being in the Christ." *Loc. cit.*

117. *Ibid.*, p. 134.

118. *Loc. cit.*

119. *Loc. cit.*

120. *Loc. cit.*

121. It is Jesus' voluntary acceptance of these negativities that apparently makes the crucial difference. See Tillich, "Psychotherapy and a Christian Interpretation of Human Nature." *Review of Religion*, XIII (March, 1949), 265. "Loneliness and insecurity, strangeness, disease and death are conquered permanently in the measure in which they are voluntarily accepted as the heritage of all creatures. But they can be accepted only on the basis of an undisrupted unity between man and the infinite ground or *telos* of his being—religiously speaking, God."

122. *Systematic Theology*, II, 153-54.

123. *Ibid.*, p. 154.

124. *Ibid.*, p. 155.
125. *Ibid.*, p. 153.
126. *Ibid.*, pp. 155-56.
127. *Ibid.*, pp. 156-57.
128. *Ibid.*, p. 157.
129. *Loc. cit.*
130. *Ibid.*, p. 155.
131. *Loc. cit.*
132. *Ibid.*, p. 159.
133. This, Tillich insists, *is* a myth, and one, moreover, "the symbolic value of which must be seriously questioned." *Ibid.*, p. 160. Cf. *Theology of Culture*, p. 66, where Tillich again asserts the story of the virgin birth to be a legend and criticizes it on the theological ground that it takes away the full humanity of Jesus.
134. *Systematic Theology*, II, 159-64.
135. *Ibid.*, p. 165.
136. *Ibid.*, p. 147.
137. *Ibid.*, p. 148.
138. See Thomas J. J. Altizer, "The Incarnation," *A Handbook of Christian Theology*, pp. 187-88.
139. *Systematic Theology*, II, 94-95; 148-50.
140. *Ibid.*, pp. 95, 149. Tillich's conception of the Incarnation has close affinities to that of Irenaeus, Athanasis, and the Cappadocian Fathers who looked upon the Incarnation as the restoration of the human race to the divine life. Cf. Thomas J. J. Altizer, "The Incarnation," *A Handbook of Christian Theology*, pp. 186-87.
141. *Systematic Theology*, II, 93.
142. *Ibid.*, p. 94.
143. *Ibid.*, p. 169.
144. *Ibid.*, p. 166.
145. *Ibid.*, pp. 166-67.
146. *Loc. cit.*
147. *Ibid.*, p. 167. Tillich emphasizes that even in estrangement life is not unambiguously evil. "Man is estranged from the ground of his being, from himself and from his world. But he is still man. He cannot completely cut the tie with his creative ground, he is still a centered person and in this sense united with himself. . . . Life is not unambiguously good. Then it would not be life but only the possibility of life. And life is not unambiguously evil. Then nonbeing would have conquered being. But life is ambiguous in all its expressions." *Love, Power, and Justice*, pp. 115-16.
148. *Systematic Theology*, II, 168.
149. *Loc. cit.*
150. *Ibid.*, pp. 176-80.
151. Elsewhere Tillich describes the elements of Salvation through

the New Being as reconciliation, reunion, and resurrection. See *The New Being*, pp. 20-24.

152. These processes he promises to delineate in "Life and the Spirit," the next and, as yet, unpublished part of his *Systematic Theology*.

153. *Systematic Theology*, II, 177.

154. *Loc. cit.*

155. *Ibid.*, p. 178.

156. *Loc. cit.* Cf. *Theology of Culture*, pp. 142-43.

157. *Systematic Theology*, II, 178.

158. *Loc. cit.*

159. *Loc. cit.*

160. *Ibid.*, p. 179. The crucial importance of Justification is also stressed by Tillich in *The Courage To Be*. In this book be emphasizes that it is Justification alone which conquers not only the anxiety of guilty and condemnation (p. 166), but also of fate and death (p. 170). But the acceptance of being accepted, though it is here declared by Tillich to be possible only if the power of grace is effective in man (p. 187), is not held by him to derive from the New Being in Jesus as the Christ. Indeed, rather than indicating that it is mediated by specifically Christian faith, Tillich maintains that it is an element of that absolute faith which comes to man when he is grasped by a sense of total doubt and meaninglessness (p. 177). Cf. Tillich, "Psychotherapy and a Christian Interpretation of Human Nature," *Review of Religion*, XIII (March, 1949), 267, for a further discussion of the idea of justification through faith.

161. *Systematic Theology*, II, 179.

162. *Ibid.*, pp. 179-80.

163. *Ibid.*, p. 180.

164. *Systematic Theology*, I, 238-39.

165. "The Ontology of Paul Tillich," in Kegley and Bretall (eds.), *The Theology of Paul Tillich*, p. 161.

166. *Systematic Theology*, I, 243.

167. Tillich, of course, claims that it is an ontology that he has developed, but we have raised the question whether it is properly to be regarded as anything more than an anthropology.

168. In Kegley and Bretall (eds.), *The Theology of Paul Tillich*, pp. 164-95.

169. "Tillich's Theology of Correlation," *Journal of Religion*, XXXVI (July, 1956), 150.

170. *Systematic Theology*, I, 86.

171. Which Tillich cavalierly dismisses as misguided attempts at "self-salvation."

172. *Systematic Theology*, I, 47-52.

173. "Three Critical Issues in Tillich's Philosophical Theology," *Scottish Journal of Theology*, X (September, 1957), 236. Italics mine.

174. *Systematic Theology*, II, 126.

175. *Loc. cit.*

176. *Ibid.*, p. 168.

177. *Loc. cit.*

178. Particularly in *The Courage To Be*, p. 177ff.

Bibliography

BOOKS BY PAUL TILLICH

Biblical Religion and the Search for Ultimate Reality. Chicago: University of Chicago Press, 1955.

The Courage To Be. New Haven: Yale University Press, 1952.

Das Dämonische, ein Beitrag zur Sinndeutung der Geschichte. Tübingen: Verlag S.C.B. Mohr, 1926.

The Dynamics of Faith. New York: Harper and Bros., 1957.

The Interpretation of History. Part I, translated by N. A. Rosetski; Parts II, III, and IV, translated by Elsa L. Talmay. New York: Charles Scribner's Sons, 1936.

Kairos, Zur Geisteslage und Geisteswendung. Darmstadt: Otto Reichl Verlag, 1926.

Love, Power, and Justice: Ontological Analyses and Ethical Applications. New York: Oxford University Press, 1954.

The New Being. New York: Chas. Scribner's Sons, 1955.

The Protestant Era. Chicago: University of Chicago Press, 1948.

Protestanisches Prinzip und Proletarische Situation. Bonn: Friedrich Cohen, 1931.

Religiöse Verwirklichung. Berlin: Furche-Verlag, 1929.

The Religious Situation. Translated by H. Richard Niebuhr. New York: Henry Holt, 1932.

The Shaking of the Foundations. New York: Chas. Scribner's Sons, 1948.

Systematic Theology. Vol. I. Chicago: University of Chicago Press, 1951.

Systematic Theology. Vol. II. Chicago: University of Chicago Press, 1957.

Das System der Wissenschaften nach Gegenständen und Methoden. Göttingen: Vandenhoeck und Ruprecht, 1923.

Theology of Culture. New York: Oxford University Press, 1959.

ARTICLES BY PAUL TILLICH

"Autobiographical Reflections," in *The Theology of Paul Tillich,* edited by C. W. Kegley and R. W. Bretall. New York: Macmillan, 1956.

"Being and Love," in *Moral Principles of Action,* edited by R. N. Anshen. New York: Harper and Bros., 1952.

"The Conception of Man in Existential Philosophy," *Journal of Religion*, XIX (July, 1939), 201-15.

"Conscience in Western Thought and the Idea of a Transmoral Conscience," *Crozer Quarterly*, XXII (October, 1945), 289-300.

"Estrangement and Reconciliation in Modern Thought," *Review of Religion*, IX (November, 1944), 5-19.

"Existential Analyses and Religious Symbols," in *Contemporary Problems in Religion*, edited by H. A. Basilius. Detroit: Wayne University Press, 1956.

"Existential Philosophy," *Journal of the History of Ideas*, V (January, 1944) 44-70.

"Existential Thinking in American Theology," *Religion in Life*, X (Summer, 1941), 452-55.

"Faith in the Jewish-Christian Tradition," *Christendom*, VII (Autumn, 1942), 518-26.

"Freedom and the Ultimate Concern," in *Religion in America*, edited by J. Cogley. New York: Meridian Books, Inc., 1958.

"Freedom in the Period of Transformation," in *Freedom: Its Meaning*, edited by R. N. Anshen. New York: Harcourt Brace & Co., 1940.

"The Idea of a Personal God," *Union Review*, II (November, 1940), 8-10.

"Man and Society in Religious Socialism," *Christianity and Society*, VIII (Fall, 1943), 10-21.

"The Nature and the Significance of Existentialist Thought," *Journal of Philosophy*, 53 (1956), pp. 739-48.

"The Nature of Man," *Journal of Philosophy*, XLIII (December 1946), 675-77.

"The Problem of the Theological Method," *Journal of Religion*, XXVII (January, 1947), 16-26.

"Psychotherapy and a Christian Interpretation of Human Nature," *Review of Religion*, XIII (March, 1949), 264-68.

"Redemption in Cosmic and Social History," *Journal of Religious Thought*, III (Autumn-Winter, 1946) 17-27.

"Redemption of Nature," *Christendom*, X (Summer, 1945), 299-306.

"The Relation of Metaphysics and Theology," *Review of Metaphysics*, X, 57-63.

"The Relation of Religion and Health," *Review of Religion*, X (May, 1946), 348-84.

"Religion and Secular Culture," *Journal of Religion*, XXVI (April, 1946), 79-86.

"Religionsphilosophie," in *Lehrbuch der Philosophie*, edited by M. Dessoir. Berlin: Ullstein, 1925.

"The Religious Symbol," *Journal of Liberal Religion*, II (Summer, 1940), 13-33.

"Reply to Interpretation and Criticism," in *The Theology of Paul*

Tillich, edited by C. W. Kegley and R. W. Bretall. New York: Macmillan, 1956.

"Theology and Symbolism," in *Religious Symbolism,* edited by F. E. Johnson. New York: Harper and Bros., 1955.

"The Two Types of Philosophy of Religion" *Union Seminary Quarterly Review,* I (May, 1946), 3-13.

"Die Ueberwindung des Religionsbegriffs in der Religionsphilosophie," *Kantstudien,* XXVII (1922), 446-69.

"What Is Wrong with Dialectical Theology," *Journal of Religion,* XV (April, 1935), 127-45.

SECONDARY BOOKS

ADAMS, J. L. *Paul Tillich's Philosophy of Culture, Science and Religion* (Typewritten thesis). University of Chicago Library, 1947.

ALLPORT, GORDON W. *Personality.* New York: Henry Holt and Co., 1937.

BAILLIE, JOHN. *The Idea of Revelation in Recent Thought.* New York: Columbia University Press, 1956.

BARRETT, WILLIAM. *Irrational Man: A Study in Existential Philosophy.* Garden City: N. Y., Doubleday and Co., 1958.

BARTH, KARL. *The Doctrine of the Word of God.* Edinburgh: T. and T. Clark, 1936.

————. *The Word of God and the Word of Man.* The Pilgrim Press, 1928.

BERDYAEV, NICOLAS. *The Destiny of Man,* (4th ed.). London: Geoffrey Bles, 1954.

BLACKHAM, H. I. *Six Existentialist Thinkers.* London: Routledge, 1952.

BOBBIO, N. *The Philosophy of Decadentism: A Study in Existentialism.* Oxford: Basil Blackwell, 1948.

BROCK, WERNER. *Existence and Being.* Chicago: Henry Regnery, 1949. (Contains translations of Martin Heidegger's *Was ist Metaphysik? Vom Wesen der Wahrheit,* and *Erläuterungen zu Hölderlins Dichtung,* together with an "account" of *Sein und Zeit* by Brock.)

————. *An Introduction to Contemporary German Philosophy.* Cambridge: Cambridge University Press, 1935.

BRUNNER, EMIL. *Christianity and Civilization.* Nisbet and Company, 1948 and 1949. 2 vols.

————. *Revelation and Reason.* Philadelphia: The Westminster Press, 1946.

BUBER, MARTIN. *At the Turning.* New York: Farrar, Straus, and Cudahy, 1952.

————. *Between Man and Man.* New York: Macmillan, 1947.

————. *Eclipse of God.* New York: Harper and Bros., 1952.

————. *I and Thou.* Edinburgh: T. and T. Clark, 1937.

————. *Images of Good and Evil.* London: Routledge and Kegan Paul, 1952.

BULTMANN, OSCAR and JASPERS, KARL. *Christianity and Demythologization.* New York: Noonday Press, 1958.

BURTT, E. A. *Types of Religious Philosophy* (Revised Edition). New York: Harper and Bros., 1951.

COCHRANE, ARTHUR. *The Existentialists and God.* Philadelphia: Westminster Press, 1956.

COHEN, ARTHUR. *Martin Buber.* New York: Hillary House, Inc., 1957.

COLLINS, JAMES. *The Existentialists.* Chicago: Henry Regnery Co., 1952.

DIAMOND, MALCOLM. *Martin Buber: Jewish Existentialist.* New York: Oxford University Press, 1960.

GRENE, MARJORIE. *Introduction to Existentialism* (originally published under title, *Dreadful Freedom*). Chicago: Phoenix Books, 1959.

FROMM, ERICH. *Psychoanalysis and Religion.* New Haven: Yale University Press, 1950.

HALVERSON, MARVIN, and COHEN, ARTHUR (eds.). *A Handbook of Christian Theology: Definition Essays on Concepts and Movements of Thought in Contemporary Protestantism.* New York: Meridian Books, Inc., 1958.

HARPER, RALPH. *Existentialism: A Theory of Man.* Cambridge: Harvard University Press, 1948.

HEIDEGGER, MARTIN. *Kant und das Problem der Metaphysik.* Bonn: Verlag Friedrich Cohen, 1929.

————. *Sein und Zeit.* Erste Hälfte, Halle: Max Niemeyer Verlag, 1927.

HEINEMANN, F. H. *Existentialism and the Modern Predicament.* New York: Harper Torchbooks, 1958.

HERBERG, WILL (ed.). *Four Existentialist Theologians: A Reader from the Works of Jacques Maritain, Nicolas Berdyaev, Martin Buber, and Paul Tillich.* Garden City: Doubleday Anchor Books, 1958.

JASPERS, KARL. *Man in the Modern Age.* New York: Doubleday Anchor Books, 1957.

————. *The Perennial Scope of Philosophy.* New York: Philosophical Library 1949.

————. *The Way to Wisdom.* New Haven: Yale University Press, 1951.

KAUFMANN, WALTER. *Critique of Religion and Philosophy.* New York: Harper and Bros., 1958.

KAUFMANN, WALTER (ed.). *Existentialism from Dostoievsky to Sartre.* New York: Meridian Books, 1956.

KIERKEGAARD, SOREN. *The Concept of Dread*. Princeton: Princeton University Press, 1957.
————. *Concluding Unscientific Postscript*. Princeton: Princeton University Press, 1941.
KILLEN, R. *The Ontological Theology of Paul Tillich*. Kampen, The Netherlands: J. H. Kok, 1956.
KUHN, HELMUT. *Encounter With Nothingness: An Essay on Existentialism*. Chicago: Henry Regnery, 1949.
LANGAN, THOMAS. *The Meaning of Heidegger: A Critical Study of an Existentialist Phenomenology*. London: Routledge and Kegan Paul, 1959.
LEFEVRE, P. D. *The Nature of Personal Existence* (microfilmed thesis). University of Chicago, 1951.
LEIBRECHT, WALTER (ed.). *Religion and Culture: Essays in Honor of Paul Tillich*. New York: Harper and Bros., 1959.
MACKINTOSH, H. R. *Types of Modern Theology*. New York: Charles Scribner's Sons, 1937.
MARCEL, GABRIEL. *Being and Having*. Boston: Beacon Press. 1951.
————. *Homo Viator*. Chicago: Henry Regnery, 1951.
————. *The Mystery of Being*. Chicago: Henry Regnery, 1951.
————. *The Philosophy of Existence*. Chicago: Henry Regnery, 1952.
MAY, ROLLO; ANGEL, ERNEST; and ELLENBERGER, HENRI F. (eds.). *Existence: A New Dimension in Psychiatry and Psychology*. New York: Basic Books, 1958.
MAY, ROLLO. *The Meaning of Anxiety*. New York: Ronald Press Co., 1950.
MICHALSON, C. (ed.). *Christianity and the Existentialists*. New York: Chas. Scribner's Sons, 1956.
MURDOCK, IRIS. *Sartre: Romantic Rationalist*. New Haven: Yale University Press, 1953.
NIEBUHR, REINHOLD. *Moral Man and Immoral Society*. New York: Charles Scribner's Sons, 1932.
————. *The Nature and Destiny of Man*. New York: Charles Scribner's Sons, 1941 and 1943. 2 vols.
OTTO, RUDOLF. *The Idea of the Holy*. London: Oxford University Press, 1923.
ROBERTS, DAVID E. *Existentialism and Religious Belief*. New York: Oxford University Press, 1957.
————. *Psychotherapy and a Christian View of Man*. New York: Charles Scribner's Sons, 1950.
SARTRE, JEAN-PAUL. *L'Etre et le néant: Essai d'ontologie phenomenologique*. Paris: Gallimard, 1943.
————. *Existentialism*. New York: Philosophical Library, 1947.
————. *Existentialism and Human Emotions*. New York: The Wisdom Library, 1957.

SCHELER, MAX. *Die Stellung des Menschen im Kosmos.* Darmstadt: Reichl, 1928.

SOPER, D. W. *Men Who Shape Belief.* Philadelphia: Westminster Press, 1955.

————. *Major Voices in American Theology.* Philadelphia: Westminster Press, 1953.

STEINBERG, MILTON. *Anatomy of Faith.* New York: Harcourt, Brace and Co., 1960.

TROISFONTAINES, R. *Existentialism and Christian Thought.* London: A. C. Black, 1950.

WAHL, JEAN. *A Short History of Existentialism.* New York: Philosophical Library, 1949.

WIEMAN, H. N. *Man's Ultimate Commitment.* Carbondale: Southern Illinois University Press, 1958.

WILD, JOHN. *The Challenge of Existentialism.* Bloomington: Indiana University Press, 1955.

WILLIAMS, D. D. *What Present-Day Theologians Are Thinking* (Revised Edition). New York: Harper and Bros., 1959.

WOLFSON, HARRY A. *The Philosophy of the Church Fathers*, Vol. I: *Faith, Trinity, Incarnation.* Cambridge: Harvard University Press, 1956.

SECONDARY ARTICLES

ADAMS, J. L. "Tillich's Interpretation of History," in *The Theology of Paul Tillich*, ed. by Kegley, C. W. and Bretall, R. W. New York: Macmillan, 1956, pp. 294-309.

BECK, S. J. "Implications for Ego in Tillich's Ontology of Anxiety," *Philosophy and Phenomenological Research*, XVIII (June, 1958), pp. 451-470.

BOAS, GEORGE. "Being and Existence," *Journal of Philosophy*, LIII (1956), pp. 748-59.

BURNABY, J. "Towards Understanding Paul Tillich," *Journal of Theological Studies*, N. S., V (October, 1954), pp. 195-205.

CROSS, W. O. "Some Notes on the Ontology of Paul Tillich," *Anglican Theological Review*, 39 (October, 1957), pp. 297-311.

DAUBNEY, R. H. "Preface to Paul Tillich," *Church Quarterly Review*, CL (1950), pp. 1-36.

————. "Some Structural Concepts in Tillich's Thought and the Pattern of the Liturgy," in *The Theology of Paul Tillich*, ed. Kegley, C. W. and Bretall, R. W. New York: Macmillan, 1956, pp. 268-91.

DEMOS, RAPHAEL. "Review of Paul Tillich's *Systematic Theology, Vol. I*," *Journal of Philosophy*, XLIX (1952), pp. 692-708.

————. "Tillich's Philosophical Theology," *Philosophy and Phenomenological Research*, XIX (September, 1958) pp. 74-85.

DILLENBERGER, J. "Tillich's Use of the Concept 'Being'," *Christianity and Crisis*, XIII (1953), pp. 30-31.

DOWEY, E. A., JR. "Tillich, Barth and the Criteria of Theology," *Theology Today*, XV (April, 1958), pp. 43-58.

EMMET D. E. "Epistemology and the Idea of Revelation," in *The Theology of Paul Tillich*, ed. by Kegley, C. W., and Bretall, R. W. New York: Macmillan, 1956, pp. 198-214.

————. "Review of Paul Tillich's *Systematic Theology, Vol. I*," *Journal of Theological Studies*, N.S., IV (October, 1953), pp. 294-98.

FERRÉ, N. F. S. "Three Critical Issues in Tillich's Philosophical Theology," *Scottish Journal of Theology*, X (September, 1957), pp. 225-38.

————. "Tillich's View of the Church," in *The Theology of Paul Tillich*, ed. by Kegley, C. W. and Bretall, R. W. New York: Macmillan, 1956, pp. 248-65.

FREEMAN, D. H. "Tillich's Doctrine of Revelation," *Christianity Today*, II (July 21, 1958), pp. 12-15.

GREENE, T. M. "Paul Tillich and Our Secular Culture," in *The Theology of Paul Tillich*, ed. by Kegley, C. W. and Bretall, R. W. New York: Macmillan, 1956, pp. 50-66.

GRENE, MARJORIE. "The German Existentialists," *Chicago Review*, XIII (Summer, 1959), pp. 49-58.

HARTSHORNE, CHARLES. "Tillich's Doctrine of God," in *The Theology of Paul Tillich*, ed. by Kegley, C. W. and Bretall, R. W. New York: Macmillan, 1956, pp. 164-95.

HEIMANN, EDUARD. "Tillich's Doctrine of Religious Socialism," in *The Theology of Paul Tillich*, ed. by Kegley, C. W. and Bretall, R. W. New York: Macmillan, 1956, pp. 312-25.

HORTON, W. M. "Tillich's Role in Contemporary Theology," in *The Theology of Paul Tillich*, ed. by Kegley, C. W. and Bretall, R. W. New York: Macmillan, 1956, pp. 26-47.

KAUFMAN, C. D. "Can A Man Serve Two Masters?—Philosophy and Theology in the Thought of Tillich," *Theology Today*, XV (April, 1958), pp. 59-77.

KAUFMANN, WALTER. "Existentialism and Death," *Chicago Review*, XIII (Summer, 1959), pp. 75-93.

KEENE, J. C. "Existential Theology," *Journal of Religious Thought*, X (1952-53), pp. 56-73.

KITAGAWA, J. M. "Theology and the Science of Religion," *Anglican Theological Review*, 39 (January, 1957), pp. 33-52.

JOHNSON, R. C. "Theologian of Synthesis," *Theology Today*, XV (April, 1958), pp. 36-42.

LOOMER, B. M. "Tillich's Theology of Correlation," *Journal of Religion*, XXXVI (July, 1956), pp. 150-56.

MOLLEGEN, A. T. "Christology and Biblical Criticism in Tillich," in

The Theology of Paul Tillich, ed. by Kegley, C. W. and Bretall, R. W. New York: Macmillan, 1956, pp. 230-45.

NIEBUHR, REINHOLD. "Biblical Thought and Ontological Speculation in Tillich's Theology," in *The Theology of Paul Tillich,* ed. by Kegley, C. W. and Bretall, R. W. New York: Macmillan, 1956, pp. 216-27.

RANDALL, J. H., JR. "The Ontology of Paul Tillich," in *The Theology of Paul Tillich,* ed. by Kegley, C. W. and Bretall, R. W. New York: Macmillan, 1956, pp. 132-61.

ROBERTS, D. E. "Tillich's Doctrine of Man," in *The Theology of Paul Tillich,* ed. by Kegley, C. W. and Bretall, R. W. New York: Macmillan, 1956, pp. 108-30.

ROGERS, CARL. "Persons or Science? A Philosophical Question," *The American Psychologist,* X (1950), pp. 267-78.

RUDICH, NORMAN. "The Individual as Myth," *Chicago Review,* XIII (Summer, 1959), pp. 94-119.

SANDERSON, J. W., JR. "Historical Fact or Symbol? The Philosophies of History of Paul Tillich and Reinhold Niebuhr," *Westminster Theological Journal,* XX (1958), 158-69; XXI, 58-74.

SALZMAN, L. "Observations on Dr. Tillich's View on Guilt, Sin, and Reconciliation," *Journal of Pastoral Care,* XI (Spring, 1957), 14-19.

SCHRADER, GEORGE A., JR. "Existence, Truth, and Subjectivity," *Journal of Philosophy,* 53 (1956), pp. 759-71.

SCHRAG, C. O. "Existence and History," *Review of Metaphysics,* XIII (September, 1959), 28-44.

SELLERS. J. E. "Five Approaches to the Human Situation," *Theology Today,* XV (January, 1959), 521-30.

SIEGFRIED, THEODOR. "The Significance of Paul Tillich's Theology for the German Situation," in *The Theology of Paul Tillich,* ed. by Kegley, C. W. and Bretall, R. W. New York: Macmillan, 1956, pp. 68-83.

SKINNER, J. E. "Critique of Tillich's Ontology," *Anglican Theological Review,* 39 (January, 1957), pp. 53-61.

THOMAS, J. H. "Some Notes on the Theology of Paul Tillich," *Hibbert Journal,* 58 (April, 1959), pp. 253-58.

TIEBOUT, H. M., JR. "Freud and Existentialism," *Journal of Nervous and Mental Diseases,* 126 (April, 1958), pp. 341-52.

————. "Tillich, Existentialism, and Psychoanalysis," *Journal of Philosophy,* LVI (July, 1959), 605-12.

WATSON, M. "The Social Thought of Paul Tillich," *Journal of Religious Thought,* X (1952-53), 5-17.

WIENPAHL, PAUL. "Philosophy and Nothing," *Chicago Review,* XIII (Summer, 1959), 59-74.

WRIGHT, C. J. "Courage and Systematic Theology: Paul Tillich's Existentialist Apologetic," *Modern Churchman,* 43 (December, 1953), pp. 275-83.

Index